MW00778731

Raising Elite Athletes

A Parent's Guide To Develop Elite Performance

By

Dr. Malcolm Conway

www.TotalPublishingAndMedia.com

Table of Contents

Introduction... xi

Chapter 1: Developing an Elite Athlete.. 1
- No Such Thing as a Bad Athlete 2
- Five Steps To Becoming an Elite Athlete 5

Chapter 2: Parents of Athletes 8
- Five Types of Sport Parents.. 9
- What Sport Is Right for Your Son or Daughter?.................. 11
- Early Stages of Development 14
- Parents and Tempers... 16
- Different Sports Have Different Parents to Deal With........ 20
- A Coaches View of Parents... 21
- Emotional Abuse 29
- Parents Behind Closed Doors 30
- How Common Is Abuse in Youth Sports? 30
- Looking for the Money.. 32
- How Can A Parent Help Their Athlete................................ 33
- When Parenting Is Too Much or Too Little 34
- When the Athlete Decides to Take the Path Less Traveled . 35
- How You Can Become an Elite Parent 42
- Dr. Conway's Top Ten Tips to Becoming World-Class
  Sports Parents.. 44

Chapter 3: What It Takes to Become an Elite Athlete...................... 47
- Working at Wimbledon 47
- Learning from the Players 50
- You Have to Make a Decision… Do I Want to Be a Jock
  or an Athlete? 54

   - Training Comparison 56
   - Dealing with Hardship 58
   - Looking to Science to Help Develop Elite Athletes 60
   - Natural Talent vs. Hard Work 62
   - Elite Athletes and the Choke Factor 62
   - Different Sports… Different Challenges… Or Are There?.. 65

Chapter 4: Pain 73
   - What is Pain? 74
   - Delayed Onset Muscle Soreness 79
   - So, what can you do for the pain? 81
   - Understanding Fatigue 81
   - Injury and Damage 84

Chapter 5: Asking the Experts Questions 86
   - Matt Stover (Indianapolis Colts, NFL) 87
   - Mike Bryan (Professional Tennis, WTA) 91
   - Qadry Ismail (Baltimore Ravens, NFL) 95
   - Bethanie Mattek-Sands (Professional Tennis, WTA) 102
   - Raghib "Rocket" Ismail (Dallas Cowboys, NFL) 106
   - Nadia Petrova (Professional Tennis) 111
   - Leonard Wheeler (Carolina Panthers, NFL) 114
   - Jon Drummond (U.S. Olympic Gold Medalist, Track) 122
   - Marquis Mathieu (Professional Hockey) 126
   - Adam Archuleta (National Football League) 131
   - Coach Robert Johnson (Cornell University, Track and
      Cross Country) 136
   - Stella Sampras-Webster (Head Coach, UCLA Women's
      Tennis) 140

Chapter 6: The Mind & The Elite Athlete 146
   - Pressure 150
   - So How Do You Prepare for Success and Leave The
      Pressure Behind 152
   - Visualization 153
   - Develop a Strategy of Success 156

- How To Turn Luck From Superstition To Reality 158
- Dr. Conway's Top 7 Rules for Luck 160
- Keys In Developing a Strong Mind That Can Attract
      Anything.. 161
- Create Your Own Energy 162

Chapter 7: Coaching 165
- So What Makes a Good Coach? 165
- Parents: Let The Coaches Coach 167
- Parents as Coaches.................................... 169
- Coaching Today.. 176
- Sighing Up For The First Time To Play Sports.......... 177
- How Much Do You Really Know? 179
- Coaching Styles 180
- Different Levels of Coaching 182
- Every Sport Has a Different Coach...Or Do They?....... 186

Chapter 8: Sports Training................................ 188
- The Phelps Phenomenon… 190
- Times Have Changed.................................... 195
- Know Your Limits...................................... 196
- Training at the Higher Levels......................... 197
- How Are You Training?................................. 198
- My Theory of Training in the U.S...................... 199
- Identifying Athletic Weaknesses....................... 200
- Gym Rats vs. Athletes 204
- Training for Your Sport............................... 205
- Schroder Training 208
- Interview with Jay Schroeder 210

Chapter 9: Sports Injuries: New Paradigm of Injury Treatment...... 219
- Evolution of Sports Injury Treatment.................. 223
- New Thinking Brings About New Ways of Treatment,
      Rehabilitation, and Sports Performance Training…...... 224
- Back to School.. 227
- Let's Go Over the Basics of Injury.................... 229

- Times Are Changing... 232
- The Exam.. 235
- New Thinking for New Treatment (MFDT)...................... 237
- New Treatment for Soft Tissue Injuries 238
- MyoFascial Disruption Technique (MFDT).................... 240
- The ARPWave.. 245
- The Sacred Myth of Stretching – Shattered! 249
- Neurological Muscle Injury..................................... 250

Chapter 10: Nutrition 101 253
- Athletes Nutrition 256
- Protein vs. Carb's 257
- Advanced Nutrition 262
- Hydration.. 264
- Water or Sports Drinks.. 266
- Energy Drinks... 268

Chapter 10: Steroids, Drugs & Alcohol............................ 271
- Parents Learn What Is Going On............................... 277
- Getting It Straight From The Source 279
- Alcohol 285
- Interview With A Drug & Alcohol Rehabilitation Expert . 287

Chapter 12: Recruiting.. 294
- The Business of Division I Sports... 295
- The Process.. 297
- How Do I Know If My Son/Daughter Is Getting
  Recruited? 300
- What Questions Do I Ask?...................................... 301
- Pro's & Con's Of Choosing A School 303
- Watch What You Ask For....You May Just Get It! 305
- Recruiting By the Numbers 310
- Good Character... 312
- Don't Get Greedy 312
- Things You Need To Know About The NCAA 314
- The Dark Side.. 320

- Father and Son Recruiting.... 325
- Revolving Door of Coaching.. 327
- Early Recruiting... 328

Summary & Frequently Asked Questions (FAQ)........................ 330

ACKNOWLEDGEMENTS

I dedicate this book to my wonderful wife, Mary Catherine, which without her patience, encouragement and understanding, this book would have never been written. "Thank you for allowing me to do my thing, enabling me to help others do their thing."

I have been blessed with a family that is the center of my universe and for that I thank you. With that said, I know that much of my knowledge has been taught to me from my two discerning children, Shannon and Malcolm, Jr. - who never met a line in a movie they couldn't imitate. Cherishing the gift of laughter, these two have supplied me with a life time of happiness, humor and wisdom which has given me the inspiration to succeed.

Also special thanks to my Mom who made it all possible providing a family environment that was my stability growing up. To my Dad who has passed, his wisdom and common sense allowed me to respectfully question authority, while providing me with the proper boundaries of life. Not a gentler man has ever walked the earth. To my departed brother Jim who listened to Sinatra by doing it his way and to brothers Bob and Tom, for keeping the Irish proud by allowing me to learn and observe from their successes. To my wife's mother Lucy, a proud mother who is the rock to her family, and a breath of fresh air to all that surround her. To my departed father-in-law Richard, a man who would give anyone the shirt off of his back...I sincerely thank you all.

Also an overall thanks to my assistant in the office Dorothy DePhillips who does a magnificent job assisting me with patients. And to all who have helped me over the years in all aspects of my professional and personal life...Thank You.

Introduction

*R*aising *Elite Athletes* is written with the sole intention to hit you right between the eyes with honesty. My intention is to assist parents to better understand how to help their children succeed in sports. The information in this book is an honest observation, experience and opinion based on 26 years of clinical practice, in treating sports injuries and studying sports performance. On top of that, I'm a parent of two athletes. If you are serious in learning how to be a better coach to your son or daughter, as well as becoming a better sports parent, you chose the right book.

Raising Elite Athletes will help educate parents and athletes alike to the 'reality' of sports. The information is intended to help educate parents on how to help their sons or daughters excel in sports no matter what was previously learned. "Don't let anyone tell you different - your child can improve." With the right motivation and passion anyone can succeed to levels never thought possible. The material in this book will arm you with the necessary information, strategy and tactics needed for success.

I've had the opportunity to work with thousands of athletes in my career. Each athlete that I've worked with has possessed a unique passion about their ability and their sport. *Every athlete is silently begging to be led to success.* No matter their present talent level, they feel that with the right direction they can make it to the top. All athletes want to succeed - they are looking for someone to give then direction. That's where the parents can help the most by listening, guiding and motivating.

I've seen some kids that have very little talent but posses a heart bigger than the Grand Canyon. Believe me when I tell you - some of these kids have accomplished heights in sports that I never thought possible. With less talent that their competitors, I've watched athletes work harder and longer than anyone else around them, "willing" themselves to success. This can be a very rewarding experience for all involved to have someone who is willing to put it all on the line to succeed.

"Most people who participate in sports don't realize how much more they can develop if they just dig down deep to see what they can really accomplish."

Unfortunately, I've also been around athletes that were truly gifted and because of a negative attitude and poor work ethic, I've watched them throw their entire sports career away. Talent that the average kid would die for, wasted on laziness and ego. Believe me when I say this, helping your child develop a sound, positive mental attitude is the best thing you can do for them. The difference between success and failure is a highly developed positive attitude. If your child develops the right attitude everything else will fall into place.

The same goes for parents. There are different levels of sports parents who decide to help (or not help) there youngster succeed. I've been privy to meet with many parents that ranged from the "I don't care parent" to the "over the top, razors edge parent". Most parents want the very best for their kids and sometimes without their knowledge they tend to go way to far attempting to push their athletes to success. This book will help you see through the veil of your relationship with your child, helping you in developing them into an elite athlete.

There are certain athletes that have an internal drive that CANNOT be coached. They have a passion for excellence that is fueled by an internal psyche that no coach on this earth can answer how to develop. When you have an athlete that is self motivated and has a "drive" for success you will have a champion on your hands. If you have to continually prod your young athlete to practice or play, it's time to look into another sport. They either have "it" deep inside or they don't. If they don't have it, it's okay. Just realize that the chance of getting to the very top of their sport is not as good. Not every kid is destined to play sports in college or in the professional ranks. Not every kid has the passion or the work ethic necessary to move on to the next level. Let me let you in on an inside secret…it's okay if your child admits to you that a particular sport isn't right for them. They'll find their niche eventually.

A few years ago I attended the Masters Golf tournament in Augusta Ga. I worked my way through the beautiful fairways and greens of this magnificent golf course following the players. I observed the best golfers in the world working at their given craft. Note: WORKING at their craft - not playing. As a professional, the game is a job and every detail must be attended to so that the athlete puts themselves in a position to win. In some instances when parents and athletes watch professionals play they get caught up in the game itself. The get caught up in the pageantry, the hype, the T.V. lights, the fame and the glory. Professionals are not playing, they're there to compete and win. Professional sports are a very serious business to the athletes because they have a limited time to make it to the top. It's dead serious work. In individual type of sports like golf and tennis you are not protected by a team and if you don't win you don't eat.

After walking the entire course I ended up at the practice range. I was fascinated watching the players come off the course after playing 18 holes and going straight to the practice area. Can you believe it? They just completed playing in the most prestigious golf match in the world and where do they go - the practice range. The players along with their caddies and instructors laid down hundreds of balls and began to hit all types of shots that probably mimicked the playing conditions of the course. In the old days, many of the players would come off the course and head for the bar to socialize. Now, professional golfers either head for the practice range or the therapy trailers to get worked on by chiropractors, physical therapist or personal trainers.

I study body mechanics, injury and performance for a living. After watching every movement of the golfer's swings I noted that each individual golfer has the same swing close to perfection. One thing was perfectly clear; these elite players were given a special gift to play the game of golf. When God was making golfers he said to his assistant, "Yep you're going to be a pro golfer – Conway, we have other intentions for you, and pro golf isn't one of them."

"There are athletes and then there are the rest of us that participate in sports."

Yes we all love various sports and many of us play them very well. However, there are the chosen few that rise above other athletes and have the unbridled talent that allows them to have thousands upon thousands of people pay good money to watch them play.

Whatever type of athlete you are you've been given a gift. It may or may not be in the particular sport that you are participating in at this time. Your gift may be in something totally different from the sport you love so much. But you need to fully grasp your limitations no matter what they are. This goes particularly for parents who are attempting to help their children succeed in sports. If your son or daughter is heads and shoulders above their competition at every level, than you can begin to recognize they may be on their way to the top. But please understand the stats of sports – 1 in 2500 student athletes will be offered a complete scholarship and 1 in 290,000 will be offered a professional sports contract.

Each level that the athlete strives for has its own particular barriers of competition, physical demands, psychological demands and worst of all 'political' demands. The better prepared the athlete is for all of these demands the better off they will be in the long run.

It's important for the athlete to constantly strive to find a way to improve. Find a mentor, an honest friend or qualified coach that can help you do one thing...GET BETTER! Parents, be real about the entire journey and take one day at a time. This book will be a good start to help you on your way to success to guide you through the ups and downs that sports have to offer.

Work hard, play hard and find ways every day to make it fun.

Chapter 1

Developing an Elite Athlete

I t's 7:30 a.m., a normal Saturday for Sandra and Bill, and they're waking their kids for the usual weekend day of sports. They have three children ranging in age from 6 to 12, and all are involved in different sports. The oldest is a baseball player who has practice at 9 a.m., the second child has a softball game at 10 a.m., and the youngest has a soccer game at 11 a.m. The children are also involved with tennis, basketball, karate, ballet, and swimming. Juggling participation in this many sports in a family is a full-time job. Husband Bill has charted out his weeks and months by using a spreadsheet on his computer. This helps him know when and where he has to be each day. He also uses that same spreadsheet to document his children's achievements.

Many parents today are waking up to the reality that their children's involvement in organized sports is akin to a full-time job. They are learning the hard way that to keep kids involved in as many sports as possible is going to takes a serious commitment.

In an article written by Laura Hilgers for CNN, she states that there are an estimated 41 million American kids playing competitive youth sports. The number of children involved in youth sports has risen significantly over the last 10 to 20 years, according to Dr. Steve Carney, a professor of sports management at Drexel University in Philadelphia. In soccer, for instance, which remains one of the country's most popular youth sports, numbers have risen from about 15 million in 1987 to more than 17.5 million in 2002, the latest date for which numbers are available, according to U.S. Soccer. In Pop

Warner Football, participation has nearly doubled in the last 15 years, from about 130,000 players to 260,000 players, according to the organization. The cheerleaders, who have competitions of their own, are now 140,000 strong.

With an ever-increasing number of players getting involved in sports, it brings along a quiet storm with it. That storm is called "parents." In the same article, Hilgers quotes Dr. Dan Guold, the director of the Michigan State University Institute for the Study of Youth Sport, "We see a lot of kids, even young kids, doing it just for the scholarship now." One of the biggest concerns in youth sports, Gould says, is parents who push their kids into "premature specialization," in which kids focus all their skills on one sport and endure year-round training. This can lead not only to burnout but also to sports injuries. As the competition heats up, so do the parents. Stories of over-training, fights, arguments, and some even leading to death have taken place all across the country. Is it just over scholarships or have we developed a new type of angry parent?

Parents and Athletes: Most parents and kids have no idea what it takes to become a "real athlete." But worse, very few understand what it takes to become an "elite athlete." This book will allow you to better understand what it takes to become a true athlete.

> **Parents:** By putting this information to correct use, you can assist your son(s) or daughter(s) to rise to the top of their sport.

> **Athletes:** Learn the details provided in this book, and it will allow you to push past your competition while creating a meaningful experience in competition.

No Such Thing as a Bad Athlete

The competition out there is getting tougher and tougher. With young children beginning to specialize earlier and earlier, the bar is being raised ever so slightly each year.

Here is my fundamental belief about all athletes.

"There is no such thing as a bad athlete. There are some athletes who mature faster, some athletes that develop faster, and some athletes that figure it out faster. But given the chance to properly develop, recruit, and hold muscular positions in the manner a muscle was intended, any athlete can improve to a level way beyond his or her expectations or the expectations of others."

There are some kids who "just have it." Some kids just seem to be able to do it all. They seem to have been given a little bit more in their snack packs when they were born. You've seen them, the kids who can do anything on the field or court and make it look easy. There are many reasons for this that scientists are still arguing over. It's the same as the kids in school, who can just pick up a book, read it once, take the test, and get a perfect score. They've been given an extra gift.

If your child doesn't have it, don't worry. It's no indication that your child can't or won't succeed to high levels in sports. There are no scientific indications that your son or daughter can't succeed to higher levels. It just may take longer.

I can show you countless number of kids who started out labeled as young "phenoms," and as time went on, they ended up fizzling out. The reason for this is that some kids mature faster than others, and at an early age, that makes a big difference. Some children advance quicker physiologically than others, giving them the appearance of being gifted. But as time continues on and the other kids begin to mature, the playing field starts becoming more level. When these types of players rest on their laurels, thinking that they are the next Cristiano Ronaldo, their talent levels slowly erode as time goes on. They need to learn the discipline of hard work to continually take their talents to the next level. I've seen firsthand young, less-than-average players work their way up to Division I scholarships. They understood that, through endless hard work, they could develop the talent needed for that level of play.

Let's face it parents, we'll do some crazy things for our kids. If you really want to help your children become better athletes, help them believe in themselves. This is by far the number one thing you can do to help them. This is more powerful for your children to learn early than hiring a dozen personal trainers.

To become any type of true athlete, it is going to take hard work. Nothing, but nothing, takes the place of hard work...nothing. Success can be achieved by both proper mental and physical preparation. Most athletes don't understand what it takes to become a real athlete. Most athletes think that because they spend an hour or two in the gym working out a halo instantly arises over their heads.

"Real Athletes Do The Things That Other Athletes Don't Want To Do"

As helpful as many parents are to their children, there are other parents who push them way too far in practice and in life. Some parents I've witnessed refused to feed their children who they thought were not at an acceptable weight to play competitive tennis. Another athlete told to me that, in order to prepare the young tennis player to become more mentally tough, the European parents put him in the closet for up to two days in order to learn to not to show weakness on the court. Can you believe that? I mean I thought some of the U.S. parents were crazy. Well, I still do, but that's another story. Locking your child up in a closet or refusing to feed them — my God, what's wrong with these people?

As I've gotten to know numerous professional athletes, it is apparent that some of this parental "passion" can and has left long-lasting mental scars on some of these athletes. The last time I looked, a child is still a child, and children continue to require motivation, compassion, discipline, and love. In the immortal words of my dad, Robert T. Conway, Sr., "I've never seen a child die from too much love." I'll be the first to tell you that I believe in hard work, mental toughness, and desire, but there is a fine line that can be crossed in attaining those goals with a young athlete. When that line is crossed not from good intention but by being over-bearing or degrading in coaching, pathology can set in, and long-term harm can take place.

There are certain athletes that have internal drives that *cannot* be coached. They have a passion for excellence fueled by internal psyches that no coach on this earth can answer how to develop. When you have an athlete that is self-motivated and has a "drive" for success, you will have a champion on your hands. If you have to continually prod your young athlete to practice or play, it's time to look into another sport. They either have "it" deep down inside, or they don't. If they don't have it, it's okay. Just realize that the chance of getting to the very top of the sport is not as good.

One athlete who comes to mind who I feel has "it" is a young girl who wakes up every day at 4:30 a.m. and travels two hours one-way to practice. She is a highly skilled figure skater with aspirations of making the Olympic team. The two-hour drive to practice and the two-hour drive back from practice doesn't allow for much more time for her in her schedule. She is home-schooled and must give up many of her favorite activities to pursue her dream. She also has a sister with Down's syndrome, whom she helps when she gets home, so her mother and father can go to work. A purely delightful child, you'll never hear a single complaint from her at any time. She always has a smile on her face and something nice to say, and she goes about her day like any other thirteen-year-old. The odds of becoming an Olympic champion are stacked against most, but for some reason, after sitting down and talking with this girl for an hour, you can see that her passion and determination are going to raise her above the normal odds of making it.

As parents, we all want the best for our kids. But you have to keep everything about your child's sports rational. If your child is good, bad, or even elite, keep it in perspective. It's a long, long road to the college or professional level. You have many hurdles to overcome to make it to the next level.

Five Steps To Becoming an Elite Athlete

One: Education and understanding. Be realistic about your son's or daughter's athletic talent. Just because he or she does well at a certain level doesn't necessarily mean that they can make it to the next level. There are definite signs that will point out if your young athlete is in fact elite. Educate yourself on the sport that your son or daughter is aspiring towards.

Two: How to work WITH the athlete, NOT against them. It's all about your kids — not you. Don't be living your lives through your children. You had your chance when you played, and now it's time to let them have their time. Help them...don't haunt them.

Three: If your athlete is above-average or elite, understand that he or she still has a ton of work to do. Each level that an athlete aspires to will become more and more difficult. Keep them working hard, keep them mentally focused, and keep them humble.

Four: This book is intended to educate you as the parent and your child together on what it takes to become a "real" athlete. The fully understand this you must first accept the fact to the realities of sports. Right now, there is some kid that is working his or her ass off trying to better themselves. Just understand there there are kids out there willing to do anything to make it to the top.

No matter if you're average or elite, there is a way to become a better athlete. I believe that there is no such thing as a bad athlete. But without desire or passion to become better you might want to choose other goals.

Five: Accept it if your athlete is just an average [or even below average] athlete. That's okay...not everyone can be the next coming of Michael Jordan. It doesn't mean that they can't strive or work towards getting to the next level.

Becoming a top athlete is a combination of self-determination, passion, and an ability to push through stress and discomfort while learning how to have fun playing. It's not just talent, because there is going to come a day when your athlete looks around, and they are surrounded by talent equal to or greater than they are.

When I was in college, I came across a framed photograph of three horses at a photo finish line. The picture taken at a horse track showed the photo finish line across the track with each horse's nose perfectly aligned squarely on the finish line. Picture in your mind three horses nose-to-nose-to-nose perfectly even at the finish line. What made this picture so unique was that one horse had his tongue out. The horse with its tongue out won the race.

My question to you is what are you going to do to get your tongue out?

Parents: There is a lot of information in this book that will inform you and help you to help your athlete become better. Be responsible to become a great parent. With good planning, good humor, and a good outlook on life, you can help your athlete get to the top of his or her sport.

Athletes: There is a lot of information in this book that will inform you and help you to become a better athlete. It's up to you as athletes to make your own success. Not your coach, not your trainer, and not your parents…you. Learn to take responsibility for yourself, and the road to success will become easier.

"Work smart, work hard, and work with a purpose."

Chapter 2

Parents of Athletes

I understand how difficult it can be to raise children today. Don't mistake this for parental advice. More importantly, look at this information as a way to help develop a solid strategy to optimize your child's performance in sports. I am a proud parent of two children who played sports in high school and college. Sports in our family are right up there with education and our belief in God. But it *isn't* our God.

Because I'm involved full-time in treating and training athletes, I enjoy being around most sports activities. I like everything about sports — the winning, the losing, the stress of competition, the intellectual side of strategy, and the interaction between all of the athletes and coaches.

Many parents take a combative approach to their children's athletics. It has become more commonplace to see parents mentally pushing their kids, taunting them, and sometimes even verbally abusing them in a backward attempt to "inspire" a better athlete. Whether you are a good or bad athlete, it takes a lot of work to get out there and play. What truly drives me crazy is to hear a fan negatively screaming at players about their athletic ability, yelling obscenities, or threatening others during an idiotic rage because he or she didn't agree with a play, the performance, an official's call, or the coach's decision. Quite often, this type of fan never played any sports, or if they did, they weren't all that good, but for some reason they feel they have the right to degrade others. Unfortunately, many times that fan turns out to be a parent of an athlete on the field.

Here is a great example of this type of behavior. At a local mini-football game, a father grabbed a player who wasn't his son and lifted him off of the ground while threatening him in front of the other parents and players. Why such an insane outbreak of temper? Because this young boy was better than his own kid who was playing in the same game, and he couldn't take watching him making all of the big plays. This man was taken away that day by the police.

Five Types of Sport Parents

I have dealt with hundreds of parents of athletes, and through clinical experience in my practice, general observation, and personal interaction, I have found that most parents are the same throughout the country. After observing parents for many years as I stood on the sidelines, sat in the stands, and interacted with them in my office, I have broken parents down into five separate categories.

The Commando Parent: The overzealous parent that always has something to say to the referee, an athlete, or the coach. This type of parent shows up for practices and other uninvited events to put his or her "two cents" in. These parents always have advice for everyone except themselves. Nothing is ever right, and they are there to make sure they get it right — mainly for their own kid's benefit only.

The Covert Pushy Silent Parent: The "covert pushy silent parents" lurk in the shadows waiting for their chance to make sure their kids aren't getting ripped off. They're the ones who are all smiles to your face but have developed a covert, military-like plot to advance their kids in any way possible. They're the ones who are quietly relentless on their kids to excel on a daily basis behind the scenes. Yep, they're the "ass kissers," the ones who just happen to always be in the coaches' ears.

The Supportive Parent: The supportive parents are those who understand that their athletes are there to have fun, and if more comes of it, then that's great. They know that their athletes are good in their eyes no matter what happens. They show up, they cheer, they volunteer if needed, and they leave it on the field and go home when it's over. The unfortunate part about this type of parent is that they are becoming extinct. As time goes on, there seems to be fewer and fewer of these types of parents on the sidelines.

The Absentee Parent: The parent who never has the time of day to come out and watch their athletes because of some excuse or another. Possibly, it's their career that is more important to them, or in their minds, they have more important things to do. Sometimes, it comes down to downright laziness. It's a shame because, whether they understand or not, the young athletes feel very secure when Mom and Dad attend their sporting events. Don't mistake the absentee parents for the parents struggling to make ends-meet by working several jobs. These hard-working parents are hustling a living in any way they can to make things better for their family, and there are only so many hours in a day.

The Totally Clueless Coaching Parent: No one is better than his or her kid. From the crib, the child began receiving letters from Notre Dame, USC, and Florida State. This parent has absolutely no clue about anything in sports. They're clueless about sports training, sports nutrition, or anything else in sports, but they try to come across as outright experts. They think that, since they played sports when they were young, they are the top experts in the land. No one else can coach except them because they are the experts, or they will constantly be in the coaches' ears, lending them their expert advice on how the team should run. No one is better than his or her kid because they are their offspring. They put enormous amounts of pressure on their own kids, mainly to hide their own inadequacies.

In order for you to become a helpful parent, you have to be "real." You need to become real with yourself, real with your children, and real about your expectations.

Definition   Real: Genuine; not counterfeit or artificial

Why are you getting your son or daughter into sports? Is it for exercise, social interaction, competition, or the love of the game? If the answer is yes to any of these questions, you are on the right road. If you are getting your children in for other reasons, such as scholarship money, popularity, keeping up with neighbors, or unfulfilled personal accomplishments, then you may be in for a rude awakening.

Some parents will do whatever is necessary for their children to succeed. Some parents have moved to other towns or even to other states to give their children a better opportunity of getting a scholarship. I've seen parents move their kids around from school to school in the same year to make sure they get to play and get noticed by coaches. Some of these kids have changed schools over five times until the parents were happy they were getting what they felt was needed. The sad thing about this is that the young athlete was average and ended up not playing sports anymore because there was no interest at the college level.

There are times that some athletes who show huge potential in their sport need to move to a location that is better suited for them to get the proper instruction. Some kids need more intense coaching or training based on their talents. Whatever the case may be, get involved with your child. Provide the necessary opportunity for your son/daughter to flourish, but keep it sensible. Let your athletes have fun, let them work hard, let them enjoy their childhoods, and you will enjoy your parenthood much more.

What Sport Is Right for Your Son or Daughter?

The answer to that question really comes down to one thing — what does your son or daughter enjoy? If it were up to me, and yes, I did this with my kids, I would let them try as many sports as they wanted.

Here are the three top strategies you can use to help your young athlete:

#1. Choose as many sports as possible that your son or daughter seems to be interested in. Find the sport that comes easiest to the child, and choose the sport that he or she enjoys the most. There are many athletes out there who love a particular sport, but that sport doesn't necessarily come very easily to their physical makeup. This doesn't mean that they can't play that sport. It just means they are probably not physically developed to meet the demands of that sport.

#2. Parents sign their kids up in a variety of sports, including soccer, t-ball, swimming, tennis, and gymnastics. Parents often times feel that a particular sport is better for a child based on what "they, the parent, think." Granted, no one has a crystal ball to know exactly what sport is perfect for your child, but that's why letting him or her try various sports is better in the long run. Kids will gravitate to sports that come easier to them than others.

#3. Many parents get too involved in trying to make everything perfect for their children at this young age. The athlete must find out on his or her own how to "feel" the sport as an individual. I've seen some kids involved in too many sports, and in some cases, this has led to increased stress in their lives. Be careful about putting them into any specialized training unless you can honestly recognize that they have a unique talent. Many times, at young ages they don't need specialized camps, so save your money. As they get older, you can think about sending them to a camp, but again, be careful, as many of these camps aren't as good as they claim.

There have been a number of prodigy athletes that have graced us with their talents. Tiger Woods, Michael Phelps, Lebron James, Jim Thorpe, Babe Ruth, and many others have changed the landscape of sports. So how do parents know if they are raising the next Phelps or Jordan? The problem is that, when your children are really young, you probably won't have any idea. There is an indication, though, that may shed some light on the possibility that your son or daughter will excel to the top levels in a sport. A study from the University of Montreal found a common link between youngsters that were passionate about their particular sport. The key finding they found was that, if children developed a passion about the sport on their own, they were more likely to stay with their sport for a much longer period of time. The study surveyed nearly 600 people between the ages of 6 and 38 and found the key was, children choosing the sport that they had a passion for, not what their parents thought was best for made them better athletes. The study found that overbearing parents made children more anxious about their playing skills. It found that as the anxiety grew players talents began to diminish over time. It also produced an apprehensive effect towards the success of themselves and the sport itself.

The key message here is that, if you have to push your child to go out to practice or to play a game, it may be time to change that sport. If you as the parent find that you are constantly pushing your child in the sport, then you have to seriously reevaluate the situation. It's pretty simple — they either want to do it on their own, or they don't. Obviously, there will be times when they get in a little rut, and you will have help them get out of it. That is expected. It's the constant nagging and prodding that should not exist. The study points out that, if your child makes the decision "on his or her own" regarding playing and practicing, then you may have a possible future pro on your hands. If your child gets up on her own or is reminding you that she has to go and practice, then there is a high probability that she is destined for success.

A sport should be something that a child wakes up for in the morning and wants to do — having fun with friends, enjoying the competition, and most importantly, feeling good about him- or herself when the day is over.

On the other hand, for some kids, sports aren't fun. It's something that doesn't come easy to them and it makes them feel uncomfortable. They may enjoy music, art, dance, or other types of activities. That's okay. Organized sports are not a necessity; however, general and consistent exercise is important to a child's overall health. Your children should be physically active from the day they begin to walk. Get them involved in physical activities that they enjoy. Physical fitness at a young age will help them grow not only as an athlete but also as healthy individuals. The body was designed to move, not to sit on the couch playing video or computer games.

"I believe that the best exercise is the exercise that you enjoy — and will do on a regular basis."

Early Stages of Development

Some children develop slower than others from infancy to toddler stage, which can have an impact later in the teenage years when attempting certain sports. Some infants may not have had the opportunity of being held enough by their mothers or fathers or didn't have sufficient interaction with their parents or siblings. As toddlers, some children may have been put in a jumper for long periods of time, inhibiting their crawling skills. Crawling has a direct affect on neurological and muscular development. According to the Committee for Sports Medicine, "Providing a stimulation environment for an infant's development is extremely important. Environmental deprivation will impede the developmental progress of an infant. There is some evidence that conditioned responses can be elicited in the newborn period."

If you ever wondered why some kids are more adept at certain sports than others, there could be a direct link to how they were raised when they were infants and toddlers. P. Royer noted in his article in the *Scientific Foundations of Pediatrics*, "The bones of infants are more susceptible to trauma than those of older children and adults. The skeletal system of a child in the first year of life is less than optimally ossified." So if you feel that you must develop a system of drills for your infant, I can tell you now — don't. The possibility exists that adults may inadvertently exceed an infant's physical limitations by using structured exercise programs.

Infants develop gross motor skills from the large muscle groups in the arms and legs. Fine motor skills involve smaller muscles in the hands and fingers. Early infancy activities serve as the basis for skillful movement for activities such as sports, dance, and exercise in later childhood and adulthood. The opinion of the Committee on Sports recommends that an infant should be provided with the opportunities for touching, holding, face-to-face contact, and minimally structured playing with safe toys.

If your child wasn't provided this type of interaction, it doesn't necessarily mean that he or she is out of contention for advancing in sports. It just means that the child is going to have to work harder to meet the demands of the sport that he or she is participating in. It seems that the early connections laid down in the nervous system to the muscles helps set the stage to assist the young athlete with motor skills early on.

Some children are more sedentary at a younger age than others. These kids get too hung up watching T.V., playing electronic/video games, or just being protected by an overly cautious parent. They won't get the same strength gains or neuromuscular development as the kids that are outside climbing, running, jumping, and generally playing. Whatever type of young athletes you have, help them as much as you can, but let them develop for themselves. When they're young, encourage them to get involved playing and having fun. It really doesn't matter if it's sports or games. Just get them outside and play! When it comes to sports, let them try a sport first to see if they enjoy playing it. They'll never know if they're good or not if they don't try. If you feel that they are struggling, then by all means get them help, but don't go over the top. Help is one thing, but some parents become obsessed in pushing their kids to become the best on the block.

One problem that I see over and over is when you have an exuberant parent who is thinking too much about the sport and not enough about the child. Not having any background in sports, the parent will sign their kids up for a particular sport, not taking into consideration if the young athlete is ready to play that sport. Many times, the youngster doesn't want any part of the sport but will do it to keep the parents happy. I've seen enthusiastic parents sign their kids up for multiple sports at once. This can be a real strain on not only the parent but the young athlete as well. One mother seriously thought that, by entering her daughter into multiple sports at once, she would be cross-training her child.

There are a whole host of sports that every kid should try, time permitting. It's one of the only ways young people can know if they get pleasure from them or not. I personally enjoy football. I liked playing football, watching football, and talking football. I was average at best when I played, but I enjoyed playing the game. Football has become the national sport and is getting more popular every year. In my opinion, football is great, but the game isn't for everyone. The game of football can be very violent, and for some kids, it just isn't for them. If your son or daughter doesn't like a particular sport, especially football, let his or her try another one. There are plenty of other sports that may be well-suited for him or her to play.

Studies have shown that children who actively participate in sports develop better motor skills, improve critical thinking, improve strategic thinking, improve social interaction, and improve their fitness capabilities. If your child gets involved in sports, you don't have to show up at every practice. The fact is it is better if you don't. If properly organized, you can find the available time to watch your child play their games. It may be hard at times, but it's well worth it.

I took care of Reggie White once for a football related injury. I met his family, including his wife, Sara, and his son Jeremy, and his daughter Jecolia. His son at the time was a tall, thin young man. I found out that during my stay that Jeremy didn't want anything to do with football at that time. Later that day, I was working on Reggie, and he asked me what I thought about his son not having any interest in football. I said it's not what I think; it's what your son thinks that is important. Reggie agreed. All Reggie wanted was to have Jeremy to be happy. Reggie White was one of the best football players of all time, and his son at that time was more interested in playing chess than playing football. Reggie and his wife had absolutely no problem with him not playing football. They never pushed him. They felt that he could make that decision on his own if he ever did.

Parents and Tempers...

Let's face it we all know of 'that parent' who is way over the edge with their kids. We all have seen them, yelling, screaming, at both referee's their kids and anyone else who got in their way. Throughout the country, a code word has popped up regarding overzealous parents — "THOSE parents." Parents that live vicariously through their children's lives, push the edge of the envelope when it comes to attending their children's games. "Those parents" are the parents who can't keep their mouths shut no matter if someone duct-taped their lips together. They not only comment on their own kids, but they go after coaches, referees, and other parents. This has become a national phenomenon that has gotten severely out of control. I've personally seen umpires tell parents to leave the premises because of their obnoxious behavior. There have been parents who went after the referees following the game in an attempt to physically confront them because the umpire made a call against their son that they didn't like. There have even been reports of death between two fathers fighting after their sons' game, when one father took it too far and shot the other one.

How Serious Is It? Here Are Some Eye-Opening Facts:

According to Gwen Moorison in *Giving Back the Game to Our Children,* "the emphasis on winning gets out of control when overzealous parents become aggressive in their quest for being number one. Recent events show that parents have become increasingly hostile at youth sporting events, and the results can be devastating."

Survey USA took a poll of 500 parents in Indianapolis, Indiana, in May of 2001, asking about views of parent violence in youth sports. The survey found the following:

- 55 percent of parents say they have witnessed other parents engaging in verbal abuse at youth sporting events.
- 21 percent say they've witnessed a physical altercation between other parents at youth sporting events.
- 73 percent of those polled believe that parents who become verbally or physically abusive during games should be banned from youth sports.
- 22 percent would allow aggressive parents to remain in the stands.

- 5 percent aren't sure what to do about parents who are prone to sports-induced tantrums.

In July of 2000, during a youth hockey game in Reading, Massachusetts, two fathers started brawling after arguing over rough play. One of them ended up dead, and the other, a man named Thomas Junta, ended up being sentenced to six to 10 years in prison for involuntary manslaughter.

Less dramatic, but still horrifying, a father from California was given 45 days for beating and berating a coach for taking his son, a pitcher, out of a baseball game. According to police, the man was heard screaming, "How dare you make my son a three-inning player?" Steven Booth, *Ventura County Online*

How about the 36-year-old father from Stockton, California, who, after his son was the recipient of a late hit in football, ran onto the field and blindsided the kid with a devastating hit from behind. Yep, you read that right... the father ran onto the field to tackle the opposing football player.

Here are more stories reported to the National Association of Sports Officials and reported by Bill Topp:

A parent body-slammed a high school referee after he ordered the man's wife out of the gym for allegedly yelling obscenities during a basketball game. The referee was treated at a hospital for a concussion and released after the February 6 attack. Charged with simple assault, assault on a sports official, reckless endangerment, and disorderly conduct is Peter J. Dukovich, 47, Hampton, Pennsylvania.

Nicokla Antuofermo, 39, of Old Bridge, New Jersey, was indicted on November 21, 2003, by the Manmouth County grand jury and charged with assault at a youth sports event for an incident that occurred on July 11 during a Babe Ruth baseball game. Antuofermo allegedly bumped and then punched the umpire during an argument. Under New Jersey law, he could face up to 18 months in prison and $10,000 in fines.

James Camden, 43, of Tennessee was charged with two counts of aggravated battery and one count of battery after allegedly charging onto the field and attempting to choke game official Mike Byrne, a 27-year officiating veteran. Franklin County assistant state attorney Aaron Hopkins said that battery is a misdemeanor, and aggravated battery is a Class 4 felony, which could include prison time if convicted.

The parent of a Davenport, Iowa Assumption basketball player turned the team's final game of the regular season into a boxing match by assaulting a referee who was getting ready to shower after the game, police said. Assumption parent Daniel Ewen, 47, of Davenport, went down the stairs and began pounding on the glass near the referee locker room, upset about a call at the end of the game, police said. Referee Timothy McCann, 46, of Eldridge, wore only a towel when he opened the door to ask Ewen to leave, police said. Ewen leaped through the opened door and assaulted McCann, who was treated and released at Genesis Medical Center-East Campus for injuries to his right arm and face, police said. Police cited Ewen for assault with injury, a serious misdemeanor.

Dontravian Evans, 29, received a sentence of nine months in jail following his felony assault conviction for punching a referee at a recreational basketball game in Long Beach, California. In addition to the jail sentence, Evans received three years' probation and must pay $3,400 to the victim, referee Kevin Robinson, for medical bills. The incident happened on September 13, 2000, early in the game, when the score was only 2-0. Evans, who was upset about a call, struck Robinson when he was looking at the scorers' table. Robinson didn't see the punch coming. The blow caused permanent damage to Robinson's eye.

A co-ed softball game turned violent when 34-year-old Charles J. Mitchell (Boca Raton, Florida) allegedly assaulted and battered 74-year-old volunteer umpire Les Barr during a recreational game in Coconut Creek, Florida. Barr suffered a fractured kneecap and inflamed a World War II army injury during the fracas. According to eyewitnesses, problems began after the second inning, when Mitchell objected to Barr calling a teammate out at second base and used a common vulgarity. Mitchell took his position at first base for the next inning while continuing to berate Barr with vulgarities. Barr issued a warning and then ejected him. Mitchell then spat in Barr's face, according to police. When Barr turned to wipe his face, police said Mitchell jumped the umpire from behind, putting him into a chokehold and wrestling him to the ground. As Barr lost consciousness, two players pried Mitchell off the umpire. Mitchell was booked for aggravated battery on the elderly, a first-degree felony.

Different Sports Have Different Parents to Deal With

Tennis parents have their own type of strategies to help their children. If the child is exceptional, there is a high possibility that the child will enter a tennis academy. These academies are extremely intense and make the athletes commit their entire lives to the sport. They practice six to eight hours per day along with schooling. There are strong indications that many "academy" players have a hard time dealing with the rigors of academy life. The vast majority of them never make it to the top levels in the sport of tennis.

Many gymnastics parents have unrealistic dreams of their kids making the Olympics. One parent that was in my office with his young daughter made the comment, "I hope you pulled your date page off your calendar today. There are only 1,000 days left until the next Olympics." The girl was 10 years old. The father didn't understand that his daughter had to be older to participate in the Olympics. I've seen other parents yell and scream at their kids even after it was apparent a child was injured. The parents felt that they weren't being "tough enough," even though they could see the child was in appreciable pain. The funny thing is that many of these parents never attempted playing any type of sport when they were young.

A Coaches View of Parents

I interviewed a coach in gymnastics who coached at a top level of competition. She reported to me that she wanted to explain to the parents what it's really like on the other side of the bleachers. His/her name was left out on purpose so that there would be no repercussions in the gymnastic world.

What is the thought process behind coaching in gymnastics?
Answer:

As a coach when I see a kid come into the gym the first thing we do is size up the child. Height, weight, movement and then I take a look at the parents. I want to size up the physical aspect of the kid before anything else.

So let's say Suzie who is 8 years old is muscular, physical in movement, very coordinated and it seems things come really easy to her I will then go over and look at her parents. If the parents are both over six feet then I know that this girl may grow too tall for the sport so we may not want to spend the quality time with her. If the parents are shorter than that is a much better in this sport.

The next thing we want to know is what type of money they have. Can they afford to do this for the next 10 years? The average cost in a bigger gym is about $10,000.00 per year when it's all said and done. That is with travel, entry fees, dues and other items needed to do this sport. For some elite international gymnasts it can go up to $15,000.00 if the governing body of gymnastics doesn't pick up part of the expense.

A young gymnast has to be fearless and have a desire if they want to succeed in this sport. And you have to have this at a very early age for example eleven years old.

What are some things you see developing in the sport which you don't like?

Answer:

I don't like that many of the coaches are ego driven. A lot of the owners of the gym's want to produce scores so that their club gets recognition and to become known. What you begin to see is that you have 30 kids but the coach is only really coaching 5 out of the 30. Keep in mind that everyone is paying the same. Even when it's early on when it's costing you less you as the parent are still paying the money but your kid is being treated like a second class citizen. That goes all the way up to the top levels.

There are some coaches who won't take some of their kids to a meet because they don't feel they will score high enough and bring the team score down. Even though that kid put in the same amount of time as everyone else but for now isn't just up to the rest of the top performers.

I don't like that they don't provide the conditioning to keep the kids injury free and get them to the level they need to be to properly compete. They look at it like the conditioning isn't going to keep the kid in the sport so we won't have the numbers. It's all about keeping the numbers in the gym to support the upper levels (more advanced gymnasts). So they aren't really creating any athletes most of the time they're just taking your money. When it comes down to it there are only a few in the gym that they want to promote at the regional and national levels. The rest of the kids are there to create the money to support the upper levels.

You'll hear the owners say... "oh gymnastics is for everybody...we love everybody...we're a big family." That's not what I see, yea they love you if you keep paying, or you can bring recognition to the gym but that's where it ends. The more publicity a kid gets in competition from winning the more new kids join the gym as a result.

Why do you say that conditioning is down? Don't coaches need better conditioned kids to do better?

Answer:

There are always a couple of kids that are so durable, so naturally strong, so naturally flexible that there successful without that kind of conditioning. They can get these kids up to a higher level without it so they will do a minimum amount. Many coaches don't understand that if they better conditioned these upper level athletes they would not only do better but would reduce their injuries.

What many coaches don't really get is that now they have let's say three or four upper level athletes in a group that excel. If they really conditioned better they could probably get an extra 5 or 6 up to the upper levels. And on top of that the injury rate would drop.

Many of the owners and the coaches don't fully understand when a gymnast crosses that line at around eleven to thirteen years old things change in the body. Hormones are different, the skeleton changes, muscles are different they aren't as resilient as they were when they were really young. At this age when you keep pushing and pushing now you're in danger of really hurting them if you don't properly condition them. If you slow them down and condition them properly you can reduce injury and create a better athlete. So now we get back to the numbers again. They push them, and keep pushing them until they break. When they break – oh, well. Let's get the other up here and keep going. It's numbers, if you keep the numbers coming in then you can keep repeating this over and over.

Owners then to be different and I'm not sure what makes them tick. Not many look at the individual child to say, what type of human being will she/he grow up to be, how will this help he in life. No they want to know how hard can we push her/him, what can they produce for the gym?

Out of all of the coaches that you've worked with and all of the coaches that you've watched coach from all over the country how many are truly competent to take a young athlete to the top?

Answer:

Geez, for all the time that I've been doing this there has only been a hand full. There are a few gyms that I've seen where all of their kids do amazing, not just a couple. There are a few gyms that come to mind that excel at every level and do this year in and year out so they know what they are doing. It doesn't matter if its one kid or 20 kids at each level they all do very well.

How can coaches harm kids in this sport?

Answer:

When coaches coach on demand it can cause harm meaning that they attempt to bully you to do skills you may not be ready for. Instead of looking at each kid individually or looking at each kid to see what they are lacking as far as strength or skill is concerned. Figuring out how they are mentally or what technique is wrong - instead of trying to fix it they just attempt to push them through. Most coaches don't have the upper level experience to teach correctly.

So when a kid doesn't produce then they start berating the kid. The will start telling them that they are lazy, their weak and not realign it may be them that have the problem not getting to the real answer. There is always a push on because time is against you in this sport so if you don't get to a certain level by a certain age you are over with as far as the coaches and owners are concerned.

What is your opining of parents are in this sport?

Answer:

It the parents that I see that seems to me that develop a 'cult' like mentality or some kind of disease going on by living vicariously through their kids. Parents will punish their kids for not being successful in this sport. I've seen them totally neglect the other kids in the family. Their happiness lies within the success of their child week by week.

Parents feel that they are doing everything for their kid the least they can do is win every meet. They take it to such extremes. Some kids change their minds when they hit a certain age. They say, "I know I wanted the sport but now I don't know if I want to be in this gym 5 hours a day, six days a week." The parents will say, "Absolutely not, I'll give you an IPod or I'll give get you new clothes or you'll be punished if you don't continue." I've seen them bribe them to unbelievable extremes basically imprisoning them to the sport. Then you begin to see the fire go out of the kids eyes and they begin to go downhill from there. No matter how many hours they put in they just end up mediocre because there is nothing in them that really wants to do it anymore.

I see many parents home school their kid, get them in the gym 45 hours per week then do more conditioning at home, they don't feed them, they want to keep them under weight and they let them do only a half an hour of school per night. Make the older sister do the homework and half these kids end up being illiterate. The driving force for many of these parents are … "you go in there and win, win, win. This happen much more than people know or are willing to admit to.

There are parents out there doing the homework for the kids every night or someone on in the house will do the homework for them while one of the parents will condition them all night long. This is after the kid being in the gym for five hours. Kids are held back on purpose not just one year but many times two years. They get so dead set on their kid becoming a champion that they forget about the rest of their life.

If 100 kids come into the gym to train for gymnastics how many would you say in your experience are going to the Olympics?

Answer:

Probably none. It takes a special type of person to put it all together to get to that level.

In my opinion to get to the Olympics you have to have a really super fit, naturally gifted child who has the right type of training, the right type of instruction, the right type of coaching with parents who can financially support it. The child has to have the right type of personality that is self-motivated and self-driven. I don't care how talented you are, I've seen a lot of talented kids, if you don't have that drive you'll never make it. It's ok if you don't you'll do well and get on in life without any problems.

I have met very few kids that have that kind of drive, talent and motivation that can get to the top.

So what would you say about the parent who get too involved?

Answer:

Well there are the kids who sacrifice an education because of their parent's overzealous attempt to get them to the Olympics. I know one little girl that when she was young it was told to her mother that she had all the talent to become a world class gymnast. Some of the best people in the sport thought early on that she could be the best. She is tiny, strong, and flexible but she really never liked the sport and didn't want to be in it from when she was young. Right now, it seems that the mother is pushing her so hard it seems that the kid is being held against her will. She is at the gym 40 hours a week, the coaches don't really want her there because she's not a worker because she doesn't want to be there. But her mother insists that she must be there because she is going to be an elite athlete some day. They end up getting in trouble because they hate what they're doing. You get kids in the gym that come in and cry everyday but the parents just blow it off like its nothing.

How about eating and food with coaches, parents and the kids.
Answer:

I don't think the coaches have too much of a problem with food. We have to weigh the kids all of the time but overall it's not too bad of a problem. I've seen kids who have been over weight and needed to lose weight because it's hard on them to do this sport if you are overweight. We've had kids under weight and I've heard about parents locking food up at home so they couldn't eat. I witnessed one mother wave a Hershey's bar from the stands telling her kid that if she did well she would let her eat the bar.

In swimming, I personally witnessed a father screaming at the top of his voice at his son not to go over to the coach until he came to talk to him first after he swam. The father had to make sure that he had to go over the young swimmer's poor technique with him immediately after the event. The young swimmer didn't have a good race, so the overbearing father had to berate this kid in front of the parents, fans, teammates, and the official's right as he got out of the water.

In baseball, I witnessed a father scream from the bleachers at his son after striking out. He actually was walking down the side of the field yelling at his kid, and he walked back to the dugout. "Can't you see? Are you blind? I told you not to swing at those high pitches!" The poor kid was scared to come up to bat the next time for fear of his father yelling at him again.

Football parents can be as intense as anyone in sports. At one high school football game, there was a young player who wasn't playing up to what the coach thought was his potential. The coach decided to pull him out of the game and put another player in. The father of the son who was pulled went wild. He began a tirade of screaming and yelling at the coach from the stands. Now keep in mind that the stands were crowded with hundreds of people, a band playing, and people cheering. You could still hear this guy screaming and yelling at the coaches. He kept it up over and over until they had to call the police to have him taken out.

An obsessed parent, unable to deal with his son not being a perfect mini-football player, lashed out at his son on the sideline during a game. The player's father was a coach, and his son was a running back. On one particular play, the son fumbled the ball. When he came to the sideline, the father made him give him his mouth piece. The father took the mouthpiece and threw it in the dirt and mud, and he stomped on it, pushing it deep into the ground. He then made his son pick it up, without wiping it off, and put it back into his mouth and go back in the game. This insane action by the father was supposedly to toughen his son up.

Some parents can really hurt their kids with the notion that they are trying to help. Take the case of the parent who came into my office bragging to me how he was really helping his young wrestler because the coach didn't know what he was doing. The coach wanted the young wrestler to drop weight so that he could wrestle at a weight below, which would help the team win. The young wrestler was having a difficult time losing the weight, so the mother told me that she knew better, and she had a better way than the coach did. The two genius parents decided that they were going to help their son get that weight off so he could wrestle at the lower weight. These two brilliant parents took it upon themselves to take their son and put a plastic sweat suit on him. They then took him to the laundromat and put him inside the dryer. Yep, you read that right! To help their son lose weight, they put the kid in the dryer to help him lose weight faster.

The pressures that some parents put on their kids can be overwhelming. In fact, many kids develop feelings of inadequacy and tend to drop out of sports. According to Dr. Michael Goldberg in *Pediatric News*, February 2002, "Twenty-five million children aged 6-18 years play organized sports in the United States, but 35% drop out annually. This is really startling, because if we look at sports as an educational program, we would hate to see 35% of kids dropping out of the seventh grade."

Twenty million kids register each year for youth hockey, football, baseball, soccer, and other competitive sports. The National Alliance for Sports reports that 70 percent of these kids quit playing these league sports by age 13 and never play them again. According to Michael Pfahl, executive director of the National Youth Sports

Coaches Association, "The number one reason (why they quit) is that it stopped being fun."

Emotional Abuse

According to the National Youth Safety Foundation, Inc., in Boston, Massachusetts, emotions, as defined by Richard Lazarous, professor emeritus at Cal-Berkeley, are as follows: "Negative emotions include: anger, anxiety, fright, sadness, guilt, shame, envy, jealousy, and disgust. Positive emotions we would like developed include: relief, hope, happiness/joy, pride, love, gratitude, and compassion."

Emotional abuse occurs when an individual treats a child in a negative manner that impairs the child's concept of self. This group of individuals may include a parent/guardian/caregiver, coach, teacher, brother, sister, or a friend. Emotional abuse is, perhaps, the most difficult abuse to identify and the most common form of maltreatment in youth sports. Examples include rejecting; ignoring; isolating; terrorizing; name-calling; making fun of someone; putting someone down; saying things that hurt feelings; and/or yelling.

Additional examples of emotional abuse:

- Forcing a child to participate in sports
- Not speaking to a child after he/she plays poorly in a youth sports game or practice
- Asking a child why he/she played poorly when "it meant so much to you"
- Hitting a child when his/her play disappoints you
- Yelling at a child for not playing well or for losing
- Punishing a child for not playing well or for losing
- Criticizing and/or ridiculing a child for his/her sports performance

Statements such as "You're stupid," "You're an embarrassment," and "You're not worth the uniform you play in" are damaging and hurt a young athlete's self-esteem and his or her perception of value as a human being. If said long and strong enough, these statements or other negative statements like them may become beliefs held by the athlete and may carry forth into his or her adult life.

Parents Behind Closed Doors

There have been parents who, behind closed doors, push the envelope of sports in order "to help the athlete" achieve the best in his or her sport. I've witnessed parents stop feeding their children because they were too "fat" in the sport of gymnastics. The girl weighed less than 95 pounds. If you looked at the girl, you would think that she could have possibly come from a third-world country. The mother was practically teaching her how to develop an eating disorder. Another gymnastics parent waved a Hershey's Bar in the air as a type of reward if the girl did well in a particular event. This particular athlete would sneak behind her mother's back and have other girls bring her a couple of hot dogs from the food stand because she was so hungry.

There are examples of child abuse going on in sports all over the country. On one particular YouTube video, a parent is caught with his arm around his son saying, "I'm going to get you tonight because you let me down." The son asks him why, and the father says, "I don't care what the f*%# you say. You let me down. If you're not going to play 100 percent, I'll get you buddy... cry about that." This was at a Little League baseball game.

How Common Is Abuse in Youth Sports?

The Minnesota Amateur Sports Commission conducted a survey in 1993 and found the following incidences of abuse in sports in Minnesota:

- 45.3% of males and females surveyed said they have been called names, yelled at, or insulted while participating in sports.
- 17.5% of people surveyed said they have been hit, kicked, or slapped while participating in sports.
- 21% said they have been pressured to play with an injury.

- 8.2% said they have been pressured to intentionally harm others while playing sports.
- 3.4% said they have been pressured into sex or sexual touching.
- 8% of all surveyed said they have been called names with sexual connotations while participating in sports.

Children who have had strong reactions to viewing violence or aggression could develop post-traumatic stress disorder. The trauma associated with witnessing violence can adversely affect a child's ability to learn. Childhood abuse increases the likelihood that the youth will engage in health-risk behaviors including suicidal behavior and delinquent and aggressive behaviors in adolescence. Abuse in childhood has been linked to a variety of adverse health outcomes in adulthood. These include mood and anxiety disorders and diseases.

Violence is a learned behavior. Our children are often learning violence from places where they should be learning positive life skills. Abuse will "turn the child off" to exercise and sports participation and prevent the development of healthy lifestyles that will promote wellness throughout the lifespan.

Can you imagine that, after a major presentation at work in front of your office workers, your boss comes to you in front of everyone and starts screaming and yelling at you? "What the hell was that? Haven't I told you over and over never start a sentence with 'however'? What the hell where you thinking about? If you can't do this, I'll get someone else!"

Sports is the only area of our lives where we feel that we can just empty out our bad feelings towards athletes in an abusive manner. Fans yell and throw things at players, while other fans sit in the stands. The fans are so bad in Philadelphia that they installed a judge and jail right in the stadium. Sports are different, and for some reason, people think that they can do whatever they want at sporting events. I'm sure you remember the father and son who attacked the baseball manager on the first base coaching box and began beating him up. Kansas City first-base coach Tom Gamboa was attacked from behind and began hitting the defenseless Gamboa. The bare-chested father, identified by police as 34-year-old William Ligue Jr. of Alsip, and his 15-year-old son were led off the field in handcuffs.

There is a growing controversy on protecting players from out-of-control fans. How much is too much? Most recently, a fan got loose on the field in Philadelphia, and the security guards trapped and tasered him to the ground. More aggressive measures are being taken all over the county to protect professional players from harm.

Why is it that in sports we lash out so excessively? I submit to you that, after watching hours and hours of sports on T.V., we've all become closet athletes and coaches. So we all think we can do it better. I've always said, it's pretty easy to coach sitting in the stands with a beer in your hand. What I find funny is that I've never seen the fans at the Academy Awards red carpet start screaming obscenities at the actors. I've never heard of reports of a fan yelling, "My God, you blew that sentence in the second scene on the bridge. You suck!" I know that John Travolta has made some pretty bad films, and Alex Rodriguez has had plenty of errors at third base, but I don't see people screaming at John Travolta.

Looking for the Money...

Many overzealous parents are looking for a free education in college for their children. Statistically, the chances for college scholarships are slim. The numbers don't lie. According to John Millea of the *Star Tribune* in Minneapolis, Minnesota:

- For every 100 high school athletes, there is one full athletic scholarship available.
- More than 60 percent of all NCAA athletes receive no athletic scholarship aid. This includes Division III, which does not give out athletic aid.
- The average NCAA athlete on scholarship gets, per year, about $10,000 less than the value of a full scholarship.

What most parents don't know is that most scholarships are given at Division I. There are some scholarships given at Division II and

Division III, and the ivy leagues do not give out athletic scholarships. In fact, some/most schools have to split up their scholarships between all of the players. For example, at the University of Minnesota, the baseball team had only 11.7 full-ride scholarships. The problem was that they had 35 players looking for the free ride. In actuality, the 11.7 scholarships have to be split between most of the 35 players. It gets much worse for tennis, field hockey, and other sports. There are other sports that say that they give complete scholarships like track and field, but in reality, those athletes are getting a very small portion of the athletic money.

How Can A Parent Help Their Athlete

Support your sons and daughters. Be there for them when they win, and be there for them when they lose or when things get tough in their lives. They are looking for some support and attention to talk and be listened to. It's tough with the stresses of today to be dealing with academics, sports, practices, coaches, and fans. The last thing they need is to have someone busting their chops when they walk through the door at the end of a day.

Most kids would much rather have their moms or dads say to them, "Hey, we're really proud of you," then have all of the fans stand up and cheer for them at a game.

Mom and dad, you know what it's like to have pressure from work follow you around. You know what it feels like to have the boss breathing down your back. I'm here to tell you that your kids can feel the same pressure from you if you repetitively brow-beat them about doing better. Can you imagine after working all day you come home to someone who begins to yell at you because you didn't put in a good enough effort? Or if you didn't get the raise you wanted, and someone in the house starts hounding you over and over that you're not dedicated or that you didn't want it bad enough.

Change the picture for a second. It's been one of those weeks at work where mostly everything went wrong, and by this time of the week, you are drained. You pull into your driveway, and all you hear is that you are a loser and that you won't make anything of yourself.

That you're not tough enough like the other workers in your job and that you have become soft.

How would you feel? I'm sure not so good.

Talk "with" your children, not "at" them. Listen to them and what they have to say. Many times, you're too busy thinking what you want to say next without fully listening to them complete their thoughts.

Lighten up and enjoy what they do on the field, in the gym, on the soccer field, in the swimming pool, or whatever sport it is. Don't take things so damn seriously because it's a game they're playing. Enjoy the games now because you're not going to have these games forever. If every sport was easy, every player would be a superstar. Professional baseball players still make errors, pro football players still drop the ball, and professional soccer player still get carded. You don't think that is going to happen to your teenage son or daughter? Take a step back, and try to better understand what your child is going through before you become "one of those parents."

When Parenting Is Too Much or Too Little

Every parent wants the best for their children. I've seen overzealous parents at games and would wonder to myself what is going through their minds. On the other hand, I witnessed other kids who never had any parents at the games at all. I began to wonder which was worse. I guess for now I feel that the overbearing parent is much better than the absentee parent. The jury is still out in my mind on this one, though.

Are you a coach or a parent? Tough decision if your child plays sports.

If you're going to be a coach of your own child, please know something about the sport. Nothing is more transparent when you attempt to become an authority of nothing. Take some time to learn the basics, or better yet, get someone else to help you who knows more about it. This way, they will make you look good.

Also, sit down with your child and let him or her know who they are talking to — you the coach or you the parent. To us older adults, in our minds, it's pretty easy to understand the difference. But keep in mind that, to a 12-year-old, it's difficult to separate the two.

Sit with your child and tell him or her that on the field you're the coach, and at home, you're the dad or mom. This way, it's easier for your child to separate the differences between both. While coaching, be a coach, not an enabler or someone just there to give more attention to. Be a coach.

When you get home, STOP being a coach and return to being a parent. Leave the sport back on the field, and let your child be a child at home. You will have plenty of time to continue your instruction back on the field another day.

As a coach, teach your athletes the importance of fitness, nutrition, hydration, and sleep. I know many young kids could care less about most of these issues, but you'll be surprised how much will be received when you attempt to teach them.

When the Athlete Decides to Take the Path Less Traveled

In one family, under one roof, three young men grew up in very tough conditions. So tough were the conditions, the mother and grandmother took those young men out of that environment and moved the family to a town that had much less violence. Under that roof, all three young men were blessed with amazing athletic talent. They all went to the same high school, they all played football, and all three ran track. Two of the young men decided to turn it into a profession. The youngest decided to turn down a different path. Many athletes have good hearts but make bad decisions, and those decisions can change lives in an instant.

Sulaiman Ismail is the youngest brother of Raghib "Rocket" Ismail and Qadry "Missile" Ismail. Rocket played college football at the University of Notre Dame, going on to play 10 years in the NFL. Qadry played college football at Syracuse University, becoming one of only two athletes in the school's history [Jim Brown being the other athlete] to become two-sport All Americans.

After having a run in with the law, Sulaiman was incarcerated in prison for allegedly committing a federal felony with the sales of illegal drugs. He has served his time in federal prison and has now gotten back with his family and is currently working at a publishing company. Sulaiman has a black belt in Shotokan Karate, judo, and jujutsu. He has fought professionally in the Mixed Martial Arts (MMA) and is currently operating a training facility for mixed martial arts, training upcoming MMA fighters. He also uses his talents to teach mini-football to kids in the small town of Kingston, Pennsylvania.

The following paragraphs are an attempt to allow you to look into the mind of a highly skilled athlete who practically threw away his talents. Sulaiman Ismail possessed incredible talent, every bit as much talent as his brothers, but he wasted it on what he thought was "the good life." The following interview will help you better understand how someone with everything to gain in life almost lost everything he ever lived for.

Conway: What type of athlete were you when you were young?

Ismail: I was a great athlete. I was a diamond in the rough, full of tons of talent, but I didn't take the time to meet the challenge of turning that diamond in the rough into the brilliant sparkling diamond I could have been.

Conway: How did you train when you were a young athlete?

Ismail: Lazily. I didn't put in a third of the work I should have. I didn't have the work ethic that was needed to propel me to the top.

Conway: What was it like growing up as the younger brother in a house with two nationally ranked athletes?

Ismail: It was great! As far as not living in their shadow, it was great. When I was younger, being the brother of two great athletes was just okay. But then as I got older, people would say, "Are you the Rocket's brother?" or "Aren't you the Missile's brother?" I would say, "They are my brothers." So slowly over time, it started to get to me. It depended on who I was talking to or what they were looking for, depending on how I would react.

Conway: When you were younger, did you feel any pressure of being the younger brother of the "Rocket" or the "Missile"?

Ismail: No, not at all. I always knew that I just wanted to do my own thing. When my brothers were younger living in New Jersey, they knew from an early age [that] they wanted to be professional football players. As a little kid, I wanted to be a fireman, policeman, the regular things that most young kids wanted to be. I remember walking to football practice with both of them in Jersey, and here I am having no interest in football at that time.

Conway: What did you feel about your brothers constantly gaining recognition as you grew up?

Ismail: I felt great. Their recognition was my recognition. I always was proud of them with everything they did.

Conway: At what point in your life did you feel you changed away from the norms of growing up and found yourself getting in trouble?

Ismail: It was gradual. Little by little, I think after my father passed, the seed was planted. Then little things happening here and there. The seed that I'm speaking of was no father figure and no guidance in my life. I was getting away with more and more and no one telling me what to do or how to correct that type of acting out.

Conway: What was your mindset when this seed continued to grow and as you found yourself in more trouble?

Ismail: Stealing came about as a kid not having anything. When we were young in the Acme market, we would steal little things because we didn't have much at all growing up. Not having any money or not having what you wanted all the time, you looked to sneak something here or there, and it got worse as time when on. Then, finally getting caught and looking at major time stopped me from stealing again. That was when I got caught breaking into the deli that I worked at. My brother threw me out of the house when I was 18, and I began to live with some friends in an apartment. I was working at a local deli but wasn't making enough money, and I couldn't make rent. So I put together a plan to rob the store after hours because I knew where the lock box was, and I knew the video and alarms weren't working. It had nothing to do with drinking or drugs at all.

Conway: When did drugs and alcohol enter the picture with you?

Ismail: I first drank a half a can of Michelob when I was 15 and threw up. I first started around marijuana when I liked this girl who used marijuana a lot, so I thought I would impress her by getting a bunch of marijuana seeds for her. [Laughing] Tells you how much I knew about drugs then. It's funny that, during any sport that I was involved with, I never partied, but when the season was over, I found myself with too much time on my hands and would play around with some drugs and alcohol. My mother was never there. She was either traveling to Notre Dame or to Syracuse. So in my senior year, I had the house to myself. That's when alcohol began to play a big part in my life.

Conway: The first time you were incarcerated was for what?

Ismail: It was for a speeding ticket. I was coming down from Syracuse [and] was pulled over from speeding, and the police said my license had been revoked. So they took me into the police station, and my brother Qadry had to come and get me to get out of jail. Believe it or not, I'm in this holding cell, and this other guy starts attacking me for no reason. I had to defend myself in that cell against this guy, thinking I was only speeding, and now I'm in the middle of all this. The whole experience was so overwhelming it was unreal. As I said before, the seed was planted, and now the flower is growing. I was put in jail a few more times for violation of my probation. I did two more five-day stints in jail. Then I ended up doing 60 days, followed years later by a five-month lock-up.

Conway: Were you not understanding the repercussions of your actions at that time?

Ismail: I didn't care at that point. I was just doing me. They said I was an existentialist. The first probation violation was about missing curfew, and I knew I was home on time. They didn't believe me and threw me in jail anyway. But I was home before curfew. I know it.

Then after that, my thought process was 'F' the police and the probation people; I'm going to look out for myself. I just didn't trust anyone anymore, so I didn't care. I didn't care about life itself, but it seemed everything was coming down around me. I got hurt, and I wasn't able to play arena football. It just seemed that adversity now was following me. My brother Raghib seemed that everything he touched turned to gold. Qadry had this unreal work ethic, and he found the gold through hard work. Everywhere I turn, some type of bad situation was somehow in front of me. So for things not to be going my way, I said, "You know, what if this is the only way I can make things go my way? Then this is the life I'm going to live." If I have to take things in control of my life, then that is what I'll do. I'll do what I have to do, and I will make things happen for myself.

Conway: What was happening in your life prior to your last incarceration?

Ismail: I wanted to make a change in my life, but I didn't know how. A couple of days later, I was moving out of the house that I was living in at that time. I was in the middle of setting up worse things in my life and couldn't break the habit of the lifestyle I was in. I was in the middle of bringing up kilos of marijuana from El Paso to Pennsylvania to sell. I got back in touch with a guy I knew from going to school down there and made a connection to move kilos of weed up here. I was moving out, and I was setting up people in different apartments for this deal to work. Then, while we were moving out of the house the one day, I had a few girls moving things out for me. They went outside to put things in the car. I was on the cell phone at the time and wasn't paying a lot of attention to my surroundings. I opened the door to let the girls in, and again I was on the phone, so I wasn't paying all that much attention. I closed and locked the door behind them, and the second I locked the door, I hear *boom, boom, boom*, "Open up. We have a search warrant." In my head, I'm thinking this is a joke, and I was about to open the door, and something told me not to open it, and I had a feeling that this wasn't a joke, that I better get out of here. There was a clear path from where I was to the back door, which was open at the time leading to a moving van. I took off running as fast as

I could to get out of the house, but in the meantime, there was a guy coming in (a federal agent). I'm running at full speed, and I see the guy coming in, and all I see [is] the guy coming up in camouflage. As I came upon him, I remember saying, "Oh God no," and just threw my arm up really fast, and he just disappeared. I jumped down on the U-Haul, jumped down, hopped the fence, and took off. I don't remember even hitting the guy. It was like a running back reacting to a defensive player. I threw my arm up and kept going straight ahead. I ended up going up to the Poconos to lay out for awhile, and five days later, I turned myself in.

Conway: Why did you turn yourself in?

Ismail: For my children. I could have been in another country or could have kept going and kept on the run for a long time. I've seen guys do [that], and I made the decision that I'm not going to live a life like that. I'm going to turn myself in and get this over with, and at the same time, I knew I didn't do what I was being accused of doing. It wasn't as bad as people made it out to be. I'm up in the Poconos, and it's on the news, so I called the news station and asked for a particular reporter that I knew, but he couldn't come to the phone. I called back after the news was over, and I said, "You have to stop running that story about me because you're telling lies. I didn't knock anybody out." They were making it out to be that I stopped and beat the guy up on the way out of the door. Anyway, I didn't want to be in that lifestyle of being on the run, and that is why I turned myself in.

Conway: When you first went into prison after turning yourself in, what did you think about?

Ismail: They told me that I was looking at 17 or more years. When I first got in the cell, that was 6 by 9. Its like putting a puppy in a cage, and he barks all night, and then he finally gets used to it. At the beginning, being locked down [with] suicidal thoughts, "This can't be it," "I'm not going to spend the rest of my life here," or "I'm going to kill somebody." Mentally, it was really tough at first. The transition wasn't that long, and in the first couple of months, I could start to see a change, although I didn't have the tools to go to where I needed to be yet. Before I got locked up, I was doing a lot of ecstasy, and my mind continued to race, and I didn't know why until I slowly began to detox, and slowly I began to get my mind back.

Over time, I began to see things more objectively. I tried to rationalize things more rather than just action out. I had the quick temper that I was getting under control. It's okay to be angry, that is a normal emotion, [but] what are you going to do when you get angry? So now, what am I going to do? Am I going to act out, or am I going to take that energy and do something positive? So I made an effort to change my mindset to turn my thinking around. So when I got challenged or confronted in the prison, I wouldn't get sucked in to the other inmates' crap. I made that decision under pressure when people were coming against me. From there, I began to work even harder on my attitude, and I remember reading Matthew Kelly, *The Rhythm of Life*. Then I just continued to read more books like that. I then started applying little things from what I was reading. I read the Bible all the way through a couple of times. I became calmer. I was able to handle stressful situations much better. I still needed work, but I was trying to make a change in my life.

Conway: So what can you say to athletes to help them avoid the mistakes that you made in your life, with any athlete who wants to better him- or herself but is going down the wrong road?

Ismail: I would ask them, what do you want? What do you want in life? What do you want out of sports, out of friends, out of school? What is the end result that you want to take out from your life experience? So let's say they respond by saying, "I want to be a millionaire. I want to be famous. I want to set these records." Well, what you are doing right now is not going to help you get what you want. If you plant an apple tree wanting to eat peaches, no matter what you do, you're not going to get apples. If your attitude is aligned on positive emotions, that will drive you towards your goals. If you keep up what you are doing now, you will never get to where you want to go. I don't how much talent you have, because you may get there on talent alone, but it sure won't benefit you once you are there, and more importantly, it's not going to last. Because you are not setting up characteristics properly that will make it last.

Conway: What would you say to parents concerning their children that are athletes and helping them become elite athletes?

Ismail: What do you feel you are going to get out of that child? Right now, if you're spoiling them, you're enabling them and holding them back. It's a matter of understanding what you want, then developing a strategy from there.

The parents need to be able to set boundaries, correct with discipline. IF the child goes outside the set boundaries, the discipline will be handed down accordingly. Another thing that is needed is consistency with what you say. The child wants all the characteristics in the parents that are transferred over to me, the child, because I'm going to be a product of my environment. So as a child, I need the same discipline characteristics from the parent to be passed down to me.

How You Can Become an Elite Parent

First and foremost, you have to develop a good communication line between both you and your athlete. The word used in the above sentence was *develop*, not try. Work with your children to set up a two-way standard of communication. You have to work with them so that both of you are on the same page. At all times, you have to be a parent, but you have to develop a mutual level of trust.

You can't be a parent and a friend at the same time. It's too confusing to the child. You have to set the rules of your home and live with them. You son or daughter is looking for direction, boundaries, and for someone to show him or her the way. It's a balance of equal amounts of praise and discipline to help them excel in life.

Don't be wishy washy. If you mean it, then carry it out. If you keep changing your mind, they will begin to feel you don't mean what you say and challenge you at every point in the future. There is an old saying… "Don't give a command that you can't carry out."

Help them with their nutrition. Make sure they are getting the right foods in them to help them develop and recover. The active rule of thumb is that, if you are getting 85% of good, nutritious foods on a regular basis, don't worry about the other 15%. The body can handle it.

Good foods are all vegetables, fruits, and lean protein sources such as turkey, chicken, eggs, fish, various red meats, and nuts. Attempt to use whole grain breads, pastas, and rice, and don't be afraid to experiment a little with new things.

- Low Sugar
- High Protein
- High Fiber

Athletes need plenty of protein and fat to help recover their muscles, tendons, and ligaments. I feel that an active athlete should be getting one gram of protein for every pound of body weight they carry. This protein will help the muscles recover so that they can continue to work hard at practice and in games.

Make sure they get plenty of water. Fifty ounces per day is a great starting point to consume if you have a high school athlete. For middle school/elementary school athletes, 20 to 30 ounces per day is a good amount. Hydration is very important in maintaining the body's systems while it is working hard and under stress. Remember that, when you sweat, you lose water that is up and beyond what you normally need in a regular day. So keep the water moving every day.

Talk with your children to see what is on their minds. Find out what they're thinking about and LISTEN! Let them tell you what is going on in their lives. Give them advice, but don't start talking down to them. Communication is a two-way street. You speak, they listen. Then they speak, and you listen.

"One thing I've learned is that it is more important to be interested than to be interesting."

This is a great way for the athlete to relieve stress and get some feedback on how they are doing. As adults, we take for granted the problems of youngsters because we've already gone through them. We as parents have been through the battles, and presently, we look down on those silly things of childhood or adolescence. Your son/daughter, however, is just going through this particular part of his or her life, and it's new and sometimes scary… and yes, it is a big deal to him or her. Just being there for your child is much, much more than you can ever expect.

Learn as much about the sport as you can. Nothing can be more frustrating to young athletes than when they try to tell their parents about their sport, and the parents have no clue about what they are talking about. They don't want to hear how happy you are that they scored a goal when you hit the ball over the fence in baseball. At least, learn the basics. You don't have to become an expert, but get to know what they are doing so you can better understand what they are going through. Better yet, go out in the backyard or the park, and try doing it yourself for an hour. It will give you a much better appreciation of what they are doing and how hard it can be.

An athlete needs sleep! No negotiation. Unfortunately, kids normally don't buy into this one because they think they're invincible. Sleep is just as or more important in sports training than working out in the gym or on the field. It's the body's way of repairing, and it allows for the mind to "re-boot," if you will, and lets the mind prepare for the next day. Sleep deprivation has been shown over and over to decrease mental acuity, reflex reaction, and decision-making, all of which are needed to become an elite athlete. As you progress through this book, you will learn all of the important aspects needed to become a great athlete and a great sports parent.

Dr. Conway's Top Ten Tips to Becoming World-Class Sports Parents

1. Get involved with your athlete and the sport. Attend games and help out when needed with concession stands, fund raising and other booster activities. Show your child that you are interested in his or her sport.

2. Know your child! Take an objective look at your son's or daughter's true abilities. If he or she has less-than-average

ability, deal with it and support it. Remember, they just want to play!

3. Listen to your kids. After a game, listen to your kids tell you about the game rather than telling them what they should have done. They already know they made some mistakes; you don't have to point it out to them... save that for their coach. They are excited about what they just did and were happy you were there to share it with them. They want to SHARE their experience with you. Please let them. Leave the critiquing up to the coach.

4. If you are a coach of your son or daughter, then sit down way before you start to coach, and explain that on the field you are not mom or dad for that time period... you're the coach. Separate your emotions from parent to coach, and explain it to your child. Believe me, they will understand if you stay fair and coach properly.

5. Lay off the referees, umpires, and officials when they blow a call. They're human, and they make mistakes. It's a part of the game. Don't get me wrong. Voice your opinion, but then cut it off. The people who continue on and on and on and on are the people who should be asked to leave the field.

6. Focus on your child's efforts rather than his or her mistakes. The mistakes should be corrected by the coach, not you. If your child is trying as hard as he or she can, then please, by all means, reinforce the good job. If the child is not putting in a valid effort, then it may be time to change sports. A young child that is happy to play a game will give it his or her all whether or not he or she is good at it.

7. Help your children be realistic with their abilities. I'm all for pumping up young athletes, but there is a fine line between deception and enthusiasm. If your son or daughter thinks that he or she is going to become a professional athlete and they are

having a hard time tying their shoes without falling over, there may be a little bit of a letdown. Some parents are consumed about "protecting" their children's emotions and will continue to tell them that they are the greatest even though they don't produce on the field.

8. Let the coach be the coach. Don't undermine them; support them. Don't be a coach from the sidelines, because this just causes immense pressure for your son or daughter and the rest of the team. If you happen to be on a team with a terrible coach or a coach that is not coaching properly, ask to speak to him or her on the side to discuss the facts.

9. Don't live your sports life through your child. Let it go. What you did was years in the past, times were different, situations were different, and you can't properly compare the past to the present.

10. Just let them have fun. You only get to be a kid for a short time in life, and sports can add so much fun, excitement, and memories that you don't want to take that away from them.

Remember one very important thing — sports are games. That's it, no more, no less. It's not war, no one is dying, no one gets shot, and at the end of every game, everyone gets to go home. So let's put it in perspective that there are more important things in life than an outcome of a game. Because when it's all said and done, no one outside of your small sports perspective really cares.

Chapter 3

What It Takes to Become an Elite Athlete

I t begins with a thought.

For many athletes, there comes a time when they realize that they are capable of accomplishing more on the field than all of the other kids around them. They slowly find out that most, if not all, of the plays, movements, and situations come much easier to them than to everyone else. In fact, they begin to think to themselves, "This so easy. Why can't the rest of them do it?" It's at that point that it becomes apparent that they have the cognition that they have more ability and talent than the athletes around them. This is the time that you have to make the realization that it will be in your best interest to break away from the competition and take it to the next level. If your child is going to continue to improve, they need a higher form of competition to not only develop their skills but to reinforce that they are, in fact, a higher quality athlete.

This is the time that you must prepare to become an elite athlete.

Working at Wimbledon

In 2009, I was hired by a few players to work at the Wimbledon Lawn and Tennis Club in Wimbledon, England, to help with injury, pre-game loosening, and post-game recovery. This was a new challenge for me, working with numerous athletes on foreign soil.

Wimbledon is hollow ground for tennis, a place where the entire tennis world takes time to watch the best tennis players in the world compete for the coveted Wimbledon trophy.

I arrived in London the weekend before the tennis championship began. As I entered the Wimbledon facility, I was told to enjoy it now because in a couple of days the place would be mobbed with fans, and it would be extremely difficult to get around. But then, it was quiet, with hardly anyone moving about the grounds except for the players and the workers. The tennis courts are all grass surfaces, cut to an impeccable height and firmness that would rival many country club golf courses' putting greens.

On the first day there, I'm standing on the practice court just taking in the surroundings. I'm tired because I flew all night from Philadelphia and didn't get a lot of sleep on the plane (thanks to a crying baby). It was typical day in Wimbledon, overcast, damp, and windy, which equals COLD. I'm a bit cranky since getting off of the plane, not sleeping, and not having a jacket. Dummy me, I'm thinking, what will I need a jacket for? It's the end of June. Maybe here on the east coast of the U.S. it's warm, but not in England.

The practice courts at Wimbledon are situated where small amounts of fans are allowed to watch, but for the most part, fans are secluded from the players. I was waiting for my players to come to court to begin practice. In the meantime, while I was waiting, I began to watch a couple of players practice on the next court. Watching one gentlemen hitting was a treat. He began hitting cross-court shots one after the other with absolute seamless accuracy. Ball after ball crossed over the net no higher than two inches while hitting the firm grass with an explosive acceleration.

As he began to speed up his place of play, I remember saying to myself, man, this guy is good. I told you that I was still groggy from the flight. I turned to the gentleman next to me and said, "Wow, take a look at this guy. He never misses." The guy looked at me like I had two heads and said that's why he's number one in the world. It turned out to be Roger Federer who was hitting, and he went on to win the Wimbledon Championship in a marathon battle over Andy Roddick.

Watching Federer play was like listening to Beethoven conduct his own music using an all-star orchestra. Not missing one ball, Federer continued to deliver shot after shot like he and the racquet were one. Observing this giant of the tennis world perform, I began to wonder if the rest of the world really understood what it takes to get to this level of performance. It was a bit peculiar to witness many of the other pro tennis players stopping to watch Federer practice. They know excellence when they see it as well.

Watching elite athletes perform can lull you to sleep by the grace and ease of their performances. The majority of amateurs have no idea the amount of work and dedication it takes to get to this level. The great ones make it look so easy, and it frustrates the rest of us. But if you can take one thing away from this, understand that it has taken them a lifetime to create a body, mind, and spirit that knows only one thing... WINNING!

Professional sports are a unique fraternity and sorority, and only the top players in the world are invited in. If your son or daughter is training to become a top-level tennis player, for example, be aware that it can be a lonely road. The travel can be overwhelming. Traveling all over the world week after week is tougher than you think. The other problem is that, if you're not in the top 100, you have to watch your expenses very closely because, after your expenses, there isn't a lot left over. Yes, you see the top players making it big, flying in private jets, and on covers of the magazines. But only the top are making the big money that allows them the freedom to do these glamorous things.

Statistically speaking, the chance of your son or daughter making it to the elite top tier of any particular sport is not good. Again, there are some players in the world that have the unbridled talent that started as soon as they began to walk, but they are few and far between. Their God-given talent has jettisoned them to the top, but they soon come to realize that, once on top, many of them have to work even harder and smarter to keep themselves at this elite level. For others, having spent their entire lives developing conditioning, reflexes, speed, coordination, and overall performance, they are still short of making it to the top. No matter how good you are 98 percent of the time, there is always a level higher that you can achieve. And, more importantly, no matter how good you are, there is someone waiting in the wings to bring you down.

Learning from the Players

The road to professional sports can be a very difficult challenge. Different sports have different obstacles to hurdle in order to reach the top. Talent is everything, but there are many other aspects needed to push though physical barriers and the political maze that awaits them.

In tennis, for example, players assemble from around the world to challenge for lucrative prize money at various tournaments. For many, it's a way out of a world of poverty and socio-economic strife. For others, it's a sacrifice moving away from your family to attend tennis academies to practice and gain the necessary experience needed to make it as a professional tennis player. Unlike other professional team sports, tennis is an individual sport. If you don't win, you don't eat. Professional players must pay for their own travel, coaches, hitting partners, and other support services, all before they even enter their first tournament. Tennis is a game of centimeters in that a centimeter in or out of the line can be the difference between a substantial paycheck or packing your bags and going home.

The team sports are run by owners who invest their money in a product — athletic competition. The owner is banking on the fact that, if they put up the money to pay athletes to play their sport, build a stadium that will hold paying customers, and offer an overall exciting experience, people will pay good money to attend. Team athletes are paid on a weekly basis and are guaranteed their pay for the year. In fact, some sports are guaranteed full pay for the full term of their contracts, no matter if they get injured or not. Many of the team sports are unionized, so there is a form of protection for their pay and benefits.

The fact is that, even if you make it, you haven't made it. Making it to the professional ranks is a huge accomplishment, but staying there is an entirely different situation. There are hundreds of athletes that make it the professional ranks every year only to learn that they didn't have enough talent to stay there. These are athletes who are far and above better than every athlete around them, except for the few that have been established in the professional ranks before them. I can't tell you how many excellent players there are who are just a hair away from making it to the top of their sport, but the talent level above them is that much greater, keeping them either in a holding pattern, waiting for their shot, or they never make it at all. Getting all the way to the top in any sport can be a monumental task. We as fans only see the top 10 percent of the professional athletes on TV, newspaper, radio, or the Internet. We don't see all of the other athletes who either make it, and you don't hear much about them, or athletes who don't make it at all.

So is it impossible to get to the top? No. Just understand that the odds are against you. The Williams sisters, Serena and Venus, came out of one of the worst environments in the world to become the best female players of their day. Because of their persistence, hard work, and never-giving-up attitude, they made it to the top. The odds stacked against them making it to the top were greater than most people realize. Not only did they have to deal with the pressures of advancing on the pro tour, but they also had to deal with the discriminatory actions of many in a "white"-dominated sport. Don't ever think that you can't make it. Just keep it realistic, in that nothing is going to be handed to you. But understand this — nothing is impossible.

Now, before we go too far, let's get one thing straight. AT THIS POINT, we're recognizing your child's talent compared to their aged peer group on a higher level. But before you start looking at the million-dollar mansions, make sure they are as good as they portray themselves to be. They might be developing faster than the other kids around them, giving the appearance that they are superior. At younger ages, some kids develop faster than others and will advance faster in sports compared to their peers. As time goes on and physiology catches up, there comes a time when all of the kids begin to even out.

It can be difficult to know whether your child has the elite qualities needed to advance at an early age. The rule of thumb is domination. If your son or daughter is making child's play out of the competition in their sport, it may be time to pay attention. If they are dominating their sport and continue to dominate no matter where they play, then it's time to pay attention. But I need to warn you about another potential problem. The fact may be that the talent level in the community that you live in may be poor. Your son or daughter may be playing against average or below-average competition, which is making them look better than they really are. If the competition in your area is really less than average, then you may perceive your child as an elite athlete when he or she is average at best. This is where travel teams come in. Travel teams will allow your child to compete against higher levels of talent throughout the state or region. The better the competition, the more your athlete will learn how to compete at a higher level. If they are truly elites, they will dominate no matter what level they play at.

It's at this point that they have to make a personal choice to become "an athlete." That decision comes down to one single-minded purpose — excellence and commitment. Commitment in the gym, the practice field, the classroom, and even in social situations is the mentality needed to achieve success. It now comes down to two four-letter words, HARD WORK!

When you chose to become an athlete, you made a decision of sacrifice. You are going to have to understand that you must be willing to do the things that the other kids aren't willing to do. When you choose to become an athlete, you are attempting something that isn't easy. That's why everyone else isn't doing it. Notice I didn't say that you've made a choice to become a "jock". I said an *athlete*. This is something that you must develop a passion for. You must be willing to give some things up in your life in order to pursue excellence in your given sport. To become an elite athlete takes drive, mental preparation, talent, skill, and heart. Yes, heart! Heart is defined as having an overwhelming persistence and commitment to generate greatness. You must be able to push though pain, stress, discomfort, and everyone else's temporary disapproval of your decision to succeed.

When you decide to turn away from the norm and direct your mind to pursue the best that you can be, it may turn people away from you. What happens is that people who strive for excellence can arbitrarily make the people around them feel average. People who feel average may begin to experience jealous emotions towards you. If this happens, it will at first become uncomfortable, but keeping your eye on your passion for excellence will help you overcome it. This is where you will find out exactly who your friends really are and which ones are not. You need people around you who can support you and understand what you are trying to accomplish.

Making the decision to take your game to the next level is a difficult decision to make. It's knowing that you have to get your butt out of bed in the morning to get your workouts completed. It's pushing yourself when you feel you can't go any more. It's having the discipline in getting the right sleep every night. It's having the discipline to eat properly and to hydrate properly every day, no matter how mundane it feels. It's taking on the responsibility yourself and making no excuses. It's doing things yourself rather than waiting for others to do them for you. It's knowing that you are personally taking full responsibility for yourself and your actions and not putting any blame on the people around you. You don't blame your parents, sisters, or brothers; you look to yourself first. Yes, it's all about you. So right now, you better take the responsibility that comes with it. It's about growing up and knowing that what you are attempting to achieve is a cut away from the norm. There are sacrifices that come with being an elite athlete. The quicker you understand that, the quicker you become a better athlete.

The student who vows to become a straight-A student must first realize what it takes to accomplish this. You can't just be the same old student anymore. You have to understand that, in order to become a straight-A student, it is going to take more study, harder work, longer hours, and constant review. There are few people who have the ability to just show up, read the book, and ace the test. Yes, you hear about a few of them, but they are a very small part of the population. Whether it's committing to straight As or committing to becoming the best athlete possible, people who make that decision to become elite must realize the massive commitment that it will take to accomplish this. The same goes for you. You need to commit yourself to what it takes to become an elite athlete. Once you've made that commitment, you will see how well you begin to succeed over time.

You Have to Make a Decision... Do I Want to Be a Jock or an Athlete?

To become the best you can be as an athlete, you have to make a mental decision to separate yourself from the crowd. I teach a lot of athletes that it takes more to accomplish great things. There comes a time when you have to make a decision on your own to become an athlete. There is a big difference when you make this decision. You have to decide whether you want to become a "jock" or an "athlete." It's a *mental* decision that allows you to burn your bridges behind you to commit to the goals you want to achieve.

Jock:
A jock is a person, either male or female, who just wants to show up and play. They don't want to do what it takes to become the best that they can be. They want the glory, but they don't want to put in the work needed to become great. Jocks tend to have egos much greater than their talents. They are more concerned about what people think about, than rolling up their sleeves and getting the job done. They are swayed by other people's opinions, and they are critical of others. They will back down when the environment gets tough. They will criticize others for working hard and doing the extra things needed to win.

Athlete:
An athlete is a special breed. They come early and leave late. They will do what others don't want to do. They are willing to do things that are uncomfortable to them both on the field and off the field. They don't have to be told what to do; they already know what has to be done in advance, and they do it. They get the work done without a lot of fanfare. They don't worry about other people's opinions. They just listen and do what is needed to win. Pure athletes are willing to do what others don't want to do to make themselves elite.

Again, it comes down to attitude. When you commit your mind in the right direction, you will see how your mind will assist you in getting what you want. A made-up mind, backed with passion and discipline, will get you the goals you want to attain.

For the first time in your life, let it be known that it is cool to be committed. And when you hear people criticizing you for working hard, just think to yourself, "What would Michael Phelps, Lebron James, Venus Williams, Serena Williams, Kobe Bryant, Ray Lewis, Derrick Jeter, and others say about what I'm doing?" Do you really think that these great athletes worried about what someone else was saying about them when it came down to working hard? They know what they have to do, and they do it. They don't worry about the temporary disapproval of others.

There will be plenty of people in your life who will begin with criticism. "Who the heck does he/she think they are? What do they think they are going to accomplish by working that hard? They're just wasting their time." Remember this — they don't erect statues for critics. Learn to work hard and not to listen to the idiots who have nothing else to do but to talk about you. You can't tell me that any great, and I truly mean *great* athlete, wouldn't or doesn't admire a person working his or her butt off trying to accomplish his or her goals. It's only the people who were or are afraid to take a chance at working hard in attempting to get to the top. If you don't believe me, go and talk to the great coaches in the world and see what they say. Talk to Bill Belicheck (New England Patriots), John Wooden (UCLA basketball), Bill Parcells (Dallas Cowboys), Phil Jackson (LA Lakers), Nick Saban (Alabama), or Joe Torre (LA Dodgers). They will have the highest respect for the kid who is busting his or her hump to accomplish something. Why? Because each and every one of them knows how tough it is to get to the top and how tough it is to stay there. They understand that it takes an extra special effort on all athletes to get to the top. Could you imagine a parent or an athlete shooting off his or her mouth against another athlete because they are working too hard, while Coach Bobby Knight sat by and listened? "Look at them! Who do they think they are? What are they trying to prove?" What do you think Coach Knight would think or say? Well, I don't want to repeat what Mr. Knight would say.

You may think that the great athletes aren't hard workers, but that is an absolute lie. Are there good athletes that are lazy? Of course! But the truly great ones are the ones who know deep down what it takes to become elite. There are countless stories of Larry Bird staying after games to practice. I've seen with my own eyes the amount of extra film work Ray Lewis and others put in to the game to be that much better. The greats have an internal drive to become the very best that they can be.

So the next time you hear a bubble-headed jock or parent criticize a player, just think to yourself how they would feel if they were sitting next to one of the greats that I've mentioned above. Do you think they would keep running their mouth? I sincerely doubt it.

Training Comparison

I truly feel that a mind made up can accomplish just about anything. In today's sports world, you have to be able to distinguish yourself against your competitors. No matter how bad you want it, you have to be able to perform to certain minimums on the field in order to advance. Parents must understand that, no matter how good your son or daughter is, the next levels of competition have their minimums that your child must be able to achieve. If you are a high school football player looking to go on to a Division I program, here are some numbers that you can compare yourself to. These are the current estimates used by coaches in evaluation to see if you have the athletic ability to play at that level. This will give you an idea of what is expected of you entering college football. If you are anywhere below the 75th percentile, consider going to a Division III school. This is the reality of football, and it doesn't pay to play at a level that you don't have the talent, speed, or strength for. Not only will it be difficult to make the team, but it could be a potentially painful experience. The level of talent at the Division I level is outstanding, and if you're not ready for it, you can get hurt.

40-Yard Dash	75th Percentile	100th Percentile
Wide Receiver	4.59	4.35
Fullback	4.63	4.50
Running Back	4.57	4.33
Quarterback	4.69	4.40
Tight End	4.91	4.65
Center	5.19	4.90
O-Guard	5.13	4.87
O-Tackle	5.12	4.93
D-Tackle	5.04	4.63
Corner Back	4.57	4.40
Free Safety	4.59	4.50
Strong Safety	4.58	4.41
Linebacker	4.85	4.64

Vertical Jump	75th Percentile	100th Percentile
Wide Receiver	33.5	36.0
Fullback	34.0	37.0
Running Back	33.0	38.5
Quarterback	33.0	36.0
Tight End	31.5	36.5
Center	30.5	35.5
O-Guard	30.0	34.0
O-Tackle	28.0	31.5
D-Tackle	32.5	36.5
Corner Back	35.0	41.5
Free Safety	33.5	37.5
Strong Safety	32.5	38.0
Linebacker	33.0	36.5

Bench Press	75th Percentile	100th Percentile
Offensive Line	330 lbs.	400 lbs.
Defensive Line	330 lbs.	400 lbs.
Linebacker	290 lbs.	360 lbs.
Tight Ends	290 lbs.	360 lbs.
Running Back	260 lbs.	330 lbs.
Corner Backs	250 lbs.	310 lbs.

If your son is playing football, the above chart will let you know if he is within range of playing at a higher level. This will take a lot of the guesswork out of it for you. No other sport uses these types of estimates to get a feel for the strength and speed of players. These are the three bell-weather tests that are used by every football coach in the country. They even use these numbers when testing football players before they turn professional.

Dealing with Hardship

No matter what level of athleticism you are at, you're going to experience losing. Everyone in sports fails. The key is how you handle that failure that makes the difference. No real athlete is ever comfortable with defeat, but if the pain and discomfort from losing continues on, then you may have a problem with properly coping.

There are many names for losing. Beaten, smoked, buried, trounced, schooled, flattened, crushed, trampled, beat down, beat up, creamed, killed, routed, whitewashed, overpowered, shit on, buzz killed, and stuffed are just a few to sum up defeat. Let's face it, losing sucks! I'm sorry for the poor grammar, but there is no other bitter pill to swallow than defeat.

In sports, losing is necessary in understanding life. Losing provides feedback that you may have to change something about your game. Losing humbles you, which allows you to properly assess your game and your competition. If you're smart enough to use the loss as a teaching tool and really learn from it, you will eventually see the results you are looking for. Muhammad Ali was quoted as saying, "For three seconds after making a mistake, I think about it, correct it, and then I move on." This is what separates the good from the elite. They find a way to win. They correct their mistakes from the feedback they receive from failure.

There is not winning without losing. The euphoric feeling that you experience is only produced knowing that, within seconds, inches, or even a point, it could have just as easily been a loss. Knowing defeat lurks around every corner makes victory that much more enjoyable. It's the lure of flirting with defeat that brings most athletes to the table.

Without losing, there is no such thing as sport. As fans, there is nothing more exhilarating as a game or a match that comes down to the wire. The ins and outs of the game creating edge-of-the-chair moments are the moments in life we all remember. The stress, the fear, and the guilt of the potential loss is what fuels our appetite for sport. The sweetest victory is the event that balances itself on the very edge of defeat. Having your toes on the edge of the cliff is how we want to experience each game we watch. The possibility of a true crash and burn is so real that it makes the victory a *real* victory. Whether it be athletes or fans, breaking it down to the least common denominator, it's the defeat or the losing the pulls us all closer to the fire. We can never have victory if losing doesn't lurk in the shadows.

Elite athletes have to plan ahead and learn how to handle defeat. This can be one of the hardest parts for elite athletes to develop. No one likes to lose, and higher achieving people have a difficult time dealing with losses. If you don't control the feeling of losing, it will eventually eat you alive. On its own, a loss is hard to take, but if you continue to dwell on it and not take the time to learn from it, you will find yourself digging a mental hole, a hole that becomes harder and harder to get out of when it becomes too big.

Recently, I heard two national radio sports personalities verbally dismantle LeBron James for not being upset after a loss in the NBA playoffs. The one commentator said that he was upset that James didn't show the emotions needed to help his team win. I'm sorry, but I don't get it. LeBron James is arguably the best player in the NBA, and we don't have to use his emotional upset to motivate his teammates. No way. Every person deals with defeat in many different ways.

Overall, is it bad to get upset if you lose? No. It's actually a normal feeling. But if you take it to the extreme where it affects other aspects of your life including family, friends, or teammates, then it's a problem. The key to losing is to learn from it. After the emotional aspect of the loss has ended, take some time to sit down and figure out any mistakes that were made and immediately figure out a way to correct them. When you return to practice, that is the time to work on the mistakes that were made. This does two things — first, it tells the mind that it was only a temporary setback and is now being corrected.

Second, it reinforces for the future what to look out for so that you don't repeat it again.

Looking to Science to Help Develop Elite Athletes

A study published in the *Journal of Applied Sport Psychology* examined the psychological characteristics of elite athletes. It revealed interesting results. Using American Olympic champions, the researchers performed various psychological tests, which revealed that these elite athletes showed the following traits.

- The ability to cope with and control anxiety
- Confidence
- Mental toughness/resiliency
- Sport intelligence
- The ability to focus and block out distractions
- Competitiveness
- A hard-work ethic
- The ability to set and achieve goals
- Coach ability
- High levels of dispositional hope
- Optimism
- Adaptive perfectionism

The study also revealed that external influences on an athlete's ability showed that community, family, and coaches had positive effects from teaching psychological lessons and indirectly from "modeling or unintentionally creating psychological environments." It isn't brought out in the study, but it is apparent that family, coaching, and other external stimuli can create negatives effects on the athletes as well. Athletes that have endured stressful childhoods while developing in their particular sport can experience a pronounced effect on their performance as well.

If you have decided to become the best athlete you can be, then you need to start planning right now. You need to plan on how many hours in a day you will need to train. You need to plan the best possible meals that will allow you to continue to train at highly intensive levels.

How many hours will you need to accomplish your studies at school? It is very important that you develop an intellectual aspect of training. It is very important in physical training to also develop high intellectual levels in the brain while you are developing your body as well. How many hours will you need for sleep? You need deep, uninterrupted sleep for your body to heal. How many hours do you need to socialize with your friends? As hard as you plan to work for your sport, you have to take time off to relax. Hanging out with friends is a great way to take the pressures off from training. The only down side to this is that these hours will probably be the least amount of time that you will have to deal with. I strongly recommend that you have friends outside of your sport. These people can give you a different perspective on your sport or life in general. When you make a choice to become an upper-level athlete, you have to deal with a word that most people don't want to deal with. That word is called SACRIFICE.

Sacrifice: To surrender or give up for the sake of something else

You can't eat the junk food that your friends might be eating. You can't stay up all night every night. You have to study when others are out with their friends. You have to get your sleep. You have to put in extra hours, miss a dance, miss a prom, and travel on days you may want to stay home. You're not the only person who has given up something to make his or her dream come true. There have been thousands of athletes before you that have made sacrifices to get closer to their dreams. They all know it was worth it. It's all part of being an athlete — not just a player on the team.

The sacrifices are many, but the payoff is exponential...

The old saying goes, "To the victor go the spoils." To the person who spent the long, hard hours working towards victory, the victory becomes the sweet taste of success.

Natural Talent vs. Hard Work

K. Anders Ericsson, professor of psychology at Florida State University and co-editor of *The Cambridge Handbook of Expertise and Expert Performance*, set out to study the effects of talent and whether it is something acquired by birth or learned. His research sought to find out what percentage of talent was "natural." He found that there is very little hard evidence that anyone is born with exceptional talent. According to Ericsson, "There is surprisingly little hard evidence that anyone could attain any kind of exceptional performance without spending a lot of time perfecting it."

Ericsson's contention is that most high-achieving performers, whether in sports, medicine, or music, are nearly always made, not born. His theory goes on to show that practice doesn't make perfect; perfect practice makes perfect. Mastery, as Ericsson explains, comes about through "deliberate practice." This is different than the typical U.S.-type of mind-numbing repetitive practice. Deliberate practice has three aspects to bring about positive change.

1. Setting specific goals
2. Obtaining immediate feedback
3. Concentrating as much on technique as on outcome

It comes down to the age-old saying that you need to do what you love. If you love what you do, then you are more likely to be able to perfect the above three techniques for honing your talent. If you don't LOVE what you are doing, you are less likely to work hard enough to get to the elite levels of that particular sport. Ericsson found that practice without attention to detail (i.e., going through the motions) does not lead to gains in development.

Elite Athletes and the Choke Factor

It seems to me that there are a host of qualities needed to help develop an elite athlete. Many things have to be taken into consideration in order to build an athlete to an elite level. Coaches, athletes, trainers, and parents don't fully understand that it takes every fiber of the athlete's being to become properly stimulated in order for him or her to respond on a world-class level.

As we've talked about in other chapters, developing a strong physiology is a must. But it goes way past just being in good shape to ensure that you are doing everything possible to optimize your athletic performance. It takes time to develop the emotional expertise to react properly in stressed situations. Seasoned athletes understand how to deal with difficult situations. The novice doesn't, so when things get tough on the field or court, they begin to question themselves. Elite athletes appear capable of regulating their reactions to anxiety.

Elite athletes understand what it takes to become winners. They prepare for their competition. They take the time to review film on themselves and become their own coach. After years and years of playing and practicing, the athlete knows what to look for. By reviewing video or film, they can make the necessary corrections needed to improve. Elite athletes watch film on their competition. They find ways to exploit any weaknesses that their competitors may have. Some of the top competitive athletes that I've been around have been masters of watching film and exploiting the weaknesses of their opponents.

Elite athletes have developed and mastered cognitive behavior thinking and reasoning. They have developed skills on remembering important thoughts to use to help them win. Based on their memories, they have developed "tactical" skills prepared ahead of time so that they have a strategy to win. Elite athletes have developed high-end "decision-making skills." They make quick decisions and live by their decisions. They don't dwell on any bad decisions that they may have made. They know that, with all of the work that they have put in, they can rely on their practice and other preparatory work to help them believe in their decision-making.

Other skills to develop to become elite:

- Study: Knowing the history of the sport that they are playing
- Goal Setting: Learning how to attain goals rather than wishes
- Coachability: Listening and understanding to the people who are coaching you
- Mental Training and Imagery: Learning how to use your mind to win

- Positive Attitude: Learning how to build a positive attitude and maintain it
- Interpersonal Skills: Learning how to get along with others and how to deal with others

On another finding, some athletes fall apart when the perceived competition is greater than them. Recent research on what is known as the "superstar effect" demonstrates that, when there is an athlete who is perceived as a superstar, the rest of the competition falls apart. You would think that superior competition would bring out the best in athletes, but some research has shown the complete opposite.

In an article written by Jonah Lehrer for the *Wall Street Journal*, the negative effect of superstars has been most clearly demonstrated in professional golf, which for the last decade has been dominated by Tiger Woods. According to a paper by Jennifer Brown, an applied macroeconomist at the Kellogg School of Management at Northwestern University, Mr. Woods is such a dominating golfer, that his presence in a tournament can make everyone else play significantly worse. Because his competitors expect him to win, they end up losing. Losing becomes a self-fulfilling prophecy.

Ms. Brown discovered the superstar effect by analyzing data from every player in every PGA Tour event from 1999 to 2006. She chose golf for several reasons, from the lack of "confounding team dynamics" to the immaculate statistics kept by the PGA. Most importantly, however, was the presence of Mr. Woods, who has dominated his sport in a way few others have. Such domination appears to be deeply intimidating. Whenever Mr. Woods entered a tournament, every other golfer took, on average, 0.8 more strokes. This effect was even observable in the first round, with the presence of Mr. Woods leading to an additional 0.3 strokes among all golfers over the initial 18 holes. While this might sound like an insignificant difference, the average margin between first and second place in PGA Tour events is frequently just a single stroke.

This may have a lot to do with athletes who seem to "choke" against stiff competition and who don't realize what their minds are doing to them. Instead of just playing and trusting their game, they begin to overanalyze, and that is when self-doubt sets in. Some players begin to subconsciously choke just at the sight or rumor of a superior opponent. I have personally been with athletes who, as soon as they learned who they were about to compete against, they began with the negative self-doubt talk.

Different Sports... Different Challenges... Or Are There?

We speak about what it takes to become a top-rated player, but do we really do the little things that it takes to put it all together? We've talked about the physical preparation, but just as important, or even more so, is the mental preparation.

What separates the best from the elite? Why are there certain people who just seem to rise to the pinnacles of their sports? I was trying to reason what all of the attributes are that it takes to become the best of the best. I looked into many different sports, including tennis, football, baseball, track, and golf, and attempted to come up with a definition of what it takes to become great. In researching the top athletes and coaches in the world, it seems that the characteristics of being a champion come down to the same things over and over.

Here are the areas I feel are necessary to becoming a top elite champion in any sport.

1. Commitment
2. Independence
3. Confidence
4. Self-determination and will
5. Competitive spirit
6. Work ethic/heart
7. Off-field/court study
8. Coping (managing emotions)

There are many aspects of being a truly elite athlete. But no matter what happens, it seems that we keep coming back to these same categories that are set above. When you study the greats, this is what you find.

1. **Work Ethic** – Champions prepare and plan well. They are **organized**. They know where they are going and how to get there. They are concerned about their schedules and peak for big events.

Organize: 1) To put oneself in a state of mental competence to perform a task; to give structure to or to form, as or into a whole, consisting of interdependent parts

Many professionals that I know have every detail worked out well in advance of game day. It is written down, it's planned, and it is formulated in an overall itinerary. This takes the stress off of the athlete, knowing all they have to do is to look at their calendar and know what is expected.

"The dictionary is the only place success comes before work. Hard work is the price we must all pay for success. I think we can accomplish almost anything if we are willing to pay the price. The price of success is hard work, dedication to the job at hand, and the determination that, whether we win or lose, we have applied the best of ourselves to the task at hand."

Coach Vince Lombardi

2. **Competitive Spirit**

Competitive: An active demand of some environment resource in short supply; to strive to outdo another for supremacy, a prize, acknowledgment, or profit

Spirit: A fundamental emotional and activation principle determining one's character; an attitude or principle that inspires feeling or action

Noted world tennis coach Tom Gullickson says that champions have a competitive spirit in everything they do. For example, Pete Sampras finds a way to compete both against himself and within himself. Other players make it a personal fight.

As you combine the words 'competitive' and 'spirit, you need to be able to understand how you can make this work for yourself. With that defined, do you fully understand this? And how can you apply this to your own way of playing? How can you use this as a part of you on a regular basis, making it a part of you when you go to play?

"When people ask me, 'Who was the toughest pitcher you ever faced?' I have to say that there has never been a pitcher who over-impressed me. That's not meant to be a bragging statement. It's just that I get up for good pitchers. Truthfully, I never faced a pitcher that I didn't think I could get a hit from."

Pete Rose, Cincinnati Reds/Philadelphia Phillies First Basemen

3. **Commitment** – Champions are focused on goals. Commitment is not just showing up to play. It's a daily commitment to winning. It's taking all of the many little parts that make up being an elite player and committing to them so that they all come together to create a champion.

Commitment: A pledge, promise, or obligation

Commitment to excellence: Never having to tell anyone about your commitment. They'll know by your actions. Never be ashamed to admit that you want to be the best. Don't ever be satisfied until you get what you want.

4. **Confidence and Self-Belief** – Champions have a great sense of themselves.

"They believe they can do it... especially when things aren't going well."

They know who they are and are not distracted by others. They don't worry about the temporary disapproval or comments of others. They know that, when things go badly, they can look to themselves to dig down and get out of trouble.

Belief in yourself is easy. Belief in yourself when things are falling apart around you is a whole other thing. This is the time that you have to have confidence and a strong belief that you can weather the storm.

Belief: Confidence in the truth; faith; trust

"It's never an upset if the so-called underdog has all along considered itself the better team."

Woody Hayes, Head Football Coach, Ohio State

5. **Determination and Will** – Champions are very determined and have great will power. Champions are willing to do the things that the people around them aren't willing to do. Champions do not give in. Champions develop resistance, and when behind, they fight until things turn around.

   Determine:To give direction to; to conclude after reasoning
   Will: The power of control the mind has over its own actions; purpose or determination, often stubborn determination

6. **Independence** – Champions take responsibility for themselves. They don't blame coaches or others for losses. They don't look to the sidelines during matches. They have support teams, but the ultimate responsibility lies with them, and they know it.

7. **Non-Field Study** – Most of the top-end athletes that I know study their opponents as much as possible. They are looking for that one edge that causes their brain to spark at the most opportune time. Hours and hours of film study is done so that they can find any sliver of an edge. Many of them told me that you may see the same thing over and over, but if you stay persistent, your brain will begin to show you things that normally you would never see in real time.

They also study themselves so that they can create their own coach inside of their mind. When they find something that isn't working (for example, an old habit creeps in), they tend to figure out other things to override it so they don't continue to repeat the same mistakes. The more responsibility they take for themselves, the more answers come to them in difficult times. They've developed a private, mental coaching manual by themselves.

8. **Coping Skills and Managing Emotions** – Golfers seem to be the best at managing their emotions better than any other athletes in the world. They know that, due to the nature of the sport, they can't get too high or too low because each and every shot has too many variables. A perfect swing and a perfect ball strike can lead to your ball hitting a small pebble or sprinkler head in the fairway or landing in someone else's divot. Every pro golfer knows that you have to keep your emotions in check.

Coping skills are acquired and learned over time. You have to work on them on a regular basis. It's no different than working out every day. As you develop your body and your game, you must continue to develop your mind. Experience shows that not dealing with your emotions can be dangerous. But on the other hand, over exaggerating your emotions can be just as harmful.

The management of emotions is how you want to feel when things are good. So when things are bad, you can "work" your mind back to that point, or as close to that point as possible, so that the severe negative emotions don't take over.

From a sports science tennis article by Jack Dinoffer:

"At the same presentation, Jack presented the results of an unusual survey compiled from videotaping 100 players getting angry after an error on a tennis court. First of all, he said that when four of them saw their video footage they denied it was even them in the first place. The other ninety-six answered that

they got angry only to show the people around them that they usually play better than they did on that missed shot. Interesting responses, aren't they?"

While looking at this paragraph, ask yourself who is the player playing for? The only person you should impress when you are playing your sport is you.

Your game will follow your emotions. When you're playing well, you feel good. When you're not playing well, your mind may begin to create negative mental patterns. When you begin to lose, many players tend to create negative emotions and then begin to play even worse. To control this, ask yourself this question: what emotion do I want when I'm playing my sport? With that answer, apply it the moment that you feel your emotions are getting away from you. You can control the way you feel if you apply the rule "not too high, not too low."

I've talked to player after player about the psychologies of their sports and how they went about getting ready for their opponents. Whether it was football, baseball, tennis, or field hockey, the overwhelming response that I received was PREPARATION. The mental preparation began after they knew that they had properly prepared physically for the contest at hand. If it was football, they needed to know that they practiced properly every day, going over and over what they needed to do in a game. So when it came time to perform, they were so confident in their ability THROUGH the repetitive preparation that the anxiety melted away. It was then that they could sit in a peaceful environment and begin to play the game in their head the way they wanted to see it. They knew they put in the blood, sweat, and tears. All they had to do was to visualize perfection, allowing the brain to "see" what they wanted to have the outcome be. As you develop as an athlete, you will begin to notice that there is absolutely no substitution for hard work. I don't care who tells you that or if they tell you there is an easier way. The bottom line is that you have no idea of the limits you have inside of you unless you take your body to the brink of failure. But it is only then when you find out where your body has been and how far you can take it.

Realize your limit. It's up to you to raise your limit. There is no ceiling except for the mental restraints you put upon yourself. It has been proven scientifically that there are no limits as far as your genes or DNA makeup goes.

In his book, *Biology of Belief*, Bruce Lipton, PhD, argues that genes cannot control life because they cannot turn themselves on or off. That is done by signals from the cellular environment. Environmental influences, including nutrition, stress, and emotions can modify genes, without changing their basic blueprint, and these modifications can be passed on to future generations. What he is saying is that how you create your environment is how your genes will react and help create you as a human. There are genes waiting for information to help develop a better you.

The mind is much more powerful than we presently understand. I have found in my practice that the power of placebo is 20 times more powerful than I've ever imagined. It has been proven over and over that placebo treatment can be more powerful than the actual treatment itself. I know of one study where they took a group of patients scheduled for lower back surgery. They prepped them as they would any other back surgery patients; however, the difference was that they opened them up and immediately closed them. They took them into recovery and told them that everything went according to plan. The majority of the patients receiving the sham operation were pain-free after the operation and continued to remain pain-free in the months of follow-up.

As powerful as a positive placebo can be, a negative placebo can have just as many devastating results. In one instance, a man was told that he was going to die from a certain form of cancer, and within a couple of weeks, he passed away. When they performed an autopsy on this man, they found that there wasn't any evidence of cancer.

There are thousands of recorded episodes of the power of the mind. People walking on hot coals, people lying on beds of nails and being hit in the stomach with a hammer, tiny women lifting automobiles to save their children… the list is endless.

"Directly influence how the physical brain controls the body's physiology. Thought 'energy' can activate or inhibit the cell's

function-producing proteins ... The fact is that harnessing the power of your mind can be more *effective than the drugs you have been programmed to believe you need. He stresses that this requires not just positive thinking, but also eliminating the habitually negative and self-sabotaging thought patterns of the subconscious mind."* Dr. Bruch Lipton

Now is the time to develop your own "mental strategy." Use the techniques that I've gone over, and make your own list that works for you. Just like any other training, you have to do this every day so that your mind understands what you want it to accomplish. You can accomplish anything that you want within the parameters of the laws of physics. We would all love to be like Michael Phelps, Lebron James, or Tiger Woods, but first and foremost, be yourself. Then develop an attitude that nothing is going to stop you, and keep on driving for excellence no matter what others say or do. It can be done.

Parents, help your children develop a sense of self-fulfillment. Help them create their own personal mental strategies that allow them to feel good about themselves and to achieve greater heights. Work with them with the tools that I've given you to develop a personal mental training program. You will soon see the results in your young athletes using these simple techniques.

Help them get over the losses. It's a natural part of life, and you have to deal with it. Prepare mentally for things to go bad, because eventually, something will go wrong. You need to be prepared to deal with the negative side of life. I've been telling my kids forever that it's not what happens to you. It's what you do about it that makes the difference. In life, things will go wrong, period. Now you have a choice — sit there and cry and play "pity poor me," or do something positive about it. I didn't say it was going to be easy, but I can assure you that, if you take a proactive stance against the negative occurrence, you're going to feel that much better.

"A Life Is Not Important Except in the Impact It Has on Other Lives... "   **Jackie Robinson**

Chapter 4

Pain

U nderstand that PAIN is a part of sports. If your child is going to participate in some type of sporting activity they will experience some type of ache or pain. Pain is an area that both athletes and parents must understand when playing sports. Learning the many differences of pain is essential in becoming an athlete. You have to develop a mind set to be able to handle a certain amount of pain if you want to become an elite athlete.

There is a major difference between feeling uncomfortable, pain from damage and experiencing muscle soreness or weakness. The key to developing an athletic body is to better understand how your body deals with the various stresses that are imposed on the body during sporting activity.

Your body has billions of receptor sites throughout the body that send information to and from the body to the brain. This communication system is designed to correct or inform any problems that the body may incur during movement. The neurological system is a system of communication in interpreting and distributing neural activity (electricity) to all aspects of your body.

The brain is the master control system in the body. It is the main electrical producer sending the appropriate signals to the organs, systems, bones, and soft tissues of the body. It acts also as a receiver of messages at the same time interpreting those messages so that it can continue coordinating the overall communication, function and movement of your body. The messages are passed through the spinal cord as a highway system from the upper and lower body. The spinal

73

cord is a long collection of nerves that attach to the brain and runs down through the spinal vertebrae.

At each level of the spinal column a nerve exits through a small hole called the neural foramen. This nerve is actually two nerves wrapped in one sheath - one part being the motor nerve (sending nerve signals) and the second part being the sensory nerve (receiving the nerve signals). These nerves send and receive messages from the external portions of the body (arms, legs, organs etc...). These messages are sent up to the brain up to the brain via the sensory portion of the spinal nerve root. The brain interprets the signal and then sends back a reply appropriate to the situation.

Let's say that you put your hand on a hot part of the stove at home. The signal of heat is picked up by your hand and that signal is immediately sent to the brain. The brain interprets the signal and sends a message back to your hand to remove it so that you don't cause major damage to your hand. The higher the heat that is interpreted by the brain....the faster and more dramatic the signal sent back to the hand. You can imagine for yourself that if the top of the stove is just warm you will move your hand in due time. However it the top of the stove is red hot then you couldn't even measure how fast you would move your hand.

What is Pain?

Pain is a sensory signal sent to the brain reporting that there is damage in a given area. Pain is something that you pay attention to so that 'damage' whether short term or long term, doesn't set in. There is a difference between pain – tightness – soreness – dull ache or just being uncomfortable.

For years the saying has gone…. "no pain, no gain."

Well, that isn't true when it comes to real pain. Most seasoned athletes understand the difference between PAIN and other sensations feeling like pain. Pain is something that you have to come to terms with if you are going to be a top athlete. Pain is a signal sent to the brain that there is damage in a particular area.

There are other signals that will be sent but not necessarily pointing out true pain.

If you are working out and you lift a weight and your muscle begins to produce a pain like feeling most experienced athletes understand that that sensation isn't really pain that can harm them. The muscle over a period of time will begin to break down metabolically (loss of fuel) and sends a message to the brain. That message is that the muscle is breaking down and you had better pay attention. Athletes that have been experienced in training and playing know how far they can take it when it comes to pain. Inexperienced athletes don't fully understand their limits. This comes with repetition and plain old doing it over and over. You will begin to understand how far you can push yourself to produce improvements in your body.

Fatigue can produce a feeling of pain. When the body runs out of fuel a signal will be sent to the brain to tell you something is going on. Most times the signal is a gentle reminder that you are running out of fuel and you will begin to feel uncomfortable. This is normal.

Soreness on the other hand will be produced when you are exerting repetitive force on your body. Soreness is okay - but if it stays for long periods of time then that can be a problem. Soreness should only stay for a day or two.

Muscles are designed to properly absorb force. Whether you are walking, running, jumping, throwing - your muscles are designed to absorb that force produced in that movement. Like the shock absorbers of your car, the muscles are designed to absorb that force before it gets to the ligaments, tendons or the joint. Those areas aren't designed to absorb force and therefore they can break down as a result. If that force ends up at the joint it can produce inflammation in that area causing pain and limited mobility. Some people go immediately to taking anti-inflammatory medication. Does it work, sure it works, but are you getting to the real problem that caused the inflammation to begin with? NO!

If you are experiencing pain then you need to evaluate the 'why' of the pain.

- Look at yourself in the mirror and see what your posture looks like

- o Are your shoulders or hips higher than the other?
- o Is your head tilted or rotated?
- Do you have poor technique in your sport?
- Are you in good physical condition?
- Do you feel grounded when you stand or walk?
- Have you lost speed or power over the last few months?

These questions can help you find out why you may have continued pain. If pain continues you need to see a qualified doctor who can help you find the imbalance or dysfunction.

If you have an imbalance then you're "leaking" energy. The body is a very solid unit that is designed to be efficient when things are working properly. But after injury or poor posture or lack of input into the system (lack of exercise) the muscles can become shortened and inhibited. When this happens the body will begin to compensate meaning that the body will call upon muscles to help. The problem with that is that these muscles called upon to help aren't designed to do that particular action which leads to further complications and injury.

An interesting thing about pain is that it can be interpreted by people differently. Some people have "high pain thresholds" while others have lower thresholds. This is a make-up that isn't thoroughly understood. It is known that some people can bear more pain than others. Why? Part of it is as a result of being introduced to pain at an early age. The pain at that point was stored away as a memory of being...'not so bad'.

Sometimes pain due to repetition to the person is delt with as the brain understands the environment and knows that real harm isn't being accrued. The brain regulates the body's response to accept more. It's been shown by various eastern types of martial arts that pain can be mentally trained. I'm sure you've seen the people walking on hot coals, lying on a bed of nails and many other forms of pain producing acts. That type of person trains themselves to deal with the pain but as a signal that they can control.

For athletes to deal with pain is just as much mental as it is physical. Pain that produces a noxious response is something to be learned to better handle. Pain that produces damage is something that has to be learned to be stopped.

So when is pain....Pain? Pain due to damage is a signal that normally will show itself as an intense feeling that doesn't go away in a day or so. Remember pain is an indicator or a signal that there is damage in one part of your body. Not all pain is bad - pain can be helpful. Without pain you would experience serious damage without knowing you ever had a problem. Could you imagine your hand on fire and you didn't feel anything?

Moreover, there are other sensory findings that can be 'learned' as pain but in reality the signal isn't causing any damage so you can deal with it as long as you confront the feelings head on.

Here is a list of inputs the brain may interpret:

- Tingling   - Ache
- Soreness   - Discomfort
- Pulling   - Tightness
- Heavy   - Restricted
- Burning   - Swollen

Many of these feelings are signals that can be attributed to the following:

- Being out of condition   - Weak Muscles
- Muscles not turning on properly - Muscles not turning off properly
- Lack of Protein   - Lack of Water
- Lack of Sleep   - Lack of Mental Confidence

So when the body runs out of fuel or your mind begins to shut down on you – your body will begin to fail. This feeling that you experience isn't necessarily pain - portions of your body are giving up. This is due to your physiology or possibly due to a lack of mental ability "feelings." Is it pain or is it something else? That is the key for any athlete to figure out so they can know when they can push through or stop to make sure they are not causing any damage.

That is the importance of working at 100% while you practice or prepare for an event. You should be able to push yourself to a point where you can better understand what your body can handle - especially your mind. To get the best out of your workouts or playing games your mind has to be at peak levels to initiate the response that you want out of it. In other words, you have to be mentally stimulated to be able to rise above the little annoyances that are produce when you workout. You have to prepare your mind to handle more than you think you can. You can't sit back and hope your mind will develop for you. In order to be able to handle increased stress and pain you have to make sure you raise your mental capacity for it. Raising you mental capacity will also raise your physiology at the same time.

Workout example of the exact same athlete on different days…..

Athlete 1:
Goes into the gym going over in his mind an argument he had with his girlfriend. He knows he wants to work out and he wants to work hard but all the time the argument is on his mind. He gets in the gym and works out but he continues to think about the argument throughout the program. His results are okay but nothing special.

Athlete 2:
The athlete is not allowed to enter the gym until he raises his pulse rate at a minimum of 5 to 8 beats per minute. By doing that he is talked to in a very loud and stern voice to make sure he is ready to go. At this point the athlete is beginning to jump around and feels really ready to get in the gym to start. Now this athlete is READY to work out. He gets to each exercise ready to go with the right mind set that he knows that he is in charge and ready to get results.

So What Was The Difference? - The Mind!

The key is that the person's ability to PREPARE to train is more important that the actual training itself. It's a mental thing and when you learn to develop a mind that can create the exact emotion needed to push your body to points you need to develop the proper results. If you're going to be in the gym for a certain amount of time - be as efficient as possible so that you are not just going through the motions. Create an atmosphere of results!!

Delayed Onset Muscle Soreness

Delayed onset muscle soreness (DOMS) is that feeling you get when you've worked out for the first time in a long time or overworked to your capacity. It's that feeling that your arms or legs feel like they are about to explode when you go to use them. It's that feeling that your legs feel like 100 pounds each - going up or down stairs. It's that feeling that when you wake up in the morning you feel like you're still lifting the weights from the day before.

Any of us who have worked out from one time to another have experienced this pain. So what exactly is this soreness and where does it come from? Delayed onset muscle soreness (DOMS) is that feeling that comes on a day or two after the workout. It's been around since the caveman and cavewoman...it was studied in the early 1900's and it continues to draw attention from the scientific community. Popular theories have been that the pain is due to a buildup of lactic acid and that has shown more recently to be Dead WRONG! This has been the prevailing thoughts since I first read about 20 years ago. The problem is that blood lactate levels rise during intense exercise however the lactate levels begin to decrease and return to normal between 30 and 60 minutes post exercise.

What is causing the intense soreness two days later?

There may be two causes. One being a high concentration of (+) positive charged calcium ions left over from the rise in lactic acid. This caused a positively charged area and can drop the normal level of blood entering in and out of the area. Blood is responsible for transporting oxygen to the muscle tissue and also carries toxins away from the damaged area. If the damaged area is positively charged then the cells can't properly communicate to one another. When communication is reduced between the cells blood flow is altered reducing oxygen. Without the normal flow of blood in and out of the area toxins are not taken away properly causing a back up.

79

The second reason is that studies have shown damage to the connective tissue structure of the muscle. This connective tissue damage includes the fascia and connective tissue matrix (the substance that binds the cells together). When the muscle and by products break down there is a breakdown of protein. This can cause cellular inflammation which can cause an increase of scar tissue build up (again positively charged) as well as increased metabolic activity including a rise in temperature. When this process advances, local receptor sites responsible for pain become excited - beginning the delayed response.

So as you can see even though lactic acid is returned to normal within 24 hours the pain from extensive training can't be directly linked to lactic acid. If the two were linked together then it would be expected that you should be sore within hours of working out...not 72 hours after. According to Jay Schroeder, "Muscles are in a constant battle between anabolism and catabolism.

(Anabolism: Anabolism, or biosynthesis, is the process by which living organisms synthesize complex molecules of life from simpler ones.)

(Catabolism: is the breakdown of large molecules down to small molecules) (Together both anabolism and catabolism equals your metabolism)

It is the ability to keep them on the anabolic side that is the goal of training. One method to assist this is to stimulate one's muscles through proper exercise; training one's muscles while in an eccentrically elongated (properly lengthened) state. This is traumatic, as exercise is always supposed to be executed at a higher level than what one is currently able to recover from in order to initiate adaptation processes. One of the benefits of this kind of exercise is that the resulting damage to the muscle fibers stimulates the release of growth hormone during pre REM sleep. In order to take maximal advantage of this, one would not like to resolve this soreness for 24 – 36 hours after its onset. [Typically 3 - 8 hours after completion of a proper stimulating exercise plan.]"

So, what can you do for the pain?

Don't think that antioxidants, vitamins or creams will help in prevention or to help you after the damage has been done. Anti inflammatories can assist. It's better to wait it out to let the discomfort go away on its own.

I have experimented with ice for 20 minutes and it does provide temporary relief but you still have to wait until the damage heals. If you have access to an ARPWave machine it can take the pain away overnight. That is a discussion I will go over in detail later in the book. The jury is still out concerning post-exercise massage, post exercise stretching and even the use of ice. But for some people these techniques work well. As you will read in an upcoming chapter - the use of ice will become obsolete. The best thing is to and works out again the next day. I don't suggest that you go as hard as you need to at least do something that will get the body moving. A light jog, a brisk walk, light exercise or even using a treadmill or stepper. Just enough to get the blood moving into the damaged area to help bring more oxygen to the area and allow it to take away toxins sitting around that aren't needed. It won't produce a complete cure but you will feel a difference.

Keep in mind that there has been no hard core scientific literature that says that you can't workout day after day. Yes there has been some articles written saying that you shouldn't lift weights every day but with proper alternating between various workouts you can continue to work out daily. The key is to work out at the same intensity as you would if you were actually in full competition. This in itself will prevent what we have come to know "burnout."

Understanding Fatigue

Fatigue has been identified as a breakdown of performance in an athlete. According to the strict definition of the word fatigue:

1. Weariness from bodily or mental exertion
2. Temporary diminution of the irritability or functioning ot organs, tissues, or cells after excessive exertion or stimulation

Fatigue can be broken down into three primary categories:

a. Neuromuscular Fatigue
b. Metabolic Fatigue
c. Neuroendocrine Fatigue

Neuromuscular Fatigue

This type of fatigue begins as a breakdown of the Central Nervous System (CNS) which is the system that provides electricity to the muscles. When this type of fatigue begins it causes a slowing and a diminished muscular contraction. Many times this is caused by an athlete not training appropriately which causes a diminished response of the nerve cells firing properly. What happens is that the nerve that provides an electrical signal to the muscle to respond to a mental command slows. This causes the muscles to contract slower and with much less force than normal.

Certain environmental stressors can be a cause - improper nutrition, lack of quality sleep - imbalances in electrolytes are causes of this type of fatigue.

Metabolic Fatigue

This type of fatigue is basically centered on depletion of the proper fuels within the muscle system. Many athletes don't fully understand how important the proper consumption of protein is for an athlete. Protein primarily fuels muscle....carbohydrates and fat do very little to supply the muscle the proper building blocks to assist the muscle repair itself.

Proper hydration is also very important in allowing the chemistry to take place within the cells of the muscles. The muscles need things like calcium, magnesium, potassium, and other minerals to allow the muscle fibers to contract properly. When these type of minerals begin to deplete the muscle will begin to slow in it contractions slowing the athlete down.

Neuroendocrine Fatigue

When you train, if you do not train at or above the intensity levels that you are accustomed to playing (in competition) your body will begin to break down in many ways. Training at high intensity 'kicks in' all of the available resources that your body needs to survive and thrive. When you work out at high intensity you force your body to kick in the vascular system, the endocrine system, the muscular system, the neurological system, the lymphatic system and even your central and peripheral nervous system. This is the way that the body designed to work. When you work at high intensity you call upon each and every one of these systems to fire up assisting you to improve what you are attempting to train.

When you train at a level that is below optimum intensity you don't turn these systems on. The theory of "what you don't use you lose" comes in. Instead of getting all of these systems turn on - you instead 'drain' the system which puts the body on defense which can create fatigue.

When you don't balance ALL of your systems and don't pay attention to proper fuels, hydration, and proper sleep, you can upset the natural balance of your body. The lack of proper deep sleep can cause a HUGE problem for the body's normal reconstruction properties. Sleep allows for the body's chemistry to make the necessary changes to repair. It eliminates from the body and allows for the CNS to "reboot" itself. This allows for the conscious and subconscious to ready itself to the day to come.

Upsetting the natural balance of the body has been termed 'BURNOUT'. This is a more of a problem with the coach, the parent or the athlete - not paying attention to detail. When you don't involve yourself with all of the details of proper training bad things can happen. I've seen burnout occur when the coach wasn't paying strict attention to the amount of work he was giving his athletes as compared to the amount of rest. It became strictly one-sided more work - and the kid's metabolism couldn't catch up.

A well-informed coach will always understand the importance of proper recovery. Good coaches know that proper recovery is just as important as a hard workout. For the athlete's body to get the full benefit of the hard training, a proper balance of rest needs to be properly calculated. Training becomes a delicate balance of intensity, rest and fuel. When you go outside of these parameters you are looking for breakdown in the system. The same if you miss handle your own automobile - you can get away with it for a short time but in the long run it will eventually break down.

If you see your athlete exhibit the following symptoms then you really need to take some time to evaluate what they are doing.

1. Loss of Appetite
2. Lethargy or Constantly tired
3. Disturbed Sleep Patterns
4. Increased Heart Rate (Pulse)
5. Longer to Recover Between Workouts
6. Increase resting Blood Pressure

If you see any signs of this you must take some action. You need to talk to your coach, talk to your athlete and back down they type of training that is going on. Most likely they are not paying attention to one or all of the above mentioned aspects of training. If this gets out of hand you will have a major problem on your hands that can take weeks to correct.

Injury and Damage

The old saying on pain no gain is nonsense. If you incur an injury and attempt to go through pain is not smart. Why? Ask your parents or grandparents and see what they say about not taking care of injuries they've had in the past. Ask them how easy it is for them to wake up on a cold or damp day.

Throughout the book I've explained in detail that when an area of the body can't properly absorb force that force will be transferred to the next area like a ligament, tendon or joint. The area that the force is transferred to normally can't absorb the force and injury occurs. Force or impact that isn't properly absorbed can in ligament damage, tendon damage or damage to the joint itself. Usually that is when inflammation beings sending a signal to the brain that damage is present - producing pain.

How does it start? Usually, in a more silent way than you think. For example, Denis Thompson and Jay Schroeder did a clinical study for the NFL regarding ankle sprains. Their theory was that instability of an ankle can lead to an inability to properly absorb force. That inability to absorb force will then transfer to somewhere else. They found that in almost every case that everyone who suffered from a previous ankle sprain led to a hamstring injury. They found that after the ankle sprain the ligament between the lower two ankle bones became less stable causing increased mobility of those bones reducing the capability of the body absorbing force in the lower extremity. This happens quite a bit with sports injuries. If any area of the body is injured and not completely rehabilitated, it can cause a breakdown (damage) in other areas of the body. It is important to make sure that if you sustain an injury of any type that you must completely strengthen the entire area. Just because you are out of pain doesn't mean that you are injury free.

Chapter 5

Asking the Experts Questions

Taking It from the Pros...

I decided to give you a little bit more insight on becoming an elite athlete by interviewing successful, world-class professional athletes and coaches. My goal is to take you inside the minds of highly skilled athletes to give you a professional perspective on how they think and how they felt about growing up and developing the necessary skills to become a professional athlete.

The following professional athletes lend their wisdom and advice:

Matt Stover (Kicker, Indianapolis Colts, NFL)
Mike Bryan (#1 in the World Doubles, ATP)
Qadry Ismail (Retired, Super Bowl Winner Baltimore Ravens, NFL)
Bethanie Mattek-Sands (Professional Tennis Tour, WTA)
Raghib Ismail (Retired, Dallas Cowboys, NFL)
Nadia Petrova (Professional Tennis Tour, WTA)
Jon Drummond (Gold Medalist, 2000 Olympic Games)
Leonard Wheeler (Retired, Carolina Panthers, NFL)
Marquis Mathieu (Retired, Boston Bruins, NHL)
Adam Archuleta (Retired, St. Louis Rams, NFL)
Coach Robert Johnson (Cornell University Track)
Stella Sampras-Webster (UCLA Head Women's Tennis Coach)

Matt Stover
Indianapolis Colts, NFL

Matt Stover is a place kicker, formerly with the Baltimore Ravens, who was scheduled to retire. However, he was proudly brought back to play in the NFL for the Indianapolis Colts that went on to play in Super Bowl XLIV. At age 42, Matt was the oldest kicker ever to play in a Super Bowl.

Matt is arguably the most accurate kicker of all time in the NFL. Matt has played in the NFL for 20 years, entering the league in 1991. Matt has been ranked as one of the all-time best kickers ever.

Conway: What does it take to become an elite athlete?

Stover: What most people don't understand is that even the very best athletes have a powerful internal drive and passion. It's working hard physically, but it's also mental as well. There is a constant persistence to win, but it has to come from inside you... It's just an overall passion.

But a lot of that is a mental psyche, too. I'll flat out tell you. Ray Lewis, he's got that engine in him. I've got that engine in me, that competitive spirit. I know Michael Phelps does. It's a competitive spirit piece that a lot of people don't put enough weight on. They put so much weight on agility and strength... A lot of people don't realize that it's that Muhammad Ali fierceness, and I can say this — either you have it, or you don't.

Conway: What do you feel was the most important thing you did when you were young to help you become a better player?

Stover: Never had anybody tell me to go out and practice.

Conway: How do you feel about coaches/trainers at all levels and how they can prepare athletes to become better?

Stover: Vital for specialty positions. Where I'm trying to go with this is, if you have to depend on a coach to get you to the next level, you'll never get there. You know what I'm saying? Coach in this aspect, politically speaking, somebody will want to put their stamp on you?

Yeah, we all need that at some point, especially when the talent is so even. So I'm trying to formulate your opinion. So let's say I'm one of four kickers, one of three kickers, one of two kickers, and it's just even-steven. Who does the coach feel most comfortable with? Who does he see the most talent, yes, but not only that, the full package? That's when you need a coach for certain things. But with regard to training and that, vital, because the knowledge of exercise training and the proper way to go about it, that stuff is extremely important, but if I'm going to depend on my coach to get me to the next level or to coach me to… then I'm not looking at it the right way. Like Tiger Woods, he goes in…I'm sure he got coached a couple of years ago and redid his swing, right? He knew he had to. It probably wasn't the coach who told him he had to. It was him, and he takes the initiative to change. He takes the initiative to get it going in that direction, and if it's not the athlete and it's just the coach, then it's reversed. That's my opinion.

Conway: When did you realize that sports were more important than other things in your life and that you had to take them more seriously?
Stover: When I was in high school, I just had that sense that I needed to work at this, so when I was in high school. I discovered I had a talent, and I needed to refine it, and I just began to work at it.

Conway: What one thing did you resent when you were young about your training or playing?
Stover: The fact that I didn't lift weights like I should have. Remember, I was raised through the '80s, okay? So remember that.

Conway: What one thing would you like to do over if you had a chance to do it all over again?
Stover: I've been trying to look back and have been asking that same question, and all the lessons from a phase perspective were there for a reason, so I wouldn't change anything other than my first two years was all about kicking for me. It was all about playing for me instead

of for the Lord and for the team, something bigger than me, so you can answer it something bigger than me.

Conway: What one thing could you tell a young athlete to help them better themselves?

Stover: The one thing that I could tell an athlete to help them better themselves is to understand that failure is a part of the game, and the ones who can deal with it the most or the best are the ones who continue to progress.

Conway: What type of training did you feel helped you become a top-level athlete?

Stover: Well, work ethic's too encompassing, but the drive to work at my position, which would be kicking, just wanting to get out there and kick. Now, I could also lump in there what has kept me in the league, of course, is performance, number one, but you have to put in there durability, which was created in the weight room.

Conway: What advice do you have for parents in helping their children to become better athletes?

Stover: Help them find what they most love to do.

Conway: Okay, and let's say they found it. Let's say the particular sport is badminton. What would your advice be for the parents in helping their kids?

Stover: Empowering the athlete to his highest potential. When you empower, you don't tell them that they have to do certain things. You don't dominate over them to say 'you have to go do this; you have to go do that.' What you do is you give them the opportunities to better themselves in that particular sport, which would be weight lifting, specialty coaching, and time. Whatever it is, it's to empower the athlete. Too many parents don't look at it as an empowerment. They look at it, from a parent's standpoint, as what they need to do. Now, of course, there's a few things that... like you probably told Malcolm, 'Hey buddy, you got to get out and work at it here, buddy, or it's never going to happen, or here's my thinking,' but it's really got to become the athlete's… he has to take the initiative. It's got to come from him.

Conway: What type of mental training or feeling did you go through to help you become a better athlete?

Stover: In college, I went to a sports psychologist, and he taught me how to visualize and have confidence in my ability.

Conway: And did you take that to a different level as you became a pro yourself?

Stover: I did. I was able to refine it and find out what worked best for me with regard to visualization techniques, relaxing techniques, how to prepare for games mentally in practice so that you are ready to go emotionally and mentally, as well as off the field. I believe the more mature you get as a person, that can also help you out on the field to perform better just because of your ability to have a better, stable mental approach.

Conway: What did you do to prepare for a game?

Stover: Well, the physical piece would be, of course, you put yourself into a routine. If you're in in-season, you have a particular routine to maintain strength and flexibility, but from a mental standpoint, you tend to take as many things off your plate as you can. You don't continue to add things onto your plate. Now, mind you, life is life, and that does happen. You do have your issues with that, but overall, you do your best to set up healthy boundaries, and then from there, you put yourself in games, and you visualize during the course of the week, so when the game does come on Sunday, you've already kicked the game. You've already kicked it, and so it's just a matter of going out there and replicating what you've already done.

Conway: How did you handle defeat, both as a youngster and as a pro?

Stover: I think pretty well. Of course, no competitive athlete likes to lose. What competition and being defeated in competition did for me was it stoked a fire in me to try harder. It didn't work in the reverse for me. It always was… it forced me to get better. It forced me never to stop working and just give up. It was always no, no, no, I've got to do my part. If it's in a team sport or if I failed individually, what do I have to do next time so I don't fail at that?

Mike Bryan
Professional Tennis, WTA

Mike Bryan has been a professional tennis player since 1998. Mike played at Stanford University before turning professional. His current player ranking is number one in the world in men's doubles, playing with his twin brother, Bob, on tour.

Between 2005 and 2006, the Bryan brothers set an Open Era record by competing in several consecutive doubles Grand Slam finals, of which they won three. They have won in excess of 57 tour titles (and climbing). They have won the French Open, the U.S. Open (twice), the Australian Open (four times), and Wimbledon. Most recently, the Bryan brothers made history at the Farmers Classic in Los Angles winning their 62nd tour title breaking the all-time men's doubles record.

Mike and Bob also are accomplished musicians. On February 12, 2010, The Bryan Bros Band, featuring David Baron, celebrated the release of their debut CD, *Let It Rip,* at a sold-out headlining show in San Francisco. You can listen to their music on their website at www.bryanbrosband.com.

Conway: What do you feel was the most important thing you did when you were young to help you become a better player?

Bryan: The most important thing I did to become a better player when I was younger was I played a tournament every weekend. Most kids today don't compete enough against the peers and gain the invaluable experience that you need to make it to the next level. You can't skip any steps along the way to becoming a top-level player, and sometimes, kids duck competing against each other because they are afraid to lose. You can't be afraid to lose. Also, I put my short- and long-term goals on the refrigerator and looked at them every day. This helped me keep my goals in plain sights and kept reminding me to work hard.

Conway: How do you feel coaches/trainers at all levels can better prepare young athletes?

Bryan: The number one thing coaches and trainers should do is be positive. There's going to be losses and injuries along the way, so it's important to have a good, positive perspective. You should never come down hard on someone for failing as long as they gave their best effort. Secondly, trainers and coaches should keep the workouts fun so that their players stay excited for each workout. This includes keeping workouts fresh and stimulating with lots of variety and fun motivational challenges. Lastly, just like the players, they should have their own set of goals and an overall plan in place for not only their players but themselves.

Conway: When did you realize that this sport was more important than others and that you had to take it more seriously?

Bryan: I realized at a very young age that tennis was going to be my primary focus, and this was paramount. I was able to log more hours of practice and play thousands of more matches than if I was splitting time playing another sport seriously along with tennis. I think it's difficult, especially in tennis, to be successful at the top level if you are a multi-sport athlete past the age of 10 to 12. From this age, the sheer amount of hours needed on court can't be split between another sport. But I do recommend other sports as fun and cross-training, as long as they're not too dangerous!

Conway: What one thing do you resent when you were young about your training/playing?

Bryan: I don't resent or regret anything about my training when I was younger because it's all been a learning experience. Obviously, in hindsight I could have done a few things better, but it's all been a journey, and I know I've given my all to be the best athlete and player I could be. Whenever I learned something or was given advice that I thought was helpful, I took it in stride and tried use it. I was never pushed into training, and it's always been my choice to step on the court or in the gym. I was lucky to have parents that motivated me to play by making tennis fun, and they instilled my passion for the game at a very young age. And I still love to play the game today.

Conway: What one thing would you like to do over if you had the chance to do it all over again?

Bryan: This is similar to the previous question. I feel that, though everything hasn't gone smoothly and I have made mistakes along the way, these tough moments have made me the person and the athlete that I am today. A few nagging injuries have popped up that I obviously wish I didn't have. I may have been able to prevent them if I had a crystal ball and pre-habbed those specific areas, but without those pains, I might not have worked so hard on getting as physically fit as I am today.

Conway: What "one thing" could you tell a young athlete to help them better themselves?

Bryan: I would tell them to find a good coach that you get along well with, a proven fitness trainer, and find a good group of friends you can train with. Training with friends will pass the time quicker, and you can push each other. Make sure that you're a well-rounded individual, and you give 100 percent into your academics and another passion that's not athletic. Example: music. This will develop other parts of the brain and make you a stronger and less one-dimensional person. Lastly, I wouldn't become overly consumed with winning or losing at a young age, just as long as you're developing the correct technique and making sure your game is improving.

Conway: What advice do you have for parents in helping their children to become better athletes?

Bryan: Parents need to motivate their kids with fun first. Developing the love for their sport is crucial. This can be done by taking their kids to professional or college sporting events or just immersing them in a fun sports atmosphere with friends. And then, once they're hooked, it becomes easy because they'll gladly want to put in the hours of practice that are necessary to improve. By taking them to watch pro and college sports, this allows them to see the highest level of their sport. In order for them to dream it, they have to see it first. And so, for them to dream big, they have to be exposed to the big time.

Conway: What type of training did you feel helped you become a top-level athlete?

Bryan: Doing a ton of core and legs exercises have been crucial in taking my game to a higher level. I know that most of power in tennis is generated from the ground up through the core, and by adding strength to this chain, I can feel more sting behind my shots. I feel more level and balanced when moving and striking the ball, and this focused training has allowed me to make the quick, subtle adjustments necessary to execute from different positions on the court.

Conway: What type of mental training did you go through to help you become a better athlete?

Bryan: Before a big match, I always like to visualize myself on that upcoming match court feeling great and playing perfect tennis. I'll do this the night before and a half-hour before competition. Within my body, I'll try to feel the emotions of winning, and I'll feel myself moving to the ball and contacting it with precise control and perfect execution. I'll also run through different possible scenarios and strategic changes and adjustments I'll have to make while competing. There shouldn't be any surprises when you step on the court. It should feel like you've been there before.

Conway: What did you do to prepare for a match?

Bryan: Preparation for a match starts in practice. You should always practice and train how you want to compete. This involves giving your all and staying focused for however long you're on court. If you're preparing for a particular opponent, then it's valuable to begin the process of exploiting weaknesses and going through patterns that will work well against that person. Eating two hours in front of a match and sleeping at least eight hours the night before are a must. I like to warm-up 20 minutes prior to a match with movement and active stretching exercises. Then right before walking out to play, I'll run over the game plan with my coach so it's fresh in my mind.

Conway: How do you handle defeat, both as a youngster and as a pro?

Bryan: Losses are always especially hard because I'm an exceptionally competitive person, and I hate losing! I try not to go over the "x"s and "o"s and what "could of should of" immediately following the match. I usually try to do the analysis of the match that night or the next day and discuss what needs to be done to improve. It takes time to get over a match. I'm usually too mad to have this discussion with my coach right after a loss. I feel losses are sometimes more important than wins because they can be a huge motivational spark. I've worked the hardest and had some of my biggest wins following a difficult defeat.

Qadry Ismail
Baltimore Ravens, NFL

Qadry Ismail, former Super Bowl champion with the Baltimore Ravens, is now an analyst for ESPN television. Qadry played 10 years in the NFL as a wide receiver. He was also an All American in track, running the high hurdles for Syracuse University.

Qadry and Jim Brown are the only two sports All Americans that ever played for Syracuse University. Presently, Qadry offers his highly qualified expertise reviewing football games and player performance for ESPN sports. Qadry also provides commentary for WBAL, the home of the Baltimore Ravens.

Ismail was brought up on the tough streets of Newark, New Jersey, before moving to Wilkes-Barre, Pennsylvania. He offers his insight on growing up in sports and realizing how they affected his life.

Conway: What is the most important thing a parent can do for their young athlete?

Ismail: If your child has the aptitude for education, then that is great. If your child has a passion to play a sport, that's great... whatever it is, help them develop that particular passion. Don't do it because you think they would like it; make sure it's something they want to do.

Don't hype them up, don't talk them up, don't think they are the gift to God's earth... let them be among other kids and hang out... let them grow up. Remember this... there is always going to be another kid that is better than yours. It's going to be a challenge for them for life... let them be a kid first, and if their talent brings them along, so be it. The athlete has to learn to recognize certain mile markers in life. I have to do certain things at that point to get to the next point. Then I have to develop from there, and I have to keep getting better if I want to succeed.

Parents understand that, by the ninth grade, you notice that your child is working out on their own and has a desire to play and doesn't need to be pushed. Then and only then, you can step in to give them a push to help them achieve the next mile marker.

It's this simple... if, by their junior year, if they aren't being actively recruited, they aren't the talk of the town, if they aren't the best [in] their conference or one of the very best in the state, then the chances of Division I schools coming after them is highly unlikely. Other than that, prepare them for the next level of sports, which would be at a lower level, either Division II or Division III.

Conway: What type of training helped you in becoming a top-level athlete?
Ismail: High school — I had the poorest training, and I'm glad I was at the right place at the right time. College — I had a strength coach and a track coach that understood the basics of strength and speed dynamics. That means that you have to get stronger and maintain your flexibility, and you have to somehow find a way to eat the right foods... even in college. That's the key — strength, flexibility, and nutrition.

Conway: What type of mental training or feeling did you go through to help you become a better athlete?
Ismail: My biggest asset was my mental toughness. The art of visualizing got me through all of my intense trials and helped me overcome some of the extreme difficulties of training in high school, college, and in the pros.

I would literally have different visualization sessions with myself in my mind and going over all of the different scenarios that [I] knew could take place and that what I wanted to happen for myself. That got me through those days through double sessions, because my legs were so dead, and because of the mental toughness that I developed and the visualization that I created in my mind got me through the toughest times.

My mental strength separated me from all of the other athletes. I recently had conversations with my past teammates, and they said, "We used to laugh at you then, but you were always able to outwork us to get you to this level (pro level), and that is what separated you."

Conway: What do you do to prepare for a game?

Ismail: By the time I got to the Super Bowl, I felt that writing goals was a waste of time. At this time in my professional life, it came down to this. You had to define who you were and by defining on who you were and visualize putting it in the debts of your mind what you wanted to accomplish. Facing your fears and your weaknesses, telling yourself that they do not exist, and if they do exist, then you can overcome them. Then you run over and over again the many plays in your mind that you needed to do for that game.

To give you an example, the night before the Super bowl, [I] had the highlight reel tape from my team video personnel, and I went into the room, put on my headset of my favorite music and put them on repeat and literally watch all of the tape of myself (the best highlights) and then the sheet that I had from the team to review as well. I then knew my number one thing that I had to do was to put my God first and wanted to bring Him glory. My number two goal was to know who I was as a wide receiver and that I needed to be consistent. I needed to be productive, I needed a big play, and I needed to 'be' a wide receiver. Once I went over this, I knew nothing could stop me, then from that point forward, I would prepare myself that there was nothing left unattended to. That included making sure my body felt great, that I was properly hydrated, that I ate the right food so that I was ready to go. My game day definition was being productive, being consistent, being a big play, and being a wide receiver.

In meetings, I would know every assignment, every route, every block, and every nuance that I had to do to prepare myself so that there was no weakness in my mind. By the time game time came around, I knew that every minute detail was confronted and ready to go. I was the person who was the first person in the seat, the first person on the bus. I was one of the first people off of the bus because I wanted to be the leader. I had a stretch routine, my catch routine, and by the time the game came, and I would then go over my game sheet and force myself to look at my weaknesses and tell myself that they did not exist. I would be in a state of 'You can't touch me, and it's time to go'... let's do this.'

Conway: How do you handle defeat, both as a youngster and as a pro?

Ismail: If I played well, it didn't bother me. Losing is a part of life, so get over it... no matter what people say. You have to understand defeat because it is going to make you better. You can take all of that other winning crap and throw it away until you learn how to deal with defeat. All I know is that you're going to have more defeats than wins, and it's how you learn to handle it [that] makes you better.

The defeats that I had when I was younger prepared me for the pros. It prepared me to be a Super Bowl champion.

As a youngster, when you get a defeat... it's tough. But when you play poorly and you have a defeat, it wears on you because you know you didn't do everything possible to overcome to help your team to win the game. That is what sticks with me in my mind the most when I look at defeat that I had in my athletic career.

Conway: When you were young playing sports in the inner city?

Ismail: Yes, my dad lived in Section Eight housing called Georgia King Village in Newark, New Jersey. Basically, the way the townhome was built, it was built on the side of a hill, and we would always with the group that was called the Top of the Hill, and there was the Bottom of the Hill. We always had an annual game called the Top vs. the Bottom. The Bottom always were the winners every year because they always had better kids on their team.

We would always be playing some type of sport every day. It didn't matter. Even if there wasn't enough kids, we would make up games. As far as crime went, it wasn't all that bad, or at least I wasn't aware of it. I had some neighbors who sold weed out of their house regularly, but I can't think of anyone else doing it. It was pretty low-key. There were no drive-by shootings or anything like that.

Conway: Do you think there was any advantage from growing up in Newark as opposed to living in Wilkes-Barre, Pennsylvania?

Ismail: There wasn't a lot of opportunity to play organized sports in my area in Newark. Once we went up to Orange, New Jersey, to play organized football, which had uniforms. I played offensive and defensive line there, but I had to lie to tell them I was from their area to be able just to play. I wanted to play so bad, but we didn't have the money for equipment.

When I got to Wilkes-Barre, it was really different. At that time, Wilkes-Barre was rated high as top places to live, but coming from Newark, you learned that you stayed in your own neighborhood, and you didn't venture out so you didn't have to fight. In Wilkes-Barre, it was totally different with my brother and I saying, 'Wow, this is going to be cool... they have equipment and coaches who really care." It was eye-opening, but it made me drool because now I could play all out with equipment that we never had before.

Conway: What kind of pressure were you under when you played youth sports?

Ismail: The pressure when we played sand lot was just being the best on the field. I don't ever remember being one of the last guys picked to play anything. I remember in Newark we went to move up to my mom's family for awhile to Detroit. That was my first experience of true ghetto living. Detroit's mentality with the kids were more edgy and violent and always wanted to do the wrong things all the time.

I remember playing where the older guys would always try to belittle you, where in Newark my "street cred" was known that both myself and my brother were better than most. Now moving to Wilkes-Barre, I'm living in a predominately community of white people in which my father had raised us to look at multiple cultures the right way. But it turned out to be a real education for me when I played my first game in Wilkes-Barre.

It was against the Hanover Mini Hawks, and I scored a touchdown and began showboating. I didn't realize I was showboating because that's what I thought you should do because I learned that from the NFL players... I really didn't know any better. So I received a 15-yard penalty. The second touchdown I scored I got another 15-yard penalty. Then I scored a third touchdown, so I didn't do anything because of the other two penalties. After the game, I was walking out of the football field, and I looked up, and there were these older white ladies looking at me, shaking their heads, saying that "He is such a bad kid." I remember right then and there that the pressure of living in a predominantly white area made me change the way I carried myself so that no one would ever say anything negative about me again.

In high school, my brother and I would be getting phone calls after the game saying not-so-kind things to us on the phone and hanging up. So I was tough in a sense growing up in a community that, because you looked different or play different, people say mean things or do mean things to you. Don't get me wrong. There were a lot of good people in our lives that helped us out, and I know there are great people living in the area. What I'm saying is that it was a big change moving from Newark, Detroit, to Wilkes-Barre.

Conway: When did you realize that you knew you had a gift to take it to the next level?

Ismail: I always wanted to take it to the next level, but all along the way, there were little mile markers of encouragement. My first mile marker was playing in Newark with my brother. Raghib and I were never able to play on the same team.

Another one was living in Pennsylvania, when the coaches of the Mini Mohawks saying, 'Where is Qadry? If he isn't here, we're not going to win.' I was thinking to myself, 'What do you mean? Why do you need me?' I didn't really realize that I was that good where people counted on me.

In high school, I knew I was good, but I didn't know how to get better because all of the focus was on my brother, Raghib. So I had to figure out ways through my own competitiveness to get better. There were key mile markers of encouragement in high school that told me that I could make it to the next level.

In my senior year, we were playing the Crestwood Comets, and the year before, they had beaten us with my brother being injured. I remember I was riding this confident wave coming out of a successful track season. I went down to the stadium, and I remember that day I knew I was going to have a big game. We get out there and start playing, and the quarterback gave me the ball, and I remember that I fumbled the ball, but it was different from other times. But this time when I fumbled, I immediately picked it up, and a kid squared up and leveled me, and I said to myself, 'No, not today.' I remember peeling off him, moving around, and breaking about four or five tackles and scoring a touchdown. I remember saying to myself that 'This year, you can say what you want, you can do what you want, but no matter what you say about me, I don't care. I'm going to show you that I can play this game.'

Conway: What can you tell parents to help them help their kids be better athletes?

Ismail: Become great listeners. Knowing I have my kids now and me back then, parents have to realize that some kids just have that "it factor"… they got it. Not every kid has big-time talent.

Guard against putting too much pressure on them, and let them have that sense of fun and excitement. Let them have that anticipation of what's next after they accomplish whatever they are playing. Ask them about their games; don't tell them about their games.

Keep in mind — win or lose — you are building your child for character. Female athletes, there aren't many pro sports you're going to get pain in, so build them to become a woman of character. Even with male athletes, please realize that it's less than one percent who make it to the pros. So help develop your children to have fun and help them to develop character.

Conway: What would you tell young athletes on how they can become elite athletes?

Ismail: Don't start narrowing your choices down in sports until you get to about the ninth grade. Play as many sports as you can or enjoy; then, if you see that you may have some extra talent at the ninth grade level, then you can begin to concentrate on that sport. Also, pick a complementary sport as well to stretch your imagination and your comfort zone to compete at something that you may not be totally good at. It helps you build adversity and how to overcome certain problems or frustrations. Learn how to overcome things in the sport that you may not be as good at... How do I interact in that sport? How can I figure out how to become better overall? How can I avoid becoming a better-bench player? Meaning, if I'm not in the game now, how can I help my team waiting until I get my chance? How can I become a better teammate?

Bethanie Mattek-Sands
Professional Tennis, WTA

Bethanie Mattek is a professional tennis player presently playing on the WTA tour. Mattek has won five singles and three doubles titles on the ITF Circuit, and her best results on the WTA Tour to date are reaching the semifinals of the tournaments in Cincinnati, Ohio, in 2005; Birmingham, United Kingdom, in 2008; and the finals of the Bell

Challenge in 2008. In doubles, she has won four WTA Tour titles. Mattek also plays for the New York Sportimes for World Team Tennis.

In April of 2009, Mattek became the first female tennis player to win both singles and doubles in a Fed Cup match after being down 2-1. The USA under Mattek's assault on the court beat top-ranked Russia to put the Americans in the finals of the 2010 Fed Cup. Bethanie has been ranked as high as 37th in the world in singles and 12th in the world in doubles. In doubles, she has won four WTA Tour titles. Bethanie grew up in the frozen tundra of Wisconsin, and her family moved to Florida to help her accomplish her dreams.

Conway: What do you feel was the most important thing you did when you were young to help you become a better player?

Mattek-Sands: The most important thing that I did when I was young was to play a bunch of different sports up to the age of 12. I'm glad I didn't specialize when I was five, like a lot of tennis players do. It made me a more well-rounded athlete in general.

Conway: How do you feel coaches/trainers at all levels can better prepare young athletes?

Mattek-Sands: I think that coaches need to help the younger athletes to begin thinking on their own. They need more about their practices, preparation, and game situations. There are too many times where the coaches just tell players what to do, rather than telling them the 'why' behind it. The players need to go out and think on their own so that they can figure things out for themselves, especially when things aren't going their way. Players now are looking at their coaches in the stands, seeing what they need to do, rather than trying to figure it out for themselves. I think that this is important so that there isn't any over-coaching.

Conway: When did you realize that this sport was more important than others and that you had to take it more seriously?

Mattek-Sands: When I was younger, at age 10 and 11, I was beating many of the older girls in my area. I was beating girls that were age 16 and 18 and began winning many tournaments. I remember at that age I won 12 tournaments both years. I knew it was time to make a decision to move to play against more of an international competition.

I had to make that decision when I was 12. I moved down to Evert Tennis Academy from Wisconsin. I went down to see if I was going to be able to make the move, because going to the Academy meant six hours of tennis per day, plus school and other workouts. So my family moved to Florida so that I could train full-time.

Conway: What one thing did you resent when you were young about your training/playing?

Mattek-Sands: I think as much as a big decision it was to move to Florida to train at the Evert Academy, if I had to do [it] all over again, I wouldn't do it. We would train six hours a day, and now looking back, that was way too much to train. It takes a tremendous toll on your body with injuries and mental stress. Knowing what I know now, I would do it much different if I had to do it all over again.

Conway: What one thing would you like to do over if you had the chance to do it all over again?

Mattek-Sands: I would have chosen one coach and not listened to anyone else. I feel I've had too many coaches, and a lot of the information that is given to you crosses over one another and can make it difficult to understand. I would pick one coach and stick with that and keep it simple.

Conway: What "one thing" could you tell a young athlete to help them better themselves?

Mattek-Sands: Have fun!

Conway: What advice do you have for parents in helping their kids become better athletes?

Mattek-Sands: Teach their kids how to have fun. But if the athlete has legit talent, then I would recommend that they need to make sure that they have the right people around them. Find people who you can trust so that they can get honest feedback. When there are too many voices lending advice, it gets too confusing. Especially when someone is good, a lot of people want to jump on the bandwagon and give advice or blow some up their dress in order to hang around the limelight. You really need someone that you can trust so that they can honestly get to the next level, rather than get distracted by the drama, gossip, or any other petty distractions. To exceed as a pro, you need to keep everything as simple as possible.

Conway: What type of training did you feel helped you become a top-level athlete?

Mattek-Sands: I've always been strong, even when I was young, so strength wasn't really an issue with me. Over the years, I did the basic training that most tennis players do. I found myself breaking down and getting injured more and more. When I started working with you (Dr. Conway) and learning your methods, I wasn't getting injured as much. Then you referred me to Jay Schroeder, whose training has helped me a ton. Also, I work with the Impulse machine on a regular basis. That really has made a big difference.

Conway: What type of mental training did you go through to help you become a better athlete?

Mattek-Sands: One thing that I've always done was to figure things out and never give up. Even as a junior, I would always be fighting through situations. If plan A wasn't working, then I would go to plan B, and if needed, I would go to plan C. My biggest mental strength was developing a never-give-up attitude. That helped me a lot.

Conway: What do you do to prepare for a match?

Mattek-Sands: By the time the match comes around, there isn't a lot you can do. As long as you've taken the time to properly prepare and do all of the things needed to compete at this level, this is not the time to start stressing. There isn't much you can do the day of a match that is going to help you. I will take a couple of minutes before my match, just going over the person I'm going to play and how I need to play against them. It's about me just being relaxed and getting into my zone.

I warm up by hitting for a half-hour before my matches, but other than that, it's all about being calm and finding that zone for me that is comfortable. Then I'm ready to go.

Conway: How do you handle defeat, both as a youngster and as a pro?

Mattek-Sands: As a youngster, I handled defeat pretty bad. I was a bad loser. I'm getting better. I've always been really competitive, either on the tennis court or even playing checkers. I don't like to lose. When I lose, I tend to go inward with myself. I will go off by myself so people wouldn't be able to find me for awhile.

All my second place trophies are damaged to some degree. They may be missing a head or an arm because I would throw it later on and tell my parents I didn't want to see it. When I was young, all I played for was trophies, and I wanted the number one trophy, not number two. As a young player, I would walk into the tournament and see the trophies all set up before the match. I would see the number one trophy as mine. But if I didn't win the tournament, I would be disappointed to say the least.

Raghib "Rocket" Ismail
Dallas Cowboys, NFL

Raghib Ismail, a legend at the University of Notre Dame, played in the NFL with the Oakland Raiders, Dallas Cowboys, and Carolina Panthers. Coming out of college a year early, Rocket accepted a position with the Toronto Argonauts for what was then the highest offer ever given to a football player. "Rocket" is known to be one of the fastest of all time players in the NFL, being timed running a 40-yard dash in 4.12. He recorded two 1,000-yard receiving seasons in the NFL and was a CFL All-Star in 1991, as well as the Most Valuable Player of the 79th Canadian Grey Cup. In 2004, CollegeFootballNews.com named Ismail as the #75 player on their list of the Top 100 Greatest College Football Players of All Time.

Conway: What do you feel was the most important thing you did when you were young to help you become a better player?

Rocket: Hanging out with friends who had common goals as me in sports. All together, we didn't think that wouldn't let us not become good athletes. That included having a bad attitude, smoking and drinking, respecting authority. We made sure that we didn't fall to the negativity of doing drugs. We all had a common vision of going as far as possible in sports beyond high school. We knew we had to pay attention in school to get to the next level.

Conway: How do you feel coaches/trainers at all levels can better prepare young athletes?

Rocket: It helps if they knew what they were doing. To be able to give the young athlete a vision of success and that they can do better. Looking back now on my youth was that some coaches were able to help me understand that I had a gift that was going to allow me to go far in life. They showed me the importance of graduating high school and to go on to a university and graduate.

Coaches/trainers need to give the athletes a vision on where they can go and what they can accomplish. They need to be able to teach discipline, teach how to respect authority, how to teach discipline, because it is extremely important to have discipline and respect authority and to teach the importance of how to sacrifice for the greater cause of the team.

I remember my last high school game I had a severe sprain of my leg/contusion. I remember missing study hall and lunch and going to you every single day to be treated. I couldn't run due to the pain, and because of the insight you had literally not saying to me 'just take some painkillers, or use ice on it, and hope for the best.' You proactively accessed what was going on and aggressively treated me where I was able to play in the game. I ended up with six touchdowns, and it was a great moment for me, but it wouldn't have happened if you didn't have the insight to find the answer to my problem.

I also remember my junior year in track where I lost the 100-meter dash. The following year, you (Dr. Conway) had the insight to develop a strength program for me for my track season. I remember that you made the decision to train us during track season when many of the coaches where against it at the time. I remember everyone was worried that you were going to bulk us (my brother Qadry) up and slow us down right before the track state championships. You stuck to your theory and continued training us two nights a week, taking us to the gym. We would do a series of weight-training exercises to increase our strength, explosiveness, and even our recovery time. I remember that it was the turning point in that the results were so staggering that I remember at states there was a silent type of talk that the Ismail boys are on steroids because the results were so staggering.

So a good trainer can be invaluable to help a young athlete in understanding how to stay hydrated, how to eat properly, and how to train properly, and teach them how to get the right rest. If they know what they are doing, then they can be a real asset to the young athlete.

Conway: When did you realize that this sport was more important than others and that you had to take it more seriously?

Rocket: I remember my junior year I knew that I wasn't getting anywhere in basketball, so I figured that I could use that time better in working on football and track. I feel it is important to play as many sports as you can, but sometimes, there comes that time when you have to concentrate on the sport that is showing the most promise for the future.

My senior year, I didn't go out for basketball because I felt that I didn't know how basketball could help me for the future. My coaches at the time relied on me for just being a good, quick athlete and not teaching me the true fundamentals needed for me to excel in this sport.

Conway: What one thing did you resent when you were young about your training/playing?

Rocket: It's not resentment; it's an eye-opener for me when I'm addressing young players now that I have to make sure that they are fundamentally sound. I look back now knowing I could have been a much better basketball player if I was taught the true fundamentals of the game. I don't really call it 'resentment.' I just look at what could have been.

Conway: What one thing would you like to do over if you had the chance to do it all over again?

Rocket: I would like to have had a better attitude in working out. My talent level was such a hindrance. Even if I didn't work hard, it didn't show at certain levels. I was able to get away with a lot because my gift was able to compensate for it. I wish I was able to apply myself physically from a working out standpoint earlier because I think it would have advanced me even more.

Another reason was that we had you to fix us. We had you to keep us aligned. We had you to keep us adjusted and correct any little injuries we had, which kept us going. All of the injuries didn't amount to anything because you were able to nip them in the bud. So it would be good for any athlete to know not to wait on injury and get them fixed.

Conway: What "one thing" could you tell a young athlete to help them better themselves?

Rocket: I don't care what they do [but] they have to learn how to identify what they believe first. They have to believe to be able to overcome whatever circumstance is thrown at them. The reason why I say that is that I learned later that you don't have to be stuck on old thinking.

They found out that in the genetic code or DNA that you were given will not limit you in any way. They used to think that whatever genes you were given at birth can't be changed. This is true in only 20 percent of the time. They found that most of the genes are sitting there waiting for instruction from your belief system to tell them what to do. So the power of belief can actually change the genetic material in your cells, so you can make real, deep changes in your makeup. So that if you can overcome strife, hardship, or other negative things thrown at you, you can make big changes in your life through the power of vision and belief.

If you feel 'I'm never going to make it,' that's what you believe. If you say, 'I can do this,' that is what you believe. Either way, whatever you believe, the cells of your body are waiting for instruction to do what you tell them to do. Do it hard, long, and strong enough, and you can change anything.

Conway: What advice do you have for parents in helping their children to become better athletes?

Rocket: Parents should not add any pressure to their kids' sporting lives. They already have lots of pressure. There are a lot of parents creating pressure for their kids when they think they are helping them.

The best thing you can do is to help them with sleeping, nutrition, watching who they are hanging out with, and just being there to guide them along. To become an athlete, it takes work, and you have to help them stay clear of outside distractions. Work their vision of their sports with them... show them how that it takes work to stay after the vision.

Conway: What type of training did you go through to help you become a better athlete?

Rocket: The best training I had in my entire life was at the Carolina Panthers. Their training system was the simplest. It was two days a week, do 15 reps on each row of machines. One day upper body, and the other day lower body, with treadmill thrown in as well. They made you rest the day after the workout; it was mandatory. It was the biggest change I had in my entire professional career because, as the season went on, I got stronger and never was injured. It went against every other NFL team out there as far as philosophy, but for me, it worked the best. I was more physical. I was more aggressive. I just felt so much better and played great.

I made sure I was properly hydrated. I ate well-balanced meals that I knew that would make me feel better. I made sure I got optimum rest and prepared to the point on what I needed to do for that day.

Conway: What type of mental training did you go through to help you become a better athlete?

Rocket: I would visualize my routes and blocking assignments over and over. When I was younger, I would listen to music that would rev me up, but I found that I was wasting energy. So I then would listen to softer music before [a] game to make sure I wasn't overpreparing and wasting energy before a game.

Conway: How do you handle defeat, both as a youngster and as a pro?

Rocket: When I was a youngster, I was a very sore loser. So I had to learn how to lose, and that led me to better understand why I lost. My attitude had to change, not to get upset and learn how to manage defeats, and more importantly, learn from what I did wrong and correct it.

Nadia Petrova
Professional Tennis

Nadia Petrova is a professional tennis player from Moscow, Russia. Nadia offers a special insight on being raised by two Olympic champions from a totally different culture. As a junior, Petrova won the 1998 French Open. And, in the same year, she finished runner-up at the Orange Bowl and also finished runner-up at the junior 1999 U.S. Open.

Overall, she has won 26 WTA titles, nine in singles and seventeen in doubles. In singles, Petrova has reached a career-high ranking of world number three in May 2006 and has reached the semifinals of the French Open in 2003 and 2005. In doubles, her highest rank was number three in the world.

Conway: What advice would you give to youngsters starting out playing sports?

Petrova: The first thing they need to understand is to enjoy what they are doing and develop a passion about what they are doing. They have to understand that they will have to dedicate a lot of time to the particular sport to develop properly. You have to be very organized and become as focused as possible in order to achieve your goal.

Conway: How did you see yourself as a young athlete?

Petrova: My life was a little bit different because my parents were both Olympic athletes. I was always around sports, and I thought I was going to follow in my parents' footsteps, but then tennis came along. So by the age of 14, I was having good results in tennis, and it was around that time I felt I wanted to become a professional athlete. Up until then, my life was around school, but when I made the decision to turn pro, my life completely changed.

It also got a bit more difficult because I had to miss certain classes to make a tournament. I would have to stay late to practice. I missed out on sleepovers. I missed parties and hanging out with my friends. My life became completely different.

Conway: When did you know that you had a chance to make it to the professional ranks?

Petrova: I knew when I began to play IVF tournaments and began beating ranked players. I played at Bolletteri Tennis Academy and beat the number one junior tennis player. I advanced all the way to the quarterfinals that tournament. That's when Bolletteri approached me to ask me to train at his academy.

Conway: What one thing was a turning point in your young career?

Petrova: In 2001, when I came off a long-standing injury, in which I worked hard to come back and made it to the semifinals of the French Open. I made a major jump on my rankings, and it seemed that all my worries and thoughts began to really turn positive, which felt like a heavy weight was lifted from me.

Conway: How do you think young athletes should train?

Petrova: Learning how to give 100 percent all of the time but understanding not to over-train. Leaving some practice undone so that you have the feeling that you need to come back again to practice more. Not being satisfied with what you just did. Being able to come back and do better than the day before.

Conway: What one thing do you regret when you were training as a young athlete?

Petrova: Not having the right coach right from the beginning. I needed the basics of tennis right from the beginning and that a lot of time was wasted in my case. It is important that the coach help you develop the proper fundamentals both physically and mentally.

Conway: What one memory stays with you as a young athlete?

Petrova: My first time playing at the big stadium at a major grand slam event. Those type of memories can never be taken away and stay with you a lifetime.

Conway: What advice would you give coaches/trainers to help young athletes?

Petrova: Make it fun!

Conway: What advice would you give parents raising young athletes?

Petrova: Before you invest the time, money, and effort in the sport, make really sure that your child wants to play this sport. Know that they are the ones interested, not just you.

Conway: What type of mental training or feeling did you go through to help you become a better athlete?

Petrova: To practice and work out is the easiest for every professional athlete. The hardest is to deal with pressure. I've tried different approaches, including seeing psychologists and doing different kinds of visualizations. At the end of the day, regardless of all [the] help you receive, you have to learn yourself how to overcome the obstacles.

Conway: What did you do to mentally prepare for a game?

Petrova: I like to start to think about the match a day before, [and] practice some tactical approaches on court with my coach. Visualize the night before and right before the game, me playing the match point by point and creating winning situations.

Conway: How did you handle defeat, both as a youngster and as a pro?

Petrova: It's changed significantly throughout the years with maturity. Some matches are more difficult than others, depending on the opponent.

Leonard Wheeler
Carolina Panthers, NFL

Playing his college career at Troy State, Leonard was drafted in the third round by the Cincinnati Bengals. A nine-year veteran of the NFL, Leonard continued his NFL career with the Minnesota Vikings and Carolina Panthers. From playing football in the NFL, Leonard now is president of Wheeler Enterprises, addressing high-power corporations and serving as a personal coach for top executives. He lectures to many business groups and corporations and has assisted in supporting survivors of the Columbine tragedy. Starring in national and local commercials, television shows, and movies, Leonard's success is well documented.

Conway: What advice would you give to youngsters starting out playing sports?

Wheeler: Create a new mentality. Young athletes are not raised the way we were in the past. We were more free to go and play from morning until it got dark. We were constantly playing some sport all day long. Times have changed, and young athletes have to create a mentality that is one of succeeding and working hard.

Most young people have a sense of entitlement in that they feel most things should be given to them. They will only give half an effort and expect the other half to be given to them. They expect to win without putting forth the right effort to win.

Are you willing to make the appropriate effort necessary to become successful? If not then you need to decide on what you want to be a part of. You see, a lot of times, kids waste their parents' time as well. The parents are trying to supply all of the necessary resources to take advantage of, but the kids aren't willing to put forth the effort needed to make it a reality.

Conway: How did you see yourself as a young athlete?

Wheeler: I was a young athlete and didn't realize my talent until I got older. I always wanted to win and be on a winning team.

Conway: Was there a piece of advice given to you when you were young, and what advice can you give young athletes right now?

Wheeler: The advice that was given to me when I was young was that, when you go on the field or the court, you're playing for everyone on your team, rather than playing for yourself. That mentality allowed me to block for my teammates better, or when I scored, I knew I scored for everyone on the team.

Even now when I coach my daughter's soccer team, I tell them that you are not on this team alone... don't get caught up that you are the only one on the field. So if you don't make a good play, don't start that 'who is me.' If you think that you are the only one out there, then you will start with that mentality, but if you know that you are a part of a team, then you won't get down on yourself so much because you will help each other out.

Conway: When did you know you had a chance to make it to the professional ranks?

Wheeler: I told my mom when I was eight that I wanted to play in the NFL. I told [my] high school coach that I was going to play there as well when I was a senior. So for me, it was always a dream, even though people told me that I had the capability. And when I got to college and began making a few plays here and there, that dream slowly began to become a reality.

Conway: What one thing was a turning point in your young career?

Wheeler: When I had to sit out one year in college, and from that, it got me really ticked off and mad that I couldn't play. From there, I had something to prove to everyone to show them that I can play. I grew up in the projects, and I was tired of failing. So that disappointment got to me to the point that I knew I wasn't going to return to the area where I grew up.

Conway: How do you think young athletes should train?

Wheeler: Smarter. What I mean by that is the athletes should take the emphasis off of how strong they can be and start studying their own body and understanding a little more about their own physiology. They need to find out how their body will adapt to certain exercises and study their body more. This way, they can feel how they react to certain situations they are presented on the field or the court.

I feel that is the reason why there are so many injuries, because they leave it up to everyone else to worry about their bodies rather than understanding it for themselves.

Conway: What one memory stays with you as a young athlete?

Wheeler: I broke a 49-yard run in high school in overtime to beat our rival school.

Conway: What advice would you give young coaches/trainers on working with young athletes?

Wheeler: For coaches, I would tell the coach to better understand the power of influence they have over the young athletes. I would make sure the influence they have over the kids in life in general and not putting all of the emphasis on the field, but helping them in life as well. I think that coaches put so much emphasis on winning that they forget to develop the athletes as people.

For trainers, I would tell them that it's not just about them getting a paycheck. They really need to better understand the individual athlete to what best fits them in preparing them properly for their sport. What is happening that trainers get stuck in a mode of the same of training, and every athlete seems [to] get the same workout. This one-size-fits-all mentality doesn't work. Each individual athlete needs to build on separate strengths and weaknesses that are individual to them.

Conway: What advice would you give parents to help their young athletes?

Wheeler: First of all, some of these parents need to grow up. That these athletes don't need over-abusive parents. The parents need to let the coaches coach and stop undermining them. They need to start trusting the coaches more. Some coaches in some towns are not playing their best athletes because of the parents' over-involvement in the athlete… it's the craziest thing I've ever seen.

> *Leonard Wheeler is the president of Wheeler Enterprises. After retiring from the NFL, Wheeler became a life coach, actor, motivational speaker, and author, optimizing people's performance in business, sports, and life. I expanded Mr. Wheeler's conversation with me to allow him to delve deeper into the aspects of what is needed to become successful.*

Conway: As a parent sitting here trying to help their child become a better athlete, what can I do to help them to develop a better attitude to succeed?

Wheeler: You're asking the wrong questions. 'How do I help my kid have a positive attitude' is tough because you can never give a prognosis without a proper diagnosis. So the same thing goes when trying to help your child's mental capacity. If you haven't diagnosed what has been going on in their lives, then you can't give good concrete information back to him. If I don't understand his thinking patterns (what he runs in his mind over and over) or his beliefs (belief systems), then it is difficult to give a prognosis of where he needs to be. Mainly because I don't know where he is (mentally) right now.

Dr. Malcolm Conway

What happens a lot of times is that you have coaches that will tell the parents what they think based on the athlete's physical prowess.

There is something that takes place when one is looking in the child's mind. That's called fear and doubt. You see, the child just shows you what he wants you to see, but that is only the tip of the iceberg. The main thoughts are much below the tip of the iceberg, in which many times the child will cover up. You will see what they want you to see.

Conway: With the pressures that the kids are under today, is there a strategy for these kids to develop to handle those pressures better?

Wheeler: There is always a strategy that will work, but the problem is that the strategy that works for one kid won't work for another, the reason being something or someone led them there to the point that they are at. Even though two people are at the same place (mentally), they probably both arrived there differently. There is no one way to fix it properly because each one person needs to have a strategy developed for them.

Generation Y are saying, 'At least tell me what I'm doing right before you tell me what I'm doing wrong first.' Other generations in the past, you can tell them anything, and they would react and do it the right way. This is a different generation now of entitlement, where many kids can't take criticism because they were raised in an increased politically correct framework.

Which is compounded by parents who are not getting involved with their kids, as well as kids not playing outside anymore, so they don't understand the interpersonal relationships needed to compete? They don't build themselves up as we did when we were kids, playing sports all day long.

Here is another example. Mark Ingram of Alabama who recently won the Heisman Trophy and a national championship; his dad is in jail, and he loves his mom. His mom was at the Heisman [ceremony] with him. He talked about his mom and dad at the ceremony, but he talked more about his dad, and he is in jail. So no matter what he did, there still was a connection with his child. What I'm saying is tying this into what I said before… it's customized because there is no one fix in teaching your kid how to deal with pressure. Without understanding, what is going on intrinsically, it's hard to understand what is going on externally.

Conway: Overall, when you were growing up, there was a point that you knew you were better than those around you, correct?

Wheeler: Um, I think that my mindset was that I began lifting weight when I was five years old. My mom always told me that I could do anything if I applied myself… so I heard that my whole life. My dad made me play football but never really came to the games. I knew I was naturally fast because I grew up in the projects, and there, you had to run, or you didn't survive.

I think what happened was that you have this false confidence that turns into real confidence. As crazy as that sounds, there is this false confidence that you have to portray in order to appear to be confident with your peers. Eventually, it turns into a real confidence. Some athletes that I know are scared, and that is why they are always talking so much. It helps them deal with the fear. And the self-talk becomes so important that it creates faith… it creates faith in yourself, and it creates faith in your abilities. It then creates faith in the people around you that you can do this. But you first have to create positive self-talk. I don't know if parents teach that to their kids.

Conway: When you were playing, where did you develop your 'nastiness' needed to play football?

Wheeler: When I was growing up in the projects, we had a game called 'Pick-Up and Run,' which was a game that you just picked up the ball and run until someone tackled you. In elementary school, we had to play with kids in the high school and in pick-up football games. The older guys would close-line you so that they could brag to their boys. So, if you didn't create an attitude of survival, you can't make it. It was a deal of survival of the fittest. So that attitude was developed young for me. And, as you grow up, it develops more because it becomes competitive. Now, if you're not aggressive and don't stand out, someone is going to take your position.

Conway: How did you know you had a special talent that you could actually go to college on a scholarship?

Wheeler: I went to a high school that didn't promote players going on to college. Coming from a small country town as an African American, you're not on the top of the list to get pushed onto college. It wasn't until my senior year when Coach Walker came, and that's when he made us believe that we could go to college. But other than that, the school wasn't pushing us to go onto college at all. They didn't care. That was real.

No one pursued me for a scholarship, so I ended up going to a junior college, paying out of my pocket. After I went there, I had to sit out a year because I had to help my mom financially at home and couldn't go back because I couldn't afford it. From there, I was tracked down by a recruiting coordinator from [the] University of Mississippi, who remembered me from visiting Florida State. He told me that he was trying to track me down for over a year and finally found my aunt and left a message with her that he was trying to talk to me.

The time that I stayed home to work to help my family, I worked out every day, seven days a week. I knew I was going back to play, and I still had the passion to play. Every day, I would work out, and I would have people yell at me out of the widows telling me, 'You need to stay right here at home. You're not going back to play anything. You're going to still be here just like the rest of the sorry ass */&#^s hanging out here.' You want to talk about a person who was driven... let me tell you something. No one wanted to work out with me at that point in my life. I'm telling you, it was game on, brother, because I was driven to make it back.

Conway: Then you went back and attended Troy State. How did you end up doing there?

Wheeler: Terrible. I was out of football for so long that my skills as a safety went way down from not playing. I had to sit out a year (NCAA rules), so now I'm out of football for two years, and I only have one year left. When I got to Troy, my skills were so diminished that you could put someone's grandmamma on me, and they would have beaten me.

I remember that I would go on the field during camp at 1:00 a.m. and run extra, when everyone else was asleep. I would go workout by myself and go back to my room and be really down on myself to the point of crying, asking God for help. My roommate still tells stories that he would wake up at two in the morning, and I would be over there doing push-ups and dips.

People want to take your place on the field, but they don't know the sacrifice that you put in. Everybody wants the fame without the sacrifice. They want to claim the fame, but they don't want to put the sacrifice in. It's not easy trying to make it in the NFL. It's not easy playing sports at any professional level, unless you're willing do something different than the others [who] don't want to do.

Conway: When did it turn around for you at Troy State?

Wheeler: I never got beat for a pass over twenty yards while playing defensive back. For the entire year, I got beat for one touchdown, and that was a 10-yard slant. My deal was that there is no way you're going to take on all of this hard work that I put in and beat me… it's just not happening. I used to go out and say, 'How many you want me to get for you today, coach?'

Conway: When you were coming out of college and entering the NFL, did you have a good or bad attitude towards life?

Wheeler: I had a great attitude for life. My mom always told me that 'Nobody owes you anything.' I came from a work ethic background. My mom was spiritual, and I knew I was being prayed for, and I just loved people. I never really got into trouble. I did have an attitude problem on the field, because I would fight at the drop of a hat. It didn't matter; I would fight anybody. Looking back, it was a feeling that you have something to prove... like someone is going to punk you for it. Also, it came from a point of where I came from, and I didn't want anything taken away from me. I would wrestle the linemen at Troy if needed, but again, I was bench-pressing 400 pounds at the time, so I knew I was stronger. But that went away as time developed and I matured.

Conway: When you went into the NFL and had to cover the best, how was your mentality then?

Wheeler: When I went to Cincinnati, I had some doubts begin to sneak into my mind. You start thinking that you came from a smaller school, you start hearing that you haven't played all that much football, and you start to hear all this stuff. It begins to settle in your mind as doubt. I had a rookie head coach, I had a rookie position coach, and their experience showed. But I continued to work as hard as I could. As I got beat on the field, I would work that much harder to show that I could stay in the league. I continued to grow in every aspect of my life, husband, father, player, friend, spiritual leader.

Jon Drummond
U.S. Olympic Gold Medalist, Track

Jon Drummond was known to be one of the fastest men in track and field during his tenure in the late 1990s into 2000. Mr. Drummond was known for his explosive starts and known as one of the fastest starters of all time. He captured the gold at the 200-meter at the World University Games in 1991. Mr. Drummond ran the opening leg for the U.S. 4 x 100 meter relay team at the World Championships, which tied the world record of 37.40. In 1996, he ran the opening leg of the 4 x 100 meter relay, which took a silver medal at the 1996 Summer Olympics and reached the semifinals of the 100 meter run. In 1999, he ran the opening leg of the 4 x 100 meter relay, capturing the gold medal in the World

Championships. He won the gold medal at the Sydney Olympics in the 4 x 100 meter relay and came in fifth in the 100.

Conway: What do you feel was the most important thing you did when you were young to help you become a better player?

Drummond: Listen and align myself with coaches who actually know what they were talking about. I was fortunate throughout my career to have a plethora of informed and educated coaches who had systems that were not only beneficial as rearing me as an athlete but also kept me focused as a person. They helped me understand discipline, commitment, and perseverance to train.

They didn't just sit there and yell and tell me to run. They explained to me why I was doing what I was doing. It was helpful in keeping me injury-free and also performing better.

Conway: How do you feel coaches/trainers at all levels can better prepare young athletes?

Drummond: If they would stop being one-dimensional. A lot of coaches think that they are the end-all, be-all to an athlete. Coaches have to understand that we are guides. We have fundamental ideologies, but it's not like we wrote the book on it. There's nothing that we've created or we're doing that is created by us. We've taken things that we've learned throughout our careers and implemented it with minuscule changes to adapt to the athlete in front of us.

Conway: When did you realize that this sport was more important than others and that you had to take it more seriously?

Drummond: Mine was always a dream, so when I was really young, I told people I was going to the Olympics. I was fortunate in the fact that I had a lot of coaches that believed in me. So when one ran out of belief, another one was there who continued to believe in me. It was real young for me when I watched the Olympics. It was at that point I made up my mind that is where I wanted to be.

Conway: What one thing do you resent when you were young about your training/playing?

Drummond: I hated practice, [though] granted it was necessary, but I hated it… it hurt. The only thing that I really resented was anyone who would tell me that I wasn't good enough to do something. I had a coach one time when I was trying to decide on college that told me that I wasn't good enough to go on to college, let alone make it at a Division I university. At the time, I was very small. [At] graduation [from] high school, I weighed about 129 pounds and [was] about 5'6" tall. I wasn't a picture perfect Division I athlete, and this guy was telling me that I didn't have what it takes for that level. I told him watch… we'll see, and the rest is history.

I resented anyone who was trying to take away from me something for their own personal gain or ideology. A lot of time, people won't invest in a person because they may not have the work ethic at the time, but it's not to say they should steal their dream from them.

Conway: What one thing would you like to do over if you had the chance to do it all over again?

Drummond: I would have taken it more serious in high school. I feel if I had really focused on the fundamentals, it would have made more of a difference. I was a well-rounded kid. I went to church, I went to school, and I was active in extracurricular activities. But I never really gave 100 percent to track and field. I did it, but I did it doing a lot of other things. I feel if I could have put more into my ninth, tenth, and eleventh grade[s], it would have gotten me a little further faster. So when I went to college, that was all I had, so I had to commit because I was on scholarship. So, if I had to do it all over again, I would have taken it much more serious in the grades in high school that I mentioned.

Conway: What "one thing" could you tell a young athlete to help them better themselves?

Drummond: It will never get easy, but you will get better. No matter what you do, the workouts will always stay hard because coaches are trying to get you to the next level. It's never going to be easy, but you will perform better, your ability will improve and expand, but you can't quit because it's not easy.

Conway: What advice do you have for parents in helping their children to become better athletes?

Drummond: A lot of parents don't understand how much at home they involve their kids emotionally. And with certain stresses dumping over to the kids, it takes away from their ability to concentrate and focus. I would encourage parents to be careful how much they share with their children. Be conscious of the fact that your kids see and hear everything, but they don't necessarily process it as an adult... they process it as a kid.

Also, if you see talent in your child, you want the talent to improve, but don't live through your kids. Your hopes and dreams are much different from their hopes and dreams. You may want them to go to college for football or basketball, but they may want to go for dance or something else. Many times, kids will get into things to please their parents, but it isn't necessarily what they want to do. Let them fulfill their dreams as they grow up.

Conway: What type of training did you feel helped you become a top-level athlete?

Drummond: I ran track my whole life, so that is where my concentration was. Mechanics was taught to me by my coach, which really helped me. Form running and special techniques in track helped me stay injury-free and become more efficient. At my high school, we barely had a weight room, so I didn't have a lot compared to others. So I got really good at sit-ups, pull-ups, push-ups, and crunches because I didn't have access to all that equipment.

Conway: What type of mental training did you go through to help you become a better athlete?

Drummond: I grew up in the hood, so the mental training was, 'Get out of the hood.' That is all the motivation I needed to keep me going.

Conway: What do you do to prepare for a match?

Drummond: I used visual imagery in preparing for a competition. I tried not to run the race in my head because I felt that I would exert too much adrenaline as I would in a race, so I wanted to conserve it. I would run through some of the things I needed to work on to put it in the subconscious part of my mind. I was coined as the "Crown Prince of Track and Field," so I would involve the crowd into what I'm doing to kind of take the pressure off of me. I would talk to people, shake hands, and get into the crowd to make jokes.

Conway: How do you handle defeat, both as a youngster and as a pro?

Drummond: I'm not going to lie… I cried like most people would. But the reality was that I would sit and look at what caused me to lose. Then I would sit with those who would be honest with me — my coach, my mom, or my dad. I would let them tell me things that I could have done better. I was lucky to have a very good support system. Unfortunately, many athletes don't have this and become loners. I always knew who to contact for certain areas of my life spiritually, emotionally, physically, so that I had someone to talk to in each of these areas. So when I had a defeating moment, I would go through those particular areas to find out did I give it my all. Second, then I would talk to someone emotionally so that they could tell me what they were hearing from me, spiritually reminding me that God is the giver [of] my gift and worship him in what we do, not the outcome of what we do. So I had that type of strong background to help me through the difficult times.

Marquis Mathieu
Professional Hockey

Marquis Mathieu came up through the junior program and the junior major programs in Canada. Starting in the Quebec leagues, he continued to work hard, then making it to the Wheeling Thunderbirds of the ECHL in the U.S. He continued to work even harder. He made it to the Providence Bruins of the AHL and then got his chance to play in the

NHL with the Boston Bruins. He then went back down to the AHL, following a year in Germany and back in Quebec, where he ended his hockey career. Marquis outlines the positive struggles he had with his career and how hard work got him to the top of his profession.

Conway: What do you feel was the most important thing you did when you were young to help you become a better player?

Mathieu: That is a tough question… for me, it would be perseverance. I had a lot I had to do to make it work. I played at some places that others wouldn't… I just kept working toward my goal.

Conway: How do you feel coaches/trainers at all levels can better prepare young athletes?

Mathieu: They need to be straightforward with the athletes. They don't really tell the players the truth, and the players end up not knowing what was going on. Being told something that isn't true causes a lot of uncertainty with a player. They need just to be more upfront and tell the player the truth from the beginning.

If I had a son playing hockey, I would certainly be a coach. You have to be now because the coaching isn't all that good, and it's the only way to protect them. I remember when I was playing pee-wee hockey, the coach said to me, 'The only thing I want you to do is to break up penalty plays.' Well, I wanted to skate and play, but the coach only had his mind made up already, and I wasn't learning how to develop correctly. Is that what I really wanted to do? No, but if I wanted to stay on his team, it was the only way. Everyone wants to play some offense and score some goals, but there can be coaches who won't let you because of their politics.

Conway: When did you realize that this sport was more important than others and that you had to take it more seriously?

Mathieu: I would say when I was about 12 years old I realized that I was a bit better than the kids I was playing with. Up here in Quebec, hockey is everything, and when I realized I could play with anyone, I began to know that I had a chance to go on to play down the road. At

127

about 17 years old, I decided to play junior major in Quebec because the school's team wasn't that strong. When I look back, I don't think it was the best decision I made because, without going on to college, I left open a chance for an education, which hurt me a little after retiring from hockey. I realized after playing [that] I didn't have a job. I didn't have any training for anything. There are a lot of players who end up settling for jobs they do not like but are stuck because they need to make a living. It's very common in Canada because a lot of guys are doing jobs that they don't like, but they are doing it because they have to.

Conway: What one thing do you resent when you were young about your training/playing?

Mathieu: The coaches took the fun part out of the game. At a young age, the game of hockey should be fun, and many coaches don't know how to coach and begin making it a job right from the start. Between the intense practices and the mental pressure they put on you, [it] takes the joy right out of it. It wasn't until I was about the age of 24 when I played for a coach who actually showed us how to have fun again. We worked hard for him, but he allowed us to have fun, which was the first time I really began to enjoy hockey again.

Prior to that, my career wasn't really going anywhere, but when I found I could enjoy the game again, my career began to take off. The fun part of hockey was taken away at an early age when I got to junior major around 17 or 18.

Conway: What "one thing" could you tell a young athlete to help them better themselves?

Mathieu: The other thing is that you have to have fun. If you're young and not having fun, it's not worth it. Do something that you like. Don't take it too serious too fast. I would have trained a lot more at a younger age. I was training, but I wasn't doing the right stuff.

When I was young, 15 to 16, all you heard was that, if you wanted a chance to play in the upper leagues, you had to have bigger shoulder and bigger legs. My knowledge of training wasn't right, so if I had to do this all over again, I would learn how to train much better. My parents made the decision for me at 16 to play hockey at the junior major level. I wanted to go to college, but I grew up in Quebec, and all we speak here is French, so there was a language barrier, and I didn't do so well on the ACT examination.

Conway: In Canada, do people take it more seriously playing hockey, thinking every kid has a shot at the NHL?

Answer: At 15 to 17, I would say so. Hockey is an obsession in Canada, but it's more with the parents that put it in the head of their kids. Just by supporting them so much (even if they try not to), they are going to create a lot of pressure on them to succeed. It is really, if you remember Alexander Daigle was a first-round pick by the Ottawa Senators about 15 years ago, but the guy [never] really liked the game, so he ended up quitting even though he was that good. After he played about five years, he came out and said he really never liked playing the game, but he was good enough, and he was pushed to play. I'm using him as an example, but if you take a lot of young kids, just because of their environment, they can't get out of it. It's just like coming out like a gay person would do, saying that you don't like playing hockey. I want you to understand that the overall pressure to play hockey has a real effect on you and your family in Canada... it can be more of a same thing.

Conway: If there was one thing that you would do if you had to do it all over again, what would it be?

Mathieu: I would have learned to fight at a younger age to be more prepared. When you are in juniors, you have to fight guys years older than you, and it's scary. I would have loved to learn different fighting styles like karate or something like that to better prepare me. There were times when I was younger I would be afraid of some of the older guys because I would lose in fights, and it hurt. I know if I knew what I was doing it would have been a lot better when I was younger. As I got older, I was fine because I could defend myself without any problem.

Also, I would have been in better condition, so that I could finish my shot around the nets and to be able to play full-out later in games when I was younger. I got away with a lot when I was younger because I was a good skater, so I didn't really get in the best shape as I could have.

Conway: What advice do you have for parents in helping their children to become better athletes?

Mathieu: Is all mental. To help prepare their kids to prepare mentally because it's not going to be a fun ride all the way. There's going to be a lot of ups and downs. I always wonder why like a guy like Tiger Woods can be so superior to his rivals. I believed someone showed him how to be more mentally tougher than others because the other people have just about the same type of physical training.

Why is Sidney Crosby as good as he is? Is it because of his skills, or is he stronger mentally? Can he react in certain situations better than everyone else? I feel that many things are mental, and you have to be able to control that to become better.

Conway: What type of training did you feel helped you become a top-level athlete?

Mathieu: We used to run up Le Relais Mountain, which is a ski hill. I would go there, and the goal was to sprint up the hill as hard as you can. We used to take some friends with us, and after about halfway, they would end up throwing up. As you can imagine how steep the hill was, and we would sprint up this hill a couple times a week.

Conway: What type of mental training or feeling did you go through to help you become a better athlete?

Mathieu: When I was 25, I went to see a sport psychologist for the first time in my career. I didn't have much money at all, and I scraped it up to work with him. At that time, seeing a psychologist was something that you weren't proud of because, back then, it was more if you had other problems. At that point, I was going to the Boston Bruins training camp, and I knew this was my final chance to make it to the NHL. I went to the psychologist right before I went to camp. I learned so much from him mentally and how to handle the pressure. From there, I ended up playing for the Boston Bruins.

Conway: What do you do to prepare for a game?

Mathieu: As I got older, I was preparing myself better. It would start a few days before a game. I would start to drink a lot of water, and my meals would be very important, so they were planned in advance. The night before a game, I would watch movies or do something to take my mind off of the game. If I didn't change my mind, I would be up all night worrying about the game. The day of the game, many coaches wanted a good pre-game skate, but for me, I just wanted to do very little because if I didn't want to get tired. Right before the game, I would go into my own zone, not talk much, and visualize a little. I wanted to be as fresh and as worry-free as possible, and then I was ready to go.

Conway: How do you handle defeat, both as a youngster and as a pro?

Mathieu: When I was a youngster, it was terrible. If I didn't play up to my capacity, I would be mad until the next game. As I grew up, I learned that defeat at times is something I couldn't control, and that life will go on anyway, and there will be another game. But if the defeat of the team was my fault, then that is really, really tough to handle... you feel ashamed.

Adam Archuleta
National Football League

Adam was an undersized walk-on at Arizona State University, not only making the team, but becoming a three-year starter at linebacker. Archuleta ranks fourth in school history, with 54 stops behind line of scrimmage. He recorded 330 tackles (202 solos) with 14 quarterback sacks, six fumble recoveries, and five forced fumbles during his four-year career.

Adam became more famous as the 1997 combine in Indianapolis, where he blew the minds of every coach in the building. At 5'11", weighing 211 pounds, he was projected as a sixth round draft choice by many with a 40-yard speed of 4.5 and a vertical leap of 34. He tested at the combine by running a 4.37 in the 40 and posted a 39-inch vertical jump. These numbers catapulted Archuleta to the first round in the NFL draft.

Archuleta spent seven years in the NFL, playing for the St. Louis Rams, the Washington Redskins, the Chicago Bears, and the Oakland Raiders.

Conway: What do you feel was the most important thing you did when you were young to help you become a better player?

Archuleta: In my opinion, whether in sports or in life is that you have to be inspired. You have to get into an environment that will allow you to live out your inspiration. I was extremely inspired from a young age to become an NFL athlete. I made a decision after watching a pro football game. I told my Dad that I was going to become a NFL player. For whatever reason, I went into a mold that drove me to the belief that I was a professional football player, but I just wasn't old enough yet. I became fascinated with working out because I wanted to get bigger, faster, and stronger. That led me to begin to study nutrition, lifting, weights, and that led me to finding key people in my life like Jay Schroeder and understand how valuable he was. My thirst for knowledge was because I was inspired to reach this goal that led me to meet the people in my life to get me there. I really feel it's as simple as that.

Conway: How can coaches at all levels better prepare young athletes?

Archuleta: That's a tough question. I think it changes between all levels. Depending on your level, coaches can influence you at different times in your life. The younger you are, the coach must really emphasize having fun. The big reason why sports is such a huge part of my life is because it was the only source of fun that I had when I was young. My source of joy was when I was on a field either playing football, baseball, or basketball. What I see in some sports you have some parents who really want their kid to make it, so they get them all of these type of coaches or instructors, which I feel really bogs the kid down. The great players that made it figured it out on their own in what they needed to do. Then the coaching and the fine-tuning should come later when your nervous system and the rest of your body is ready to handle it.

Conway: When did you realize that this sport was more important than others and that you had to take it more seriously?

Archuleta: I knew early on that I was going to be a football player. I played all sports up to ninth grade, and it was at that point I made the decision was that my dream was in football. I'm not going pro in baseball or basketball, so I wanted to dedicate my off-seasons to training. I wasn't big enough, strong enough, or fast enough to become a professional football player. I decided that I needed to train on the off-season to get there. I actually grew to really enjoy training. I spent all my time reading and studying training and trying to figure it out. That's where I got a lot of my joy from.

Conway: What one thing do you resent when you were young about your training/playing?

Archuleta: I don't resent anything. Everything in my life allowed me to learn, and my thirst for knowledge allowed me to meet people who were instrumental in my development. I had very supportive parents that emphasized the important things. They weren't overbearing or pushy but emphasized the importance of working and preparation. My parents always wanted it to be my decision. I remember when I first met Jay Schroeder, and I came home to tell my mother that he spent the last two hours berating me and cursed me out for two hours. She didn't get mad and go to him and start yelling, 'Why do you talk to my son that way?' She asked me what I thought about Schroeder and his training. I told her that 'I think he's the guy for me.' My mom says to me, 'Well, that's good. I think you should do it.' My parents weren't micromanagers in my life. They allowed me to live and do what I wanted to do but were always there in a supportive role to give me what I needed in order for me to succeed.

Conway: What "one thing" could you tell a young athlete to help them better themselves?

Archuleta: I keep going back to it, but it is a buzz word for me, and that is inspiration. You need to find out whatever it is to move you and decide what you want to do. That needs to become what drives you or consumes you. You need to be willing to go distances that nobody else is willing to go. You can't live somebody else's dream. You have to have that laser focus in order to accomplish your dream.

Conway: If there was one thing you could do all over again, what would it be?

Archuleta: I don't think I would do anything over again. I look back at my life in sports, and although it was a bit [of an] unorthodox journey, many of my missteps and failures paved the way for my success. It was all a tremendous learning experience. I don't regret anything.

Conway: What advice do you have for parents in helping their children become better athletes?

Archuleta: Parents should not expect your kids to live your dream. Let them become their own individuals. Let them inspire to become great in whatever it is that they want to do. I see a lot of kids ruined by their parents becoming overbearing. Instead of the parents trying to support them or help them with the tools in whatever they want to become, they already have a predetermined expectation of what they want their kids to be. Then the kids can't ever live up to that expectation.

Conway: What type of training did you feel made you a better athlete?

Archuleta: For me, it was the training that I did with Jay Schroeder [that] was instrumental. His presence, his techniques, and his motivation really helped me to understand what it meant to be disciplined. He taught me what work ethic really meant. I feel his method of training is the finest training in the world.

Conway: What type of mental training did you go through to make you a better athlete?

Archuleta: Nothing specific.   I was blessed with tremendous will power and an ability to attain my goal at whatever the cost.   Once I figured out what I wanted to do, I just went after it.   My mental training was just a byproduct of my goals and what it took to reach them.

Conway: How did you go about preparing for a game?

Archuleta: I'm not big on superstition or rituals.   The looser I was, the less I worried, the better I focused and played.   Anytime I tried to be [or] get really intense before a game, it seemed like I got more fatigued, and I didn't play as well.   When I look back on the best games of my career, it's kind of strange, but I went into those games asking myself, 'Man, am I ready to play today?'   I just ended up being in the zone, and things happened automatically.   Nothing was forced. It just came as I played.   The more I tired and the more pressure I put on myself, the worse I played.

Conway: How did you handle defeat as a youngster and as a pro?

Archuleta: The more successful I was, the less it bothered me.   I always looked at defeat as something to work from or use it as a stepping-stone.   I would be upset, but then I knew I just had to do better.   I would go and work on it and get better and move on.   As I got older and there was more on the line, I turned into a perfectionist, and I began to take defeat very hard.   The more and more I tried becoming a perfectionist, the more mistakes I made.   That was something I grew to understand that, if you play sports, you are going to lose.   You have to accept it and move on.   I would have preferred to concentrate more on my successes rather than my losses.   I wanted my body to remember what it was like to be great, what it was like to make a big play, and what it was like to perform at a high level.   I don't want my body to remember what it was like to get beat.   I feel that that can negatively program you.

A Coach's Perspective...

I felt it interesting for parents to get a feel for how many coaches think about the recruiting process and how they view high school athletes. The following is an interview with Coach Robert Johnson, who is a coach at Cornell University.

Coach Robert Johnson
Cornell University, Track and Cross Country

(Cornell website) In just six years at Cornell, Johnson has already coached athletes to no less than 12 school records and a staggering 53 top 10 all-time Cornell performances, including school records in the 800, 1k, 3k, marathon, 4 x 800, and DMR (Ivy record), including the nation's number one time in the indoor 4 x 800 in 2005 and 2006.

His athletes have also won conference titles in the 800, 1k, mile, steeplechase, 5k, 10k, and cross-country. Over the last four years, Johnson's athletes have scored a staggering 338 points in the 800 through the 10k, a conference-leading point total that is 50 percent more than the third best mark in the conference (212 points). During his tenure at Cornell, his cross-country teams have never finished lower than they did the year before, capped off by a runner-up showing in 2007.

In 2000, Johnson cofounded the running website "LetsRun.com" with his twin brother and has seen it grow to become one of the world's most popular running websites.

Conway: As a Division I (DI) coach, what is it that you are looking for in an athlete to come to your school?
Johnson: The nice thing about being a track coach is that you recruit on time and records. You look for fast time, long throws because, in track, it's pretty subjective, quite honestly. The kid has to be at a certain level, or they really don't have a chance to compete at a Division I school because they will get eaten up at this level.

We start looking at the athlete's best times in and around their junior year in high school. If the time interests us, then we begin to pursue it more. Once we contact them, I will ask what they did in ninth and tenth grade to give me a better understanding of their development. I'm looking for a good rate of improvement over those years. On the other hand, a kid who just switched over to track from another sport and runs a good time in his junior year, it gets me interested. There is a good chance that this kid hasn't been running his whole life, so the chances of him burning out are less.

Conway: If you are looking at a miler, what times are of interest to you?

Johnson: At Cornell, we're a good track program. We're currently ranked number one in the Northeast, so we're looking for quality. For a good Division I school, you're looking at a sub 4:20 in the 1600, sub 9:30 in the 3200, and it has to be by their junior year in high school. You see, in college, if a kid can't run a 4:10 in the mile, he really can't help anyone with over that. So to improve by 10 seconds is a lot, and most runners that I've seen can't do this.

Conway: As a DI coach, what is your feeling of walk-ons?

Johnson: That's an interesting question. I've been coaching for eight years, and it's changed somewhat since I started. We've had some guys who were very slow in high school and ended up beating top recruits. We've had a few success stories that ran a 9:50 3200 run in high school and really turned it on in college. My brother, Weldon, for example, ran a 9:35 3200 runner as a senior in high school and wasn't recruited by anybody and ended up running a 28:06 in the 10k, walked on, and ended up an elite world runner.

I see why now why the really big-time programs don't really bother with walk-ons. You can work four years to develop one of these kids, and by his senior year, and [he] will end up as your fifth runner let's say in cross-country. He may be only seconds behind one of your stud recruits, but the recruit is a freshman.

I don't mind having kids walk on, and we've been fortunate to have big rosters. Big powerhouse schools like Michigan don't even bother with walk-ons. The reason I think is that it becomes increasingly more difficult to manage all of the kids on the roster. So as I get older, I'm getting a little more cutthroat because of the time intensity of having so many kids on the roster. The success rate with walk-ons is about one in 10. So you end up spending a lot of time, and many times, they don't pan out. I know that I work harder than anyone else in the country with walk-ons, but I can see now why other coaches don't bother.

Conway: What do kids in high school need to know about running in Division I?

Johnson: They need to know that it's unbelievably competitive. It takes a huge time commitment, and it can be a huge shock to these kids. Most of the kids that were battling for a top spot in their state championships come to school and end up fifth on the team or worse. That can be hard on them because of their expectations. They forget that, when they were in high school, they were the best on their team, but when they get here, it's a whole different story.

They have to have a mindset of improving every year. Then, ultimately, they will become a better performer. Many kids in high school don't work as hard as they should, and when they get here, it becomes a major shock to them.

Some kids get to a big college campus with all that it has to offer, and all of a sudden, track isn't their number one priority anymore. If that's the case, you're not going to be successful. I always tell my distance runners that they think they're working hard when they are training. In high school, 90 percent train at 30 miles per week, and now they get to college, the mileage goes up to 80 miles per week. So if you're not training at these levels, how do you think you're going to beat these other kids? Everyone that makes it to college is talented. Now, once you get here, you have to be the talented kid who is willing to work hard... it's not easy.

Conway: What can you tell parents about running at the Division I level?

Johnson: A lot of parents think they can trick the coach in recruiting their son. 'Oh, he is such a good boy. He really works hard. His coaches are really good.' We always get these letters from parents with those type of statements, but they never give us their kids' times.

If I was interested in a school for my son, I would pick up the phone and call the coach, and I would very simply say, 'Hey, I have an athlete in high school. He's a 400-meter runner or a miler. What types of times are you looking for as a junior in high school?' The coach generally knows what he is looking for, and he can tell you straight-up what he is looking for. Then tell them the truth and let them know. If he is close, they will keep their eye on him. You're not going to be able to convince this coach, because they know what they are looking for. There are parents that keep calling over and over, but in track, quite honestly, it comes down to times.

Coaches also want to know if the kid is really interested in the school. They want to know if they are serious, and then they want to know the grades and other things going on in their life.

Conway: As a young runner, how would a young runner properly train for their sport?

Johnson: As a distance runner, it's pretty simple. You have to build up your mileage. High school runners need to get their mileage up to 60 miles per week. For other events in track, you can try to get to someone who can teach you, especially in the technical events like pole vaulting and discus throwing. It's pretty simple. If you don't have a certain amount of talent, you're not going to be a Division I athlete. And to tell the parents, if your kid doesn't love the sport, they shouldn't be doing it.

Also, I think when the kid is young, they should be playing several sports. They need to have fun, and as they get older, then if their heart is in the right place, then they can think about specializing in one sport. We see some kids who have been doing nothing but running start to burn out by the time they get to college.

They need to show some potential by ninth to tenth grade for you to begin to think of dropping other sports. At that point, they need to be beating all their competition, and at that point, it may be time to get more serious. Everything in track will be summed up by your junior year in high school, so know beforehand that the coaches are looking early.

Stella Sampras-Webster
Head Coach, UCLA Women's Tennis

Stella is the head coach for the UCLA women's tennis team. After working at UCLA for the past 14 years, she has compiled a record of 229-110. In 2008, Stella led UCLA to the school's first NCAA National Championship in women's tennis. In 2008, she was named PAC-10 Coach of the Year. In 2004 and again in 2007, she guided the tennis program to a pair of second-place finishes.

She has coached a total of 16 players who have earned All-American status. A graduate of UCLA herself, she also had an outstanding career playing for the Bruins.

Stella played professional tennis, playing at the U.S. Open, the Lipton Championships, and Wimbledon. She has won three satellite tournament titles and competed in team tennis for the Wichita Advantage in 1992.

Conway: As a Division I coach, what are you looking for from a high school athlete?

Sampras-Webster: What I'm looking for [is] someone who is really committed to their tennis and continue on to become professionals. The commitment is huge. They have to love to play and love to work. The attitude and the way they compete is huge. As a college coach, I need players who can work together and compete in a way that is positive and be a good reflection on me as a coach. I want someone with a real work ethic who isn't afraid to work hard, which will produce good results.

Also, understand I don't go to high schools to look for players. I only go to national tournaments to find the best players in the country. I also go to the Junior U.S. Open to find the top players in the country.

You see, in tennis, some of the best players in the country don't go to high school. If someone calls me from a high school, I will first ask what their national ranking is. If they don't have one, I'm really not interested for my program.

Some athletes in the past get to college and stop trying. They get to college out of junior programs, and all of a sudden, they stop trying, and that can ruin a program. Some of them, by the time they get to age 18, burn out from playing. They've been playing their entire life, and when they get to college, they now see another side of life, and they're ready to have fun. I need an everyday player, someone who wants to continue on that will stay hungry. These types of players will stay motivated and will continue to work, and that is what I need.

Conway: What do young athletes need to know about playing at a Division I school?

Sampras-Webster: They need to know it is a huge commitment. Once they go to school, they're on scholarship, so there is a huge responsibility to the program. It's like a job, and it's a lot of time commitment and hard work. There isn't a lot of downtime as compared to nonathletic students. Coaches expect players to have the commitment and to look at it as a job. They're getting paid to play tennis at UCLA, so we expect a lot out of them. If they're not doing their part, we'll get rid of them.

Conway: What do parents need to know about Division I tennis?

Sampras-Webster: Parents need to know that they've done their job to get their kids to where they are at. It's time now to let them go and become an adult. Now it's up to the kids to perform, and now it's time to let the coaches coach. When you have overly involved parents in college, it doesn't let the player grow. It's a great time for the student-athlete to find out who they are [and] how to survive on their own. It's time for them to take responsibility for their tennis. Parents need to let them go and let them learn how to do things on their own, and if they fail, they fail. Parents have to trust the coaches. They've done their part, now it's time to let them go.

Conway: How should young tennis players be training to ready themselves for a Division I program?

Sampras-Webster: We have kids, before they get to our program, training four to five hours per day. Nowadays, junior players are coming in with a lot of off-court training behind them. They know what to do in the weight room. They know how to condition, doing a lot of agility, footwork drills. They have a lot more knowledge now in training coming to our school.

You have to put in the time, and you have to be in great condition. We recruit people out of the national tournaments, and they are the top players in the country/world, so they have to train and perform and get results. These kids are training six to seven days a week, playing tournaments every week. Young athletes must know that it takes a huge commitment on their part to even think about playing at this level.

When I was growing up, I would train at least three hours per day, with about 45 minutes of off-court training every day of the week. My father helped myself, and my brother (Pete Sampras) organized our practices and workouts. He would drop us off at the club and tell us what to do, and we would do it. We loved to do it, so there was never a problem getting us to get our workouts in.

Conway: Can a college tennis player realistically make it to the WTA tour?

Sampras-Webster: Most definitely. Julie Ditty came out of Vanderbilt that has been pretty successful on the tour. There are college players who have made it in the top 100. I don't know of any that played in the top ten or twenty. To make the top 100, it's about one in one hundred.

Conway: Is it better for a young player coming up through the ranks to go to a Bollettieri-type of camp or go to college?

Sampras-Webster: I would say it depends on what they are doing on the court. To go the route of the Bolletteri system, they would have had to do something special at a young age. Usually, you can tell at a young age if they have what it takes to get to that next level. My brother, Pete, had it very early, and you knew he was destined to become a pro at an early age. My route was to go to college, and after college, have the opportunity to turn pro.

The Bolletteri path, you have to be pretty special early on. But I don't think that you have to go that route to make it to the pros. They can certainly stay in their hometown if they have [a] tennis-oriented area that can produce the right coaches and playing partners. I don't necessarily think you have to be in an academy to make it to the pros. I'm not totally sold on the academy route for young players. There are just as many academy players that don't make it to the top as well, and for some of those players, it can be really sad because they have nothing to fall back on.

On the other hand, if you go to college and do well in the NCAA championships, then you can try turning pro for a few years to see how it goes. If you're not in the top 200, then you better go to college after a couple of years of playing on the tour.

Conway: As a coach, what are the demands of running a Division I tennis program?

Sampras-Webster: Recruiting is huge. The biggest thing is traveling and scouting players to see how we will use the eight scholarships available to give out. It's very time-consuming and a very long process to make sure that you are getting the very best players for the team.

Fundraising is always a big part to make sure we need additional money for travel or other incidental items needed that isn't in the school's budget.

Managing the team is very time-consuming, meeting the needs of your players. I have great assistants that help overseeing the shoes, clothes, and racquets for the players.

Managing our budget for the team is a full-time issue.

Conway: As an experienced coach, how do you deal with walk-ons?

Sampras-Webster: I've had both positive and negative experiences with walk-ons. I've had a bunch of walk-ons that want to come to UCLA and earn a scholarship, but not all make it. I've had a few experiences that have made it and ended up earning a scholarship, with a couple of them playing on my top-three list. There are others who don't get to play, and then they end up transferring. And I've had other types of walk-ons that are dying to come to UCLA and say they are committed to their tennis, and you get them into school, and they end up quitting. So some I've had bad experiences, where I've felt used by the player just to get into school.

Some don't realize how difficult the demands of playing at UCLA are, and they end up quitting. Some think that they played hard somewhere else. They don't expect it to be harder at our school. So, overall, I've had both positive and negative experiences with walk-ons.

Conway: The players you have now as compared to when you first started coaching... is the hunger and work ethic different? Are they still as dedicated? Are they harder to coach?

Sampras-Webster: It depends on the group. Right now, I have a really great group, but if you asked me this three or four years ago, I would say yes. The former coach here at UCLA told me when I took over the program that coaching is a lot harder because kids don't appreciate what they have, they don't work as hard, they don't deal with adversity all that well, and they feel entitled to everything. But right now, I'm really happy with the group that I have.

Conway: What is the difference from Division I tennis as compared to the pros?

Sampras-Webster: In college, we have limitations. The players here have to go to school, study for tests. We have limits on the players. We can only work with them for four hours per day. Some of our players that are more committed and are looking to continue on after college have to find extra time on their own to hit. The pros have the luxury of time where they can drill in the morning and play matches in the afternoon. We don't have that luxury because of classes and the stresses of college.

In the pros, they are much more accurate with their shots. They are stronger and more-fit and I would say a lot more disciplined than college players. One thing that I feel is that the pro player tends to be more mentally tough as compared to the college player. I've had players here that, in practice and drills, they look amazing, but when they get in a tight game, they seem to fall apart.

Chapter 6

The Mind & The Elite Athlete

"A Diamond is a Chunk of Coal That is Made Good Under Pressure."   **Henry Kissenger**

We've all felt it, those 'butterflies' in your stomach either before the start of the competition or during a critical time of the competition - that uneasy feeling of anxiety that comes along with playing sports.

Feeling a little excited or nervous is okay. This helps your body and mind get ready to compete. Your body makes **adrenaline** (say: uh-**dren**-ul-in), which is a hormone that gives you extra energy. But if you're getting so nervous that you aren't having much fun, it's time to figure out why.

For any athlete the most over looked portion of training is controlling your mind.

The mind is a funny thing….what you put in - it will give back to you. Like a computer, it's just a machine (or a blob in this case) until you load it with software….the software for your mind is powerful positive thoughts and images. Negative, pessimistic, fear, anxious, gloomy, depressive, fright, - these thoughts will eventually come back to you in situations that are important.

Where you are in life, is directly related to the thoughts in your mind. You may not think of that - but truly your mind sets the tone of your behavior. Your behavior will set the tone for your actions and your actions are what dictates the results that you've acquired in life. A well made up mind can do anything -overcome anything - produce anything. If you can truly set your mind right - have passion about knowing exactly what you want you will get it.

Realize this…faulty thinking, negative thoughts and poor behaviors is one of the main explanation of preventing greatness. Believe that you can do it - before you do it and you find much more success in your desired sport.

There are many ways that the mind becomes infected with what Zig Zigler calls….stinkin' thinkin'. Gossip for example is one way of polluting the mind with senseless information that is 99% negative. Stay away from it and protect your mind from it.

Worry is another plague on the mind. Worry will slowly creep in to undermine your thought process to slowly turn a positive outlook to a negative one.

Not taking responsibility is another way of playing the blame game. "She has more than me – he is faster than me – they were given more." Stop your belly aching and stop blaming others for your misfortune. Confront life on every twist and turn and take responsibility for your short comings. Once confronted, you will see that most of the negative thoughts will begin to disappear.

Stop feeling sorry for yourself and get out and make something happen. I've told my kids – It's not what happens to you it's what you do about it that makes a difference." The person who sits and continues to play 'pity poor me parties' in their mind are the type of athlete who never accomplish anything. Some use it as an excuse because they actually fear winning. You will see an athlete climb their way to the top but once they get there they forget what got them there. The scratching, clawing and crawling all the way up was the effort needed to get them up out of the lower part of their situations. They get some momentum and get up towards the top and BAM they sabotage themselves and begin to lose and fall backward. Proper thinking is a choice - you can choose to be positive or you can choose to be negative. You can make a lot of positive things happen…with the right thinking.

Winning is a mental choice. You can't win on the field until you win in your mind. "There is no I in TEAM but there is I in WIN"-Michael Jordan. You have to take care of the "I" before you can take care of the team. Too many athletes take it for granted that since they've worked out hard that they are ready for competition. A good portion of success is sports in training your mind to allow your body to endure success.

Success in many cases isn't easy. It can be tough, long and sometimes intimidating. How many football games have been lost in the last seconds? How many tennis matches have been lost after the player was dominating for most of the match? If they didn't physically break down - what was it? Success is something that must be understood - it won't be handed to you for free. Success is a state of mind. Success should be seen in your mind before you go out on the field, court or ice. Success is an everyday thing, not just a sometime thing. Success comes from your thoughts and your thoughts are something that you must control on a regular basis.

Your muscles and your mind need training. The more you workout the more you become stronger, fitter and more developed as an athlete. But what about your mind? Are you putting in the amount of work needed to develop an elite mindset?

The untrained mind can play a lot of tricks on you. It can begin to set you up for self doubt. Self doubt is the kiss of death. Doubt means that you've left the doors of your mind open after preparation. Or it can be a subconscious drain after knowing that you didn't do what you needed to do in practice or in the training room. Self doubt will question your very existence as an athlete. It will question your passion for the game, your image, your feelings - just about everything about you if you let it. If you train your mind to handle success and defeat you can push yourself across the finish line. What is it about the mind that is so elusive? Why doesn't every athlete understand how to develop a mind for success? Because no one ever teaches the athlete how to control their minds. It's as much of the game as any other part and in my opinion more important than the physical aspect of sports.

Most people feel good about themselves with success. They are happy, they are smiling, they are open - it's an overall good feeling. What exactly happens when the success begins to turn away from the athlete? Your physiology changes, you become more guarded, less open – there is a feeling of despair. One reason is that you've never prepared for the feeling and you've failed to confront the feeling when it did come. Some people run to the medicine cabinet when their feelings change to take something to make them feel better. Instead the athlete should develop a strategy on how to overcome these feelings, without the use of medications.

Change is necessary for the athlete to be successful. First stop the negative self talk. No matter what comes into your mind that is negative just counter it with something that is positive. What I'm trying to teach you are little strategies that can help you overcome anything.

Life is not fair.

Life will throw things your way that are going to be unpleasant and sometimes downright cruel. To overcome this you have to take on a mind set of being prepared. When you wake up every day expect Life to throw you a curve ball - and then deal with it and get on with life. And, here is the crazy thing about LIFE, it's going to happen again, tomorrow, next week or next month….but it's coming. I'm not saying that you have to become a gloom and doomer - thinking that everything is going to go wrong before it happens. Develop the MENTAL capability to confront the problem, handle it, and move on. That's it.

With a good self-talk strategy you can do it….no matter the task. It's the same when you bear down to lift a little more on the bench press. The same goes for your mind - you can kick out the negative self thoughts that are brining you down. I can, I will, I'm determined, I won't stop, don't give up, now, now, now. Over and over you will begin to develop your brain muscle. Once the brain becomes more developed you will see you won't have to bear down anymore - you'll just be able to do without any exertion.

Become certain that you can become better, stronger and faster. Feel good about yourself while you're doing this and believe that you can do it. Connect to the people who are striving to gain the same goals and get rid of the people who don't. Step outside of your comfort zone and attempt new ideas, new skills and stop doing the same things that got you in a rut. You need to grow. If you stay in a rut you can't develop the roots needed to prosper. If you do these things you will see how much more of an athlete you can become.

Pressure

Top notch competition involves pivotal moments which determine who wins and who loses. That's what makes sports unique - there is a winner and a loser. As the saying goes, "the winner takes the spoils."

The loser goes home to try again another day.

Lee Travino said, "true pressure is trying to make a 2 foot putt for $500.00 when you only have five bucks in your pocket."

Definition of Pressure: an oppressive condition of physical or mental or social or economic distress.

So where does the pressure come from?

It can have many sources including parents, coaches, fans, colleagues, and from the athlete themselves. Pressure is stress. Stress can be good in the right amounts. It can create an awareness that is needed to keep you alert and ready for competition. It can be overwhelming to the point that it can begin to make you irritable, nauseous, fearful, and anxious. It is somewhat of a protective mechanism that dates back to our cave man assisters. Stress is something that kept you alive back when the food you were hunting began to hunt you.

Everyone adapts differently to the pressures of sports. In some cases athletes simply fold like a house of cards, while others take that pressure and use it to their favor. The great athletes find how to take the pressure and use it to help them win championships. According to world class sprinter Michael Johnson, "It took me some time to realize, but I love pressure. If there is one thing that will really take you to another level of performance--to the plateau where your victories are measured in the blink of milliseconds--it might be the ability to embrace pressure, to understand it, to draw it in, to make it your own and use it to your advantage."

On the other hand some people can't handle the stress it takes to become a champion. "I know guys out here [on the PGA Tour] who fear success, who don't want the pressure that comes with success or the attention. Heck, I've seen guys back off on Sunday afternoon because they know if they win they'll have to give a speech and they're afraid of giving a speech," said golfer Paul Azinger.

So, what is this pressure all about? Where does it come from and how does it affect you?

Pressure, stress whatever you want to call it can tie your stomach up in knots. Mental images of defeat and all that comes with it. Mental thoughts begin to develop - "what will they think of me, everyone is going to think I'm not that good anymore, am I good enough to be here, I'm not good enough anymore." These thoughts can drive people over the edge. There have been many an athlete who has tried to injured themselves after a big loss. Alcohol, drugs and potential suicide were psychotic choices made by some athletes.

"Without stress we'd all be dead," said Stanford University neurobiologist Robert Sapolsky. "The trick is knowing when to turn it on and turn it off. One person might panic and say, 'I don't know if I can do it.' The other person says "Great, I've been preparing for this all my life." Those two people are both experiencing the same stress, but they are having very different biochemical stress responses." Whether you are good at handling pressure or not it's time that you develop a strategy to conquer the feelings that come along with athletic pressure.

Every sport has their own unique set of pressures as a part of the sport. Golf can be difficult for some. It can keep some players that are unable to conquer their stress of the game of professional golf.

David Leadbetter, a famous British golf instructor, said it helps to pretend that you're just practicing. "You can't admit that one shot means more than any other. Whether it's the tee shot off the first hole with 10 people watching or a two-foot putt on the last hole for the Masters with the whole world watching, stick to your routine." He also suggested that you remind yourself that you can handle the situation. "Don't let one bad shot affect another. If you've been putting well and miss a short one, think of it as an aberration. Don't allow doubt to seep through your game."

Here's the advice Mark Rypien (quarterback of the 1992 Super Bowl winner, the Washington Redskins) was given: "Coach [Joe

151

Gibbs] told me his definition of pressure is having a chance to prove yourself."

Choking is a slang term used for someone who is unable to overcome the pressure of the game to pull out a win. It's a cruel term but in our U.S. society, everyone wants to back a winner. The loser must go home and deal with the loss.

No one knows more about pressure than kickers in the NFL. Place kickers for example are only called when the offence is unable to produce a score. The pressure lies squarely on the kicker. Kickers become popular when they make the kick and score three points. Miss right or left and an eerie sound of silence falls over the field. What do they feel, what goes through their heads - are they nervous? The great ones don't feel anything other than it's just another kick. They know the importance - they've trained themselves not to concentrate on the moment but concentrate on their mechanics. "It's just another kick," Matt Stover said. That mindset of Stover "of just another kick," comes about after years and years of physical and mental training.

I asked Qadry Ismail how he felt before he played in the Super Bowl game against the N.Y. Giants. "I knew that I've done everything possible as far as my preparation went. I knew my assignments, I knew what routes to run, and I knew that everything down to my chin strap was correctly prepared. From there I didn't worry, I just went out and did my job."

So How Do You Prepare for Success and Leave The Pressure Behind

First put yourself under pressure at practice. Even if you do it yourself in simple drills it will teach your mind that there is a consequence for every action. This helps to deal with adversity.

Think! When under pressure what is the worst that can happen? How can you work your way out of this situations. When preparing for competition have a backup plan when the first plan begins to fail. Preparation is your first line of defense. Do what your coach tells you to do and make sure you know exactly what is expected of you. If you practice correctly every day you will develop mental toughness that will help you when the pressure is on.

Breathe! Many times with stress people stop breathing. Learn to get air deep inside you which will allow for maximum oxygen and slow your mind down. Relax and breathe and focus on one thing that is needed to be accomplished.

Lean back on your thoughts from practice that were comfortable for you. I can tell you that when I'm golfing and the pressure begins to build I take my mind back to the practice range and think how I would hit this shot if I was practicing. I go through the same set up and swing that I do on the practice range. Invariably the shot comes off with no problems. (Keep in mind I'm not in the pressure cookers that professionals find themselves in...)

Understand your competition. Knowing who you are playing against can give you a better idea of their weaknesses. Go after what you can accomplish and stay at it. Choose a strategy that you can feel good about and go with it. Either way, lay it all out on the line and go for it...that pressure may just be the spark you need to win.

Visualization

There is a story that I tell every athlete that I work with about the three horses. When I was in college I discovered a framed photograph of three horses nose-to-nose-to-nose at the photo finish line. Each horse had their nose squarely on the line with perfection except for one. The one horse had his tongue out. That was the difference between winning and losing. When you get to a certain level in sports everyone around you has the equal talent as you. What are you going to do to get your tongue out?

Visualization is a technique that has been used for years by athletes and not athletes. Visualization is a method of seeing it before it happens. The concept is that the mind doesn't know the difference between what is real and what is imagined. By 'seeing' the performance the way you want it to unfold the mind will buy into that and give you what you've seen. It's been there so it knows what to do.

The problem comes with many athletes that they will sabotage themselves through self doubt.

1% Doubt…And You Are Out.

For visualization to work you have to be 100% committed to it. I've worked with athletes for years using this powerful tool and when they buy all the way in the results are exponential. One swimmer I worked with would break out in a full sweat during simulation.

To do this for yourself; find a quiet room and lay down - without falling asleep or sit in a comfortable chair. As if you were sitting in a movie theater seeing yourself up on a movie screen performing your event you with positive results. See yourself with every detail in the movie - picking up all of the sounds and smells that come with the event. Spend time on the beginning, middle and the end with sharp detail to technique. Go over this as many times as you can to develop a clear picture of the outcome that you want.

Keep in mind, just like lifting weights for the first time you have to be patient. You can go into the gym and begin lifting tons of weight the first day. It takes time to build up your strength and it will take time for you to develop your mind to see the clear outcome that you want. Many times other thoughts will pop into your mind while you are attempting to see your picture. Stop what you are doing and get back to see your picture. Keep doing this over and over until your mind gets used to staying on point to produce the outcome that you want. It will happen - you just have to be patient and persistent. Some people like using their favorite music from their iPod or radio. It's okay to use as long as you stay focused to see what you are trying to accomplish with strict and accurate detail.

Another great time to do visualization is right before bed. This is a powerful time to perform this because it gives the brain time to work on it for you. Have a particular area of your life that you want to improve - such as speed. Before you drift off take some time to see your running in your mind. Look at yourself from every angle including the side, the front, the back and on top. Look at your arms and make sure that they are in perfect movement to your body to produce maximum speed. Look at how your legs are moving - pushing earth away from you as you begin to separate yourself from those around you.

This exercise must be done over and over until you can feel your speed increase in real life. Don't give up at the beginning because you are asking your brain to make major changes and those changes don't come over night.

When it comes to your brain there is a lot to understand. Did know that there are more connections within your brain than there are stars in the Milky Way? A computer can do a trillion mathematical calculations in a second. Neuroscience has confirmed there are nerves in your brain called "mirror neurons." There are trillions of these neurons in your brain. When an image is placed upon this neuron it will excite the other neurons in and around the learning center of your brain. What does that mean to you? Well, if your brain can see it then it will allow you to do it. Have you ever wondered how athletes can just 'see' the field and make the correct reactions at a moment's notice? These are premotor neurons that are the nerves needed to be excited to send the signal to your muscles to create movement.

A study in Italy proved that when a monkey was hooked up to an electrical receiver it would emit a noise every time the monkey would eat. One day, one of the lab assistants walked by the monkey's cage eating an ice cream. The receptor began to emit the same noise as it did when the monkey ate. It showed that the nerves began to fire just watching an activity.

They opened a bag of peanuts in front of the monkey and again the receiver began to go off. They estimate that 25% of your brain is made up of these mirror neurons. They fire watching movement or imagining movement. It comes down to the fact that if you can see it in your mind your body will have an idea on what you want to do in advance.

If you are learning a particular movement it is best to begin to watch it on as many media outlets as possible. This included pictures, movies and even sound that will allow the mirror motor neurons to 'pre-create' the movement necessary for you to succeed in your sport. Just as this can be programmed on a positive note it can be programmed as a negative program just as easy. This is why you have to be in control of your thoughts at all times. It is called non visual stimuli - which can come from sounds in the environment. There are vast populations of emotional mirror neurons that receive information from our natural senses. As an example let's say that you are in a critical part of a game and the athletes around you are sensing defeat. The 'mirror' motor neurons are already in action doing what they are picking up. This may be why in a certain games the 'momentum' can change in a game. This information shows us that the more you can create success in your mind the body will deliver. The key is creating a burning desire for success....not a dream. Develop a 'I can taste it so bad" mentality along with using your mind to see what you want and it will come.

Develop a Strategy of Success

1. Develop Self Talk: Develop a way of 'talking back to negative thoughts." If you're a teenager you're probably a master at talking back to your parents. Instead of taking it out on them learn to take it out on yourself. Stop negative emotions from entering your mind by reversing the sentence.

   Thought: you really can do that jump...so why waste your time?

   Correction: I can do this, the heck with it, even if I don't I'll keep it up until I can.

2. Confront Your Fears: Do an inventory of what you are afraid of and confront them. If you feel that you are not strong enough then find a way to correct that. If you feel you aren't fast enough design a plan to increase your speed.

   Don't take a back seat to fear. FEAR stands for False Evidence Appearing Real. If you attain the right evidence and work with it your fears will go away. But you must confront them first.

3. Stop Beating On Yourself...Don't Take Yourself So Serious.

   Laugh a little and learn how to use that stress to better your mind and body by laughing at it. I'm not saying don't be a fly-by-night person but stop beating yourself into the ground and learn to enjoy life.

4. Learn Who You Are.

   Stop trying to be everything to everybody. You are who you are so go with it. Don't try to be someone who you are not. This way you take any external stressors off of you and go back to being yourself. Too many people are trying to please everyone except themselves STOP. Work hard, understand what you have to accomplish and as Larry the Cable Guy says, "get 'er done."

5. Learn To Deal With Disappointment Correctly.
   There's a saying that I live by and have told my kids forever. "It's not what happens to you, it's what you do about it that makes a difference."

   No matter how you prepare - how positive you remain "things" are going to happen to you. Negative things will happen and its' up to you to learn how to deal with them. Stop the blame game - take responsibility and move on. Learn to look for trouble before it happens and deal with it. I know every day of my life there will be situations that I really don't want to deal with - but its life. Some of them are small and some downright hurt. I made a decision a long time ago I can cry "why me?" or get up do something about it and move on. It creates a sense of power and fulfillment. But keep in mind, as long as you're here on earth those situations will keep coming. Deal with one at a time and move on - they don't last forever.

6. Enjoy what you are doing. When you are happy that is when things are going to attract to you. The more you get down or become unhappy it's a sign of internal fear. You will push energy away from you.

7. Be Grateful For What You Have Now.

The best thinkers in the world have shown that when you are grateful for what you have now much more will come to you. Based on the laws of energy positive energy - will attract to you if you stay positive. If you are grateful for what you have you will attract much more to you because your subconscious has no barriers. It can be only blunted by negative conceited thinking.

8. Stay Humble

Be confident/cocky inside but develop a feeling of humility. Knowing what you can do without boasting about it is ten times more powerful. People know how good you are with your talent, not your mouth.

How To Turn Luck From Superstition To Reality

What is luck? Have you ever really tried to find the correct definition? Thomas Jefferson, 3rd president of the United States, who said, "I'm a great believer in luck, and I find the harder I work, the more I have of it."

One definition: the FORCE that seems to operate for good or ill in a person's life. Good Fortune; advantage or success.

Second Definition: LUCK...Living Under Correct Knowledge

Depend on the rabbit's foot if you will, but remember it didn't work for the rabbit. R.E. Shay

Most luck comes when you are making things happen. There are few if any people who are sitting idle who are lucky. When you continue to be busy and do the things that others don't want to do you will be amazed how lucky you become. You can't rely on luck. Luck will happen one way or another. When it happens great - if it doesn't don't worry about it and move on. When you put yourself in a situation that you've been properly prepared and the right opportunity presents itself - luck will show through. Until then, count on you, your mind, and your work ethic and luck will follow.

Carl Bialik wrote for the Wall Street Journal, "The Power of Lucky Charms," and showed what research shows about "luck." In a test conducted by researchers from the University of Cologne, participants on a putting green who were told they were playing with a "lucky ball" sank 6.4 putts out of 10, nearly two more putts, on average, than those who weren't told the ball was lucky. That is a 35% improvement. The results suggest new thinking in how to view luck and are intriguing to behavioral psychologists. "Our results suggest that the activation of a superstition can indeed yield performance-improving effects," says Lysann Damisch, co-author of the Cologne study, set to be published in the journal Psychological Science. The sample size, just 28 university students, was small, but the effect was big enough to be statistically significant. "Simply being told this is a lucky ball is sufficient to affect performance," Stuart Vyse, professor of psychology at Connecticut College and author of "Believing in Magic: The Psychology of Superstition," says of the new study.

According to Daniel Pink in writing "How To Make Your Own Luck," Richard Wiseman, is head of a psychology research department at the University of Hertfordshire in England. For the past eight years, he and his colleagues at the university's Perrott-Warrick Research Unit have studied what makes some people lucky and others not. After conducting thousands of interviews and hundreds of experiments, Wiseman now claims that he's cracked the code. Luck isn't due to kismet, karma, or coincidence, he says. Instead, lucky folks -- without even knowing it -- think and behave in ways that create good fortune in their lives.

Wiseman's four principles turn out to be slightly more polished renditions of some of the self-help canon's greatest hits. One thing Wiseman discovered, for example, was that when things go awry, the lucky "turn bad luck into good" by seeing how they can squeeze some benefit from the misfortune. (Lemonade, anyone?) The lucky also "expect good fortune," which no doubt has Norman Vincent Peale, author of *The Power of Positive Thinking*, grinning in his grave. According to Wiseman, what I'm arguing is that we have far more control over events than we thought previously. You might say, "Fifty percent of my life is due to chance events." No, it's not. Maybe 10% is. That other 40% that you think you're having no influence over at all is actually defined by the way you think.

Dr. Conway's Top 7 Rules for Luck

1. Take the time to listen to your mind speak to you. Through quiet time or meditation impressions will come to you that will bring success.

2. Preparation and hard work will set your life in motion and effects of luck will soon follow.

3. Ready – Aim – Fire is a thing of the past. Instead change to Ready – Fire – Aim. Make opportunity a thing that you go after don't sit around waiting for opportunity come to you.

4. Do you know what you want? If you don't it will never happen. Make sure you have a clear and full understanding what you want and relentlessly pursue it and luck will find you.

5. Take time and plan. Find out where you want to go and go after it. Expect the unexpected and watch the luck multiply.

6. Something always good comes out of something bad. Don't self collapse if something goes wrong. Prepare for the good that is about to happen and the luck to come to you.

7. Prepare for success. Don't be paralyzed by thought – prepare and see your success coming to you and then give 100% of your efforts and you can then call your success luck.

Keys In Developing a Strong Mind That Can Attract Anything

Most people don't know that properly program in your mind will attract the energy needed to develop success. Just like having a personal assistant that will do anything for you by asking. When you tell your mind that you want to do something or accomplish something you begin by putting the train in the tracks.

It will take time to get there but when you tell your personal assistant to do something it will get done because they've been trained to produce results. Well, that is how your brain is designed…once you tell it what to do it will do it. Unless - you start self-doubt-talk in your mind. When you do this it's just like telling your personal assistant that you wanted coffee - but before they go out of the room you say to your assistant no I want tea instead. Once they hear that and they begin to go out the door - you say no I think I want a soda. By now you have your assistant all confused and nothing gets accomplished. The same goes for your mind as well. The more confusing self talk you recite the more confused the brain becomes and nothing gets accomplished. You have to be consistent and positive with your thoughts.

The best way to begin this is right before you drift off to sleep at night - give your brain something to work on. The subconscious part of your brain never goes to sleep. By telling it what you want and by seeing it in your mind you put the wheels of the train on the track and motion begins. To gain speed you have to constantly repeat this over and over until the train is up to full speed. You have to stay positive and repeat in your mind what you originally intended for your mind to produce. If you don't it's the same as getting the train up to full speed and slamming on the brakes.

No matter how rough things get, if you continue to see yourself in the manner you set your goals for your mind will get you there. But it's the consistency and the dogged repetition of self talk, visualization and telling your mind before bed what it is you truly want. If worry, self doubt or anxiety seep into your mind - your brain will fulfill that line of thinking that you programmed until it gives you what you asked for. Just like your personal assistant who want to do the very best job for you it will follow your commands.

THERE IS NO LIMIT TO YOUR SUBCONSCIOUS MIND! That means that if you stay true to feeding it what you want you will create the energy that will allow you to surround you with the necessary people to help your or the actual event needed to accomplish your goals. No matter what happens to you, no matter your current situation, no matter what you think is going to happen to you, you have to believe in what you are doing. This is the key and without the key you can't open the door to get onto train.

When you worry you create what you worry about. If you get down on yourself your mind will go downhill on you. What you ask for you will get - so watch what you ask for because you will get it. You want to succeed but then you tell your brain "I can't do this" "they're better than me". This is the kiss of death for mental preparation. Once you start that the brain says…. "okay, well let's go home he/she doesn't want this anymore." It's just like your personal assistant who is out getting you lunch and receives a call from someone saying that "hey were not sure but I don't think he wants lunch anymore."

You've created doubt and when that happens your mind, just like the rest of your body is always trying to protect you - will stop everything in its tracks. You have to as much or more discipline with your mind as you are working your body out. I'm telling you it works - and it works far more than you can ever imagine.

Create Your Own Energy

Your body is made up of billions of cells that carry out multiple functions every second of the day. Those cells are electrically charged. Some cells are positively charged and some are negatively charged which is how they help the body work in harmony. Your brain is an electrical generator. It produces electricity and can send and receive frequencies or vibrations from the electricity that it produces. If you can 'tap' into that vibration you can use it as an extra piece of ammo of your sporting life to attack the things in life that you want. The key to this is creating a mindset that allows you to use that energy.

Nature shows us that energy attracts energy - so positive energy attracts positive energy and negative energy attracts negative energy. You have the ability to create the energy or the vision that will attract other visions to your physical life. From your mind you create a positive vision. That vision will create physical vibration or energy that will attract to other positive energy in the universe.

You choose the thoughts that you want. You can use other people's thoughts or create your own it doesn't matter as long as it is positive and repetitive. Either way you will begin attracting positive things to you on a regular basis. Thoughts create emotion, emotions create motion and motion creates outcome. Your mind and body will follow your thoughts creating emotion that is transformed into behavior. Once it gets logged into the subconscious mind then the wheels of positive motion will begin to roll.

You Can Change Your Own Reality....Based On The Way You Think.

You start with a thought, you create a feeling or emotion and produce action and things will begin to attract to you. The difficult part of this whole thing is getting started and staying disciplined. You will have self doubt because everything around us all day long is negative. You turn on the news – negative, you read the newspaper - negative, you listen to gossip - negative. There are tons of non-productive news that comes to you on a regular basis unless you draw the line in the sand and stop it.

With your mind made up to change - and a determination to continue - you can attract whatever you want in life....it all depends on how bad and how hard you go after it. It's up to you - and the questions you ask. I believe that every answer that we need has already been answered. We just need to ask the right question.

So what is that you want? Have you taken the time to sit down and think about that? Probably not. We have a hard time getting the family to sit down to have a meal let alone time to think. What I'm proposing to you is that you take some of time to sit down with pen and paper and ask yourself what you really want. Write it down....make sure it's complete. Begin to create the vision or the image of the end result. You need to go over this daily. The best time is when you first get up in the morning and right before you fall asleep at night. This gives the subconscious mind plenty of time to log it in and to turn it into a personal behavior. This new behavior will then attract the outcome that you are wanting.

It's this simple - it can be done. It will take work, but if you have the guts and the ambition you will become a better athlete.

Remember, You're Never A Loser Until You've Confirmed It In Your Head...

Chapter 7

Coaching

So What Makes a Good Coach?

To answer that it depends on the level of the program and the level of the athlete.

Take for example little league. A good coach will teach and drill fundamentals while making it fun to learn the game at each position. At this level you are trying to teach the game of baseball to young athletes. Teaching their position, the strategy of the game, the rules of the game, and the importance of being a team player are all a part of coaching young kids. Coaches should be teaching the principals of fitness and how important it is to become a complete athlete. Yes everyone wants to win but a good coach knows that if he can develop good fundamentally sound players the wins will follow.

At the high school level coaches are there to continue the development of players however the strategy of winning becomes more important. Less time for coddling and more time to work hard to be able to handle advance plays and positions needed to beat top opposing teams.

At the college level - it's all about winning - period. Yes they will develop you as you mature but if you don't develop fast enough you will be pushed aside and the next kid will take your place. The hand holding is over, leave your feelings at the door and get ready to be pushed, prodded, cursed at, and belittled all in the name of winning.

A coach is more than a person who knows how to draw up plays. First and foremost, a coach's number one responsibility is to develop his or her players to better execute movements properly first. They need to know what the exact abilities of each of the athletes that they have.

A good coach develops his strategies around the talent he/she has as opposed to jamming a strategy or philosophy down the throats of players he/she has.

Most kids are not in proper physical condition in the younger stages. With a good program you can develop your athlete's strengths which will help the athlete better command their bodies. By strengthening I mean, cardiovascular and muscular endurance. If the coach knows what they are doing they can take mediocre players and develop them into outstanding athletes. This is done by properly identifying each of the player's weaknesses and restrictions and developing a program to overcome them. Coaches can now begin to build a base for their team with more of the kids team developing better skills.

The coach needs to put the best players they have on the field. (field is used here as to represent all sports). Coaches and parents need to stop all of the drama and choose the best players that you have to play. Yes there will be times where two (or more) players will be close to one another in ability and it's the coach's job to choose the best.

Coaches are executives. An executive's job is to get others to get their job done. In this case, it's the head coaches' job to get their assistants get their jobs done. Some sports demand a staff of coaches to help plan, direct and implement the strategy set forth by the vision of the head coach.

Coaches need to choose good quality assistants that can and will buy into the head coach's vision and will carry out that vision on the field. Assistant coaches need to understand that there number one job is to make the head coach look good. A good head coach will test his assistants. Test them on what they are coaching (positions, techniques etc.) and not assuming that they know what the head coach wants accomplished. Overall, a good coach needs just to be fair to the best of their ability and to challenge each athlete to give their best at all times. They also need to challenge each assistant coach to become better coaches. All coaches need to gain respect of their players by leading my example so that they can guide the athletes to victory.

With respect high enough from their players the player will trust them in a way as to do anything that they want done. You've heard of some teams that would run through a brick wall for their coach. That comes from pure respect.

A good coach should be able to fit the players into a scheme that is developed to the talent at hand. Not to jam the players into a system that they like and hope it works. A coach should analyze his/her talent and understand how best to use them to advance their players to the next level. In some cases at the lower levels a good coach should forget about winning and concentrate on developing players to excel at the next level. Spend the appropriate time developing the crucial fundamentals needed at the upper level of sports. At this level, it's not about trophies, jackets or banquets...it's about development. The good coaches know this and will take the kids and properly exploit their weaknesses. This way they can properly correct them and continue on to the next level of their sport. Coaches at the upper level need to continue to develop the fundamentals but it's time to push a bit harder through competition. Allowing all of their players to get an honest chance at playing and if they are good enough then let them play.

Parents: Let The Coaches Coach

There comes a time when your influence as a parent will not matter anymore and your son or daughter will have to advance on their own merits. If you've been actively involved with your child's sports advancement there will come a time that you have to pass over the reins over to the coach at the next level. It's time to stand back and let the coach do their thing. The worst thing you can do is attempt to be a side line coach. The only thing I've ever seen by this is that it confuses the athlete to no ends. Let the coach do their thing no matter what your opinion is.

You know when we were kids playing in the park either football, baseball, basketball there was one thing understood. Every kid there knew who was good and who was bad. When you're not picked first in certain games the peer pressure alone was enough to make you play harder to prove you belong there. We didn't need a summer camp to tell us or a coach of any kind to pick sides. We chose the sides and made the best of what we had. If we were playing baseball and didn't have enough kids to make two teams we would split the kids in half to make two teams and then make rules that would help us play the game. We would adopt rules that if you hit the ball to right field you were automatically out. We didn't have anyone to play that field so we just made it an out. This way we could establish one thing – we could play. We didn't sit around worried that we didn't have enough players. We made it happen.

Times have changed and now there are camps for everyone and every sport. Good in some senses and bad in others. Camps are in business to make money. To make money you have to keep your customers happy. Many times in order to keep people happy short cuts are developed. This is the bad part in making everyone happy.

Kids truly need the harsh reality of survival of the fittest at earlier ages. As they develop and eventually get to the mid to late teenage levels it's a hard dose of reality when there is no one around to help them advance like they did when they were younger. There comes a time when you find out that you're standing all alone and the only person can help is you. I feel that if children learn this early it will make them much more secure in themselves and their favorite sports.

It's pretty funny to think back that when we played amongst ourselves there was never any type of political maneuvering - you either were good enough or you didn't come back. That was enough motivation for anyone to pick up their game, so to speak. We played all types of sports all year long and didn't have coaches. In today's day and age it's not nice to make kids quit. In fact, I'll share a story with you about my daughter's soccer team. My wife and I were watching the soccer game when one of the parents came up to us asking us to sign a petition. I asked what the petition was for and the mother responded that they started the petition so that there were no scores at the end of the game. She went on to say that they wanted to protect the feelings and the self esteem of all of the players. She felt that when someone loses they will begin to feel bad about themselves and it's time to change that. I was speechless for a brief moment and responded by saying, "lady, you've come to the wrong guy on this one. Sports are all about winning and losing and you will create anxiety ridden psychotics if you do this. As in life, people win, people lose it's the way it works – and no I will not sign your petition." Thank goodness that the petition died along the way. To my surprise many of the parents held the same view as my wife and me.

Again, coaches are there to guide the athletes not take over their lives. Coaches are there to teach the athlete a more streamline way of doing things for a better outcome. If they are organized properly and they have some talented players then they can develop a team that can win. In all fairness to coaches please understand that coaches are not there to hold day care! There not there to hold hands and there not there to do the work of an absent tee parent. From the age of 12 and up its time to teach your child that its time to begin take some responsibility in being an athlete.

Athletes: There comes a time when you have to stand on your own and take responsibility for your actions. You can't have Mom and Dad always sticking up for you. You have to learn that your decisions and your actions are your own responsibility.

Parents as Coaches

I know that I'm going to upset a lot of people in this chapter but it is a subject that really needs to be discussed – Parents as Coaches.

Its one thing to be a parent and it's a totally different thing to be a coach. When the two are mixed together it can become a real problem for both the parent and the child. If you as a parent can't separate the two – please go and do something else before you develop an irrevocable relationship with your child.

What is becoming an epidemic throughout our youth sports are overzealous parents coaching with self agendas. The agenda's that they have is to either protect their own kid from getting yelled at, to make sure that there kid plays in each game or to make sure that they make all-star team. Parents have developed a political mechanism to promote their kids advancements. In baseball I've seen fathers lobby other fathers to help promote their son to vote for their kid for the all-star team. Knowing that their votes would leave one or two players of greater talent out of the all-star line they continue to mastermind between themselves to make sure their kid makes the team.

A local hockey organization took over a junior hockey team in my town. Their first rule of order was to remove all parents as coaches. They opened the jobs for new coaches to apply. One of the main rules for the coaches was that you couldn't have your own child on the team in order to coach. I give them a standing ovation for that move. These new coaches will allow the kids to play and put the best players on the ice.

According to Fred Engh, president of the National Alliance for Youth Sports, "85% of people that coach are the parents of one of the kids on the team." Times have changed and we've adapted to the times. Years ago we had people who enjoyed the game of baseball and people who had no kids on the teams coached for the pure joy of the game. They knew much more and they seemed to care much more about teaching the kids the art of the game.

There was a time that in America we had a feeling of charity. We gave of our time, our money or our resources to others who have been less fortunate. Little leagues, football leagues and others had coaches who gave back to the game that was given to them.

Now we live in an entitlement society that it is assumed that someone else is going to do it for you. The long standing excuse I've heard over and over was that if it wasn't for Dad's coaching kids wouldn't have sports at all to play. I strongly disagree with that statement. If it is so important that Dad's HAVE to be coaches then why don't I see them volunteering for ballet, figure skating, tap dance and other less popular sports?

There is a new state of baseball known throughout youth sports known as "Daddyball." It's when a parent becomes a coach with the covert intention of showcasing his or her child. They attempt to build a team abound the child so that child stands out to potential all-star voting coaches.

In other cases how many times have you heard of a son or daughter saying, "he works me harder just because I'm his kid." If the coach was truly understanding about being a coach he would tell everyone on the team how he or she felt about the situation and the best athletes will play. The problem is that is only the case in less than 5% of the time. The other times it's a premeditated plan to get their kid in the game as much as they possibly can. Too many times parent-coaches push their children too hard because they want them to excel at every moment.

It is a fine line between being a good parent and a good coach. You must be able to allow your son or daughter to be themselves as an athlete. When the both of you hit the practice field or court you have to separate your relationship. Tell your son or daughter that when it time to practice or play I'm your coach...not your parent. Conversely, when the game is over, you're back to being a parent and stop being a coach. If you overload either side of this parent/coach equation it can turn out to be detrimental to your relationship with one another.

Most parents get involved in early stages of the kids athletic career. Most parents fill in at the youth leagues and have good intentions to help out so that the kids can play. However there are those "other parent coaches" who are there to only help advance their kid. They have a premeditated agenda to help their son or daughter crack the starting lineup. This can be a sad situation because it doesn't help anyone. If your son or daughter can't make it on their own merits you can only help them for a short period of time. There's going to come a time that you're going to have to give them up to the upper level coaches. If you've helped them along the way without letting them earn it for themselves the results down the road can be devastating.

If you're there to advance you kid - do them and you a favor and stay home. If your child is good he/she will rise to the top on their own. If you're going to be a coach then please learn something about the sport. If you're coaching at the younger levels please keep winning out of it and make sure that you teach the kids how to play properly. If they play properly they will win - it's that simple.

The best thing you can do for your son or daughter as an athlete is to develop each athlete with strong fundamentals of the sport. In the former Soviet Union for example, they would put the equivalent to our U.S. PhD's at the youth level. They knew the importance of developing the proper fundamentals. As a youth coach your job is to DEVELOP players to excel and progress to the next level. This one thing can help each athlete more than you know.

I have spoken to numerous high school coaches that have become ever increasingly frustrated with the athletes that has come up from the youth ranks over glorified and under prepared. Most coaches at the upper levels have been pulling their hair out because of the lack of fundamentals they witness when the young athletes get to their level. Coaches have told me that they have to "undue" the bad habits that were learned at the youth levels. That means they have to take the time to review the fundamentals to make sure that they know that the athletes know the basics.

As a youth coach, get organized and have a game plan for every practice. Don't have the kids there for hours on end. Train them, run them, practice them and let them get home. They don't have to be there hour after hour if you organize your schedule properly.

To make sure that you are training your athletes properly you should be training them at the same level as they would be playing in a game. This not only better cardiovascular training but it also will help your athletes decrease the amount of 'burn out.' A practice should be a no nonsense time to develop skills and conditioning. There should be a period of time to get the body warmed up then continue into actual game simulating drills and other practice skills. A practice that is intense and kept to a logical minimum to not to go over board that become unnecessary.

I have witnessed coaches having parents pull their cars up to the field to turn their lights on so that the kids could continue to practice. The problem is that this mini football team had been there for well over three hours and a half. The kids were 10 to 12 years old playing mini football! The coaches wanted to get another hour in. It doesn't make any sense because most kids don't have the attention spans to begin with needed for that length of time. Coaches, if you properly organize your time you can get much more done in shorter amount of time which will be retained by the athlete much more.

Trust me, I know and understand, every kid wants to win - I get it. But don't just win for the sake of winning without developing these kids to become better players. Develop their knowledge of the game, develop their skills and develop their work ethic. I was at a legion league baseball game and a situation came up that was unbelievable to me. A situation arose where the players didn't know what an infield fly rule was. For parents that don't know about the infield fly rule let me define it for you:

Runners are on first and second with less than 2 outs. Pop fly is hit to the third baseman. He intentionally drops the fly ball, picks it up, touches third and then throws to second for a double play. It's an easy double play because both runners are tagging up on their bases expecting the ball to be caught.

The runners on base were teenagers that have been playing baseball for years in the little league system and didn't know the rule. That only comes down to poor coaching. To allow these kids to pass up through the little league ranks' playing baseball and not teaching all aspects of the game is unacceptable.

When coaching younger athletes please don't expect perfection - you're not going to get it. Mistakes are "red flags" for the coach (and the player) to look more closely at the situation to see what is going wrong. Once that is properly confronted the player stands a much better chance of improving. If your player continues to repeat the same mistake over and over then you have to make a decision if this person is right for this position. They may have a weakness that won't allow them to perform the action that you want. The key is to test them to see what the problem is to see if you can correct it. The best time to make the corrections is at practice not in a game. If needed, while the game is going on take a few notes, so that you can pull them out the next time you have practice to review with the player. I can't tell you how many times I've seen coaches on the side lines screaming at the top of their lungs attempting to correct a situation that should have been corrected in practice. The chances of correcting it in the 'heat of battle' in the game are not plausible.

A good coach will take some notes so that they can think about helping a particular athlete do better. Screaming and yelling is so 1960 - how about we start teaching, correcting, teaching and repeating.

If the player continues to make mistakes it's up to the coach to figure out 'the why' behind the failure. Is he/she not able to play that position? Is he/she not physically fit enough to handle this particular part of the game? Was the player properly coached enough for the player to make the play? Could it possibly be a eye sight problem? Are you using words in your practices that the players don't understand?

I remember I was talking to a female basketball coach that was telling me that she was having a problem with her team fully understand what she wanted on the court. She had me come to watch a practice and the first thing that I noticed that some of the words she was using were going over the kids head. The coach would yell out "crash the point and secure the perimeter." She wanted the player to get more aggressive at the top of the key and then get back on defense. There were many other 'slang' references that she was making which were flying over the players heads faster than the stealth bomber.

The coach and I sat down and talk about what she was saying and began to write them down. As she looked at them on paper it dawned on her that what she was saying could be misconstrued. So we changed the way she communicated to her players and it made a huge difference in the performance of the team.

Take time to understand what is going on before you just stand there and yell. Yes, there are times that you have to raise your voice to get people in the game. Sometimes young players tend to 'zone out' mentally if not actively challenged on a continued basis. But at the same time, yelling just to yell without teaching is a waste of time and energy.

Upper level coaches - stop screaming and cursing and start teaching. Make sure your communication is set properly so the athletes can understand you. Many times I hear coaches using words that the people from Webster dictionary would have to spend time looking up. The key to communication is to say what you intend to say and make sure that the person that you are communicating to understands what you intentions are.

Coaches, what have you done lately to improve your coaching skills - besides go to a sports specific seminar or camp? Have you taken any organization classes? Sports psychology, sports training, sports physiology or sports injury classes? Do you need to be an expert in these areas - of course not, but have some kind of idea what is going on with the many various aspects of your team. Advancing your knowledge will help you build better athletes and better citizens of our country.

Assistant coaches need to understand that there number one job is to make the head coach look good. A good head coach will test his assistants. Test them on what they are coaching (positions, techniques etc.) and not assuming that they know what the head coach wants accomplished. It's not a test to test IQ, it's a test to make sure that the entire coaching staff is all playing from the same sheet of music. Overall a good coach needs just to be fair to the best of their ability to challenge each athletes to give their best at all times.

The coach should gain respect of their players so that they can lead the athletes to victory.

The coach needs to develop respect high enough from their players so that they can develop the players to do what they want done - when they want it done and to the level they want it complete at.

A good coach should be able to fit the players into a scheme that is developed to the talent at hand. Good coaches don't jam players into a system that doesn't fit their talent. A coach should analyze his/her talent and understand how best to use them to advance their players to the next level. In some cases at the lower levels a good coach should forget about winning and concentrate on developing players to excel at the next level. Spend the appropriate time developing the crucial fundamentals needed at the upper level of sports. At this level, it's not about trophies, jackets or banquets…it's about development. The good coaches know this and will take the kids and properly exploit their weaknesses. This way they can properly correct them and continue on to the next level of their sport. Coaches at the upper level need to continue to develop the fundamentals but it's time to push a bit harder through competition. Allowing all of their players to get a honest chance at playing and if they are good enough then let them play.

Coaching Today

Understanding that there is a shortage of coaches I applaud the parents who step up to help out. But please keep in mind, even though you have volunteered your time it doesn't make it right for you to become someone you're not. Many parents that become coaches tend to change their personalities when coaching on the field. With a little bit of power thrusted upon them they seem to forget that they are dealing with kids. It's about training, educating and motivating - rather than enabling or destroying. Some coaches do more yelling than they do teaching and wonder why they don't win. I understand there are times that you have to raise your voice to get you point across but I don't understand why some coaches scream from the time they get on the field until they go home.

I once had a patient who was an art teacher at a local school who also happen to be an assistant football coach. I asked him, why do some coaches yell so much? He said, that football is a war and you have to yell at players to motivate them. I was taken back a bit by his answer.

With a perplexed look on my face I asked, coach, if young Sally colors outside of the lines do you get right in her face and start screaming as loud as you can attempting to motivate her? He said no, because that was different. I didn't agree but I understood what he was saying. What he was telling me, without telling me, that this is what was done to him when he played football. This is how most of coaching is learned – past down from coach to coach and from team to team.

When it's all said and done – football isn't a war. No one gets shot, no one gets killed and everyone gets to go home at the end of the day. I understand why drill instructors in the military scream and yell because they are trying to save your life when you go into real combat. Some yelling in sports can be acceptable - but when it goes on and on without any educational intention it becomes brainless. Coaching doesn't give anyone the right to become a psychotic that takes their frustrations out on young men and women. It's not that I advocate that all practices need to be all sugar and spice. I'm all for working every athlete to the very end of their endurance envelopes. But there doesn't have to have an intimidation component interwoven in it. Coaching can be a rewarding experience however if taken for granted you can do more harm than good.

Sighing Up For The First Time To Play Sports

When you send your son or daughter to play a sport you are essentially sending your precious little one off to change their life. With all of the parenting, encouragement, and nurturing that you've done over the years it's now time to turn them over to someone else. Somewhat like taking your child to kindergarten for the first time but the only difference is that the teacher has been certified by the state.

Not so in the coaching world. Most of the junior or bittie league coaches are fathers/mothers who are there with their own kids. Some never played a sport in their life, some crammed the night before from a book at Barnes & Noble. I'm glad there are fathers and mothers out there who can give of their time to help the kids get playing. Some will Just know sometimes you son or daughter will be taught things that will be much different than the other kids…it's sort of the luck of the draw.

In today's sports era 90% or more of your youth leagues are taught or coached by parents, uncles, and aunts or similar. The unfortunate part of that is that the kids are being taught by someone who knows nothing about properly preparing a young child how to become an athlete. Having kids play and developing athletes are two very different areas of sports.

We can develop many more elite athletes if we just put better coaches at the earlier stages of your child's entry into sports. Quite honestly, at this mini level the only thing that coaches should be concentrating on is TEACHING the kids about the sport and TEACHING them how to have fun. Yep you heard it here first - younger kids should be having the most fun possible and enjoying the sport that they are participating in. While having fun the coach should be teaching the proper mechanics of running, jumping, cutting, changing direction and many other pivotal aspects of sports. The fundamentals of being an athlete are not being taught so therefore we have an over abundance of mediocre athletes.

Coaching in much, much more. Coaching is like being a Mom – you're a psychologist, trainer, organizer, executive, strategist and a role model. Coaching is taking a young man or young women (boy or girl in many cases) and molding them both physically and mentally as well. It's a daunting task but if done right it can be the most rewarding job in the world. On the other hand it can be the most destructive job on the face of the earth. If I've said this once, I've said this a thousand's times - in my area, we'll never put out a championship little league baseball team until fathers stop coaching their son's. Why? Well because many of them are there for a different reason than just to coach. Many see a way to watch their kids so they don't get hurt, some are there to make sure they make the All-Star team and some are there to make sure that their kid makes the starting rotation. Whatever the reason - you're not a coach, unless you are there to teach, instruct and pass on advice to help each and <u>everyone</u> on the team advance to the next level.

Is there a shortage of coaches? Probably. Do we need fathers involved - without a doubt. I would much rather see a father [or mother] involved with their child than leaving them out to fend for themselves on the street or leave them home to play video games. But just because you have decided to help it doesn't give you the right to push an agenda for your own advantage. Everyone appreciates your time that you are giving but if you're not giving it for the right reason....DON'T GIVE IT!

Most recently a parent was in my office telling me of the outrageous behavior of his daughter's softball coach. He explained that there was a play where the coach's daughter was caught up in a double play. He told me that the coach went absolutely crazy, throwing his hat, throwing the book and carrying on for a lengthily time period. Yelling at the top of his lungs saying to his daughter while pointing his finger into her chest, "are you that stupid to get tagged out after a fly ball? Oh my God, I can believe how dumb you are, I've told you over and over how to play this game." The fans became eerily quiet because they couldn't believe what they were watching. The umpire put in a formal complaint to the league about this situation and said that if he ever does that again he will be thrown out of the league.

I can't tell you how many fathers/mothers come into my office telling me how hard they push their child because they know what is best for them. With resentment written all over the child's face you can see the mental brick wall being built between their relationships without a word being spoken by the child.

I had one softball pitcher whose father thought it was fine to pitch his daughter in five straight games in a row in a local tournament. The girl was crying due to fatigue and the father stood there and told me how it was making her tougher. She was ELEVEN YEARS OLD!!!!

Coaching is a very difficult job position one that takes a lot of work, organization, talent and the ability to put in the necessary hours to make things happen. Coaching is as important as any other job when dealing with kids. As a coach, decide whether you want to leave an impression on the child for long time to come. If you do then teach - show them how to play correctly, show them how to win, show them how to lose and you will build a kid for life.

What every kid needs to learn no matter what sport their involved in are the FUNDAMENTALS of the sport. Every professional player that I know review fundamentals almost every practice before they continue to train. So, if you're going to do anything help the kids review their fundamentals over and over so that they get the basics down. This one thing will help them more than you will ever know.

How Much Do You Really Know?

If you are a coach and a parent, and in this case I don't mean a coach on the field, I mean a coach at home. Have you asked yourself how much do I really know about this sport? Do I know as much as I think? I mean a coach at home. Have you asked yourself how much do I really know about this sport? Do I know as much as I think?

If you don't know as much as you think then you can be giving your son or daughter the wrong information. What happens is that the athlete is getting information from you at home and then attempting to do it on the field which causes a problem for the coach of the team. The only thing that comes from this is confusion.

Do you have your son or daughter on specialized training programs at home? I've seen father's initiate a weight training program for their kids at ages 5. The kid couldn't even do a push up or a sit up but the father made a small bench press so that the child could start weight lifting. The father wanted to get a head start on the child's future competition. I'm going out on a limb here but the chances of this father completely understanding pediatric strength training are slim and none.

As a parent what do you really know about the physiology of strength training? Most people that get into weight lifting do so with information based on what they did when they were young. Do you really know as much as you think?

As a parent I'm sure you have good intentions but please don't go overboard. It's good to get excited about your young athlete competing in a new sport. But please let them go and just have fun in the early years. Let them get out there and discover on their own how to move, how to run, throw and kick. It's important that young athletes "feel" what they are doing so that they can make decisions on their own.

If you have specialized knowledge of a particular sport then by all means show your son or daughter some moves, tricks or drills that will help them. Don't turn into a full blown work out that begins to look like a professional workout. Make it fun, make it diverse and you will see that you child will want to do this with you on a repetitive basis.

By all means learn as much as you can about the sport that your child is involved with. Learn how you can assist your child to develop into better athlete without making it a full time job. There are tons of books and DVD's on the internet for you to read and learn from. They can be a big help to allow you to pass on solid knowledge on developing athletes who will learn and have fun.

Coaching Styles

I've personally had coaches who were screamers and yellers and I've had some coaches' that were quiet. I've been on a part of winning teams with both types of coaches. Some coaches are just gruff and have a poor way of communicating their ideas and thoughts. All I can say to you is get used to it.

I've always told my kids and my patients… "don't listen to how loud they say it….listen to what they have to say." Some coach's delivery is poor at best - but many have their hearts in the right area and truly want to do the best for the kids. Their delivery may be way off but their message might be dead on. So don't get so emotional about how they say it…listen for the content.

So what makes a good coach? That can be a really tough question to answer. When you look at the great coaches they are primarily known for one thing…winning. They can be the nicest person on the world but if they don't win they don't coach for long.

People like nice coaches….people LOVE coaches that win.

So, if you take that kind of attitude you better deal with the coach as a whole. You buy into all of their eccentricities, phobias, biases and tendencies. There are many things that make up a good coach but if I was pressed for an absolute answer I would say that a great coach builds a game plan or strategy AROUND the talent he/she is handed. Good coach's allows the talent they have be placed in the right positions to excel rather than saying that the athletes must adhere to his/her philosophy of the game. Players win games - coaches don't. I feel if you put the right kid in the right spot at the right time he/she will perform properly. If you try to force your x's and o's philosophy on the kids who are not physically capable of that philosophy, eventually you will have problems.

There are as many different coaching styles as there are sports. The bottom line for many is that at the end of the day who won and who lost. Was it the coach's fault, the player fault or both? Very few coaches don't put any blame on themselves for a team's loss – it seems that they always put it on the players. There are times that coaches blow it and the team loses. It's not the time to blame the players there are times that coaches have to take it on the chin and admit the loss.

It always amused me after a game when the coach gets interviewed nine times out of ten the coach will begin to blame the players. We didn't execute well, we didn't run the plays with the right intensity, and we didn't play our own game. Just once I would like to hear the head coach say, "wow, we (the coaches) blew that one, we had the wrong game plan and we didn't correct our mistakes as the game went on."

Yes I know many times it is the players that make mistakes but I can't tell you how many times I've sat in the stands watching a game and saying to myself boy I don't think that was the right play to run. Yep, I have an opinion, but I also understand that it's a heck of a lot easier sitting up in the stands sipping on a coke than it is on the side line enduring all of the pressures of the game. I understand, but again, all I hear with many coaches "it's a TEAM game" – so I'm assuming that the coaches are a part of the team as well. Well, I'm here to tell you it's a two way street. The captain of the ship is responsible for everyone below him/her on the organizational chart. So if coaches are good when the win - they have to be bad when they lose. That's why head coach is such a difficult position to take on.

It's a learning experience - the team wins together and the team loses together. That means that all the players accept responsibility for the loss or the win and the coaches accept the responsibility as well for the loss or win.

Different Levels of Coaching

Some coaches are there just to do the best job that they can and help the little ones do well. They may not know tons of technical information about the sport but they know enough to get the kids moving in the right direction.

Some coaches have some good experience and are there to develop solid players so that they can advance to the next level. This can be a huge asset if your son or daughter has a little extra talent and is interested in advancing in the sport. Some coaches are there just to win. Nothing else will do unless they can bring home a victory. They could care less about how they do it as long as they do it…win.

Some coaches are there just to advance their own kid. Yep, you heard that right, the only reason they are there is to make sure that there kid "gets a fair shake". While they are worried about their kids advancing many other kids are not getting the attention they need to advance. Some parents/coaches are there to make sure that they 'jam' their kid into a position of prominence even though they may not have the talent.

Politicking with other coaches to cut deals to make sure their kid advances to the next level. Whether it's a travel team, an all-star team or just a particular higher level team - these parents have an agenda and it won't stop until their mission is accomplished.

Trust me I've been there and have witnessed the self agendas of some coaches. I never got involved with my children's sports because I wanted them to develop on their own. So if they achieved the accolades in the sport they knew that they did it all on their own. The only reason why many fathers/mothers get involved is to make sure their kid is pushed to the top. In fact when my son was in his last year of little league he played well. He was hitting way above average and his fielding was good. When it came time for all-star selections my son was left off the all-star team because the one assistant coach, whose kid was on the team, who barely batted .250 and was pushed politically to secure a place on the team. My son who was batting over .500 at the time was left out of the all-star selection for a kid who had a father who could make it happen for his son off the field. The father/coach was able to do this by going to the coaches meeting and lobbying his friends to vote for his kid to make the all-star team. (You vote for my kid I'll vote for yours…) Kids are left behind all the time in sports for situations like this or similar to this. Sometimes the life lesson is difficult to swallow at the time, however in the long run, it will make your son or daughter a stronger person.

Depending on the level that your son or daughter is at you will experience different aspects of coaching. That is to say, that each coach is motivated by many different things. Some coaches are there because they love the particular sport. They were probably pretty good athletes themselves and continue to want to stay around this environment. They love the sport, they love the action, they love the stress and they like all what it takes to build a winning program. Some coaches are there as a part of their life isn't complete. They failed at their sport or multiple sports and now they are going to take on a little bit of power to show that they really know the sport. Unfortunately these types of coaches can be a problem. They tend to yell, curse, bully - they do everything but educate and coach. Why? Because they don't know enough to really teach what they are trying to get across to the athlete.

Let me tell you a quick story about a young football coach that I can across years ago. It was a warm Friday night in August and I was pulling into my driveway after work. As I was getting out of my car I heard this extreme yelling going on. It wasn't just someone yelling....it was a pathological yelling that gave me goose bumps on my skin.

As I walked around the house I noticed that there was a mini-football team practicing up in the field behind my house. I looked up to the field and the screaming became louder so I had to take a walk up to see what the commotion was all about. As I crested the small hill I could see it was a coach screaming at his players in a manner that made me uncomfortable - let alone the little kids. The sizes of these kids were at a level where their helmets came half way down their body. The funny thing about this situation was that the coach that was doing all of the yelling went to high school with me. He was the kind of kid who never played any sports while in school. I couldn't take it anymore so I decided to yell over to the coach, "hey coach, how about you and I go one-on-one to show these kids what you mean." Well that got the imbecile coach even more mad and he yelled to me, "get off of my f*%#@& field." For a second I was startled at his answer but then when on to tell the fine coach that if he would look over on the park building you will see my name as a donator to the park. As I graciously replied...."coach being that my name is on the building...technically your on my field." At that point he threw the players out of practice because as he added... "I can't take it anymore." I was glad I opened my mouth because at very least I get the kids out of practice and away from that goof ball.

These coaches are trouble for the kids, the parents and the program. They have no idea what it takes to become a leader of young men and women. They're there to create havoc because that is what they only know. They aren't organized, they scattered, they change their minds, they forget what they said and they are never happy. They need to be taken out of the program.

Excellent coaches are really hard to come by. Good coaches are out there and trust me they're trying but some fall short in one or more areas of being a complete coach. I feel like everything else, most coaches' get into coaching to enjoy the sport and the kids. However there are a small minority that should not even step on a field, court, rink or pool. I've seen them scream excessively until they've broken the spirit of the person in front of them. I've seen them use language that even Satin himself would blush over.

One coach comes to mind that told one of his players that his mother was an assh#@e for allowing him to stay up and study for an exam. The young man had a late football practice under the lights preparing for an upcoming game. He got home around eleven p.m. and had to study for some tests. The next day he was in school and came across his head football coach in the hall way. The coached asked him why he looked so tired and the player told the coach that he was up late studying for exams. The coach starts to yell at him saying that he should know better that during football season there is no time for school but only for football. He told the coach that his mom said that school was more important than football and he needed to study. That is when the coach responded with the derogatory response about his mother.

At the higher levels of athletics money becomes a very powerful motivator. Coaches who perform well will develop a reputation for winning. When this happens often enough these coaches will be sought out by others who want them on their team. The more wins, the more experience, the more money will be offered.

If you are expecting to go on to a higher level of athletics keep this one thing in mind. At the Division I and Division II levels it's all about the dollars. I've mentioned this before in this book and it bears repeating. Most coaches are there to advance themselves. You are there (or your son or daughter) to help them build a winning program for them!

Many feel that you've taken a free education so you owe the school your soul. So now they have you 24/7. Practices, meetings, travel, weight lifting, conditioning - and oh yea, don't forget about the offseason. Yep you have to be there with the team training and did I mention that most of your summers will be included as well? All of this will center around a coach or two in your life. The smaller the program the more interaction you will have with the head coach. The larger the program the less interaction you will have with the head coach. You will have to get used to this new type of program - one that I very much doubt centers around you.

Don't get me wrong there are a ton of positives about being a scholarship athlete. Besides the free education, room and board, there is the discipline of schedules. Learning how to properly budget your time between study and athletics. The lifelong camaraderie you develop between your team mates and coaches and the understanding of the discipline of hard work. I've said it once and I'll continue to say it to I'm blue in the face - there is no substitute for hard work. That is the one thing that binds all elite athletes together knowing that they had the discipline to deal with the demands of hard work.

A good coach is a motivator, an organizer, an executive, leader psychologist, strategist, a field general and above all a foundation for his or her players. Someone that they can lean on when there is trouble either on the field or off. Someone who they can look up to and admire without the fear of having mental or physical games played on them. It's a lot of hard work being a coach. There are tremendously long hours that are put in to making a season work. I've played with some figures once and my calculations showed me that some high school coaches that put in long arduous hours end up getting paid about $1.25 per hour.

Every Sport Has a Different Coach...Or Do They?

I've played a lot of sports and have been around a lot of sports and it seems that every sport has its own unique coaching temperament behind it.

Take for example junior tennis. The demands of the tennis world can be not only time consuming but outrageously grueling. The upper tier players leave home at an early age and begin to work with special coaches or training camps. Many of these camps will allow for school work in the morning or later in the afternoon and the rest of the day is devoted to tennis. Day in and day out these kids constantly prepare for match after match after match.

The vast majority of the all tennis professionals did not graduate from any college. They turn pro at a very early age and leave the schooling behind once they get their high school degree. To my knowledge the only one that acquired her college degree was Samantha Stevenson. While on the WTA Tour she continued her studies online accomplishing what other tour professionals have not – a degree from an accredited University. Most of the tennis players that I've met have been very bright people. You would think that without a formal education there would be some apparent glimpses of ignorance but what I've seen it's been different. Many of them have been educated on the road. After years of traveling worldwide they seem to develop a street education that serves them well.

I have been around some other sports where educations were sacrificed for the sport and by all accounts there is a bit of a void in their ability to reason properly. Many players on the professional tennis tour have been trained for perfection. Every ball must be hit perfectly and if not you are a failure. This mentality of training goes a long way of making mental infants out of many players. Their ability to deal with stress and allow proper coping skills to take over is complexly void. There seems to be this mentality of pure perfection on everything they do. I've witnessed players melt down just after a game or so because they couldn't properly handle how to cope with temporary defeat. Many times this has to do with coaches who lack the ability and the experience of developing the players coping skills dealing with adversity.

Chapter 8

Sports Training

S ports are the only entity that I know of in which, by a bounce of a ball or a measurement smaller than a human hair, there can be the difference between immortality or anonymity. That is why I think so many of us are so passionate about sports.

In the U.S., the two most popular sports for youngsters are soccer and little league baseball. In days past, kids would gather all of their friends from all over the neighborhoods to play sports. They played baseball, basketball, football, dodge ball, or whatever sport was popular at that time of the year. Neighborhood kids would pick teams amongst themselves, figure out the rules, and play the game. No one had to tell them who to play with or how to play. They just played. Not being picked early in the process was warning enough for you to continue to play harder to earn the respect of your friends. The peer pressure amongst friends made you a much better athlete. You didn't need fathers or coaches telling you who should be playing and who shouldn't. The kids made the decisions.

Because of the competitive nature of sports, the best athletes play. Sports weed out the good players and the not-so-good players. It's similar to the laws of nature — eaten or be eaten. In the early days on earth, you were either chasing your food, or your food was chasing you. It seems that this has been imbedded into our very nature as humans, translating over to modern day sports. Sports have a way of developing an attitude of rivalry in a way of bringing out the best in most people. Losers fall by the wayside at every level of competition, which promotes a fear of failure for many athletes. That fear of failure can develop an increased work ethic that invariably develops winners. Most top elite professional athlete have stated on more than one occasion that one of the driving forces of their success has been the fear of failure.

There has been a push to develop youth sports to become less competitive so that you don't infringe upon the losers' self-esteem. This new-age transformation is to have every youth sporting event end in a tie so each child can go home feeling good about him- or herself. Political correctness has invaded sports to the point that the emphasis is not on the trophies or jackets but whether or not little Johnny is feeling good about himself after the game. Rather than helping develop more sound, fundamental skills both mentally and physically, people have become over-sensitive, worried about children's feelings.

When was the last time you went to a professional baseball or football game or other sporting event that ended in a tie? Could you imagine if every pro football, baseball, or tennis game ended in a tie with the way ticket prices are today? It seems that the prices keep going up, and the people continue to support their favorite teams, regardless of price. Sports fans want to be entertained by the best athletes that can be put on the field. They don't want to show up to a game where no one wins because it may hurt someone's self-esteem. Fans want to witness the best of the best going one-on-one with each other, and "may the best man win."

Times have changed. Kids now are playing more sports on their couches than they are on playgrounds. Instead of kids going outside and playing either by themselves or with friends, they are sitting at home playing video games. Today, sports are specialized, including camps, seminars, and meetings. They include coaches, trainers, and other experts, but the kids aren't getting any better. Rather than figuring out the sport for themselves, they attend these camps to be told what to do or what to expect in the sport. This doesn't allow them to make the many mistakes needed to gain better knowledge of the game. Mistakes are where you learn, and it's better to get the mistakes out of the way when you're younger rather than when you get older.

The kids that are getting out of the house to play are usually playing in organized sports overseen by parents. Parents that get involved tend to produce more stress on the kids when playing. Parents tend to place more expectations on their kids in not allowing them to just be themselves.

Parents are hiring personal trainers for their young athletes to get them bigger, faster, and stronger. There is nothing wrong with that, as long as they train them for the sport rather than train them to excel in the gym. Many kids are becoming better in the gym rather than better on the field. They can pass various tests in the gym, but when it comes down to playing the sport or the position itself, the athlete's skills don't seem to match up.

In the U.S., we tend to do what was done before us. Most training has been passed down from one trainer to another. Some of the training is good, some of it is bad, and most of it is too confusing for the athletes and parents to decide which is best. When your children are young, the best thing to do is to get them out the door to play. Don't worry about specialized training until later. Make sure that they are having fun in the sport that they are playing and that they have chances to play as much as they can.

The Phelps Phenomenon...

Michael Phelps is without a doubt the best swimmer that the world has ever seen. When he accomplished his remarkable feat of winning eight gold medals in the Olympics in 2008, the phenomenon began. Everyone looked to his coach to find out how he was training Phelps. Everyone wanted to know his training regimen, including swimming, gym training, and nutrition. People were dying to see what new secrets they could discover. Phelps' coach, Bob Bowman, was portrayed as a genius and as someone who has revolutionized the sport.

I'm not going to say that Phelps' coach isn't good, but if he was as sensational as the media make him out to be, then why weren't the other swimmers who he coached just as good as Phelps? I'm a big fan of Coach Bowman in how he handles his athletes. He once stepped on and broke Phelps' swim goggles in order to see how his athlete would handle adversity. But to say that Bowman is solely responsible for the development of Phelps is far from accurate.

When someone of Phelps' caliber comes along, most coaches and swimmers rush to find out what he did in his training to make him so far above everyone else. It was learned that Phelps' training program wasn't anything different than that of most other elite swimmers of his caliber. There was no real mystery to his practice sessions. It came down to hard, intense work six days a week. He worked hard both in the pool and in the gym to produce the results.

Another problem in trying to copy Phelps' regimen is that he has a freakish body. Phelps has larger than normal feet, a wing span larger than a condor, and a cardiovascular system rivaling Lance Armstrong. When his body was analyzed by scientists, they all agreed that they had never come across a frame and body similar to Phelps.

The media investigated what his nutrition was like and found that he was eating approximately 8,000 to 10,000 calories a day. In an interview with ESPN, Michael reported that his nutritional intake included a lot of pizza and pasta. It has been noted that, just for breakfast, he ate three fried egg sandwiches, cheese, lettuce, tomato, fried onions, mayonnaise, an omelet with a bowl of grits, three slices of French toast with powdered sugar, and three chocolate chip pancakes. Obviously, this is not noted as a breakfast of champions.

When we examine his nutrition plans, we can see that these foods are available to anyone. So if his training regimen was the best in the world and his trainer was so special, there would have been several other members from Phelps' team that should have had the same type of results. It comes down to this — Michael Phelps genetically is a one in 25-year athlete. He has the genetic makeup that provides him with the widest wing span, exact muscle density, and oxygen uptake system that allows him to do things in the water unlike anyone else in the world. Michael Phelps, Michael Jordan, Roger Federer, Tiger Woods, Lebron James, Lance Armstrong, Kobe Bryant, and Usain Bolt are among the few elite athletes that separate themselves from the crowd.

It goes back as far as being an infant. Learning to crawl, learning to walk, and interacting with other humans are just a few traits that have been found to be important in the developmental stages of an athlete. Were you abandoned? Were you read to? Were you exposed to music? Believe it or not, these features have a lot to do with the overall sensory and neuromuscular development of an athlete.

Is it possible to be similar to these athletes? That has been the million-dollar question for centuries. Coaches, trainers, and scientists have been trying to solve that question forever. Statistically speaking, the odds are against you. You may develop into an elite athlete, but can you rise to the heights of Phelps, Jordan, or Armstrong? Mathematically speaking, the odds are strictly against you. However, if you feel that you have the desire, passion, and guts to achieve this, than I submit to you that, if you don't try, you will never know.

You need the perfect storm to properly develop an elite athlete. It is not only physical training, but more importantly, mental training. An elite athlete has a great attitude towards training and competing. They have a strong belief system towards themselves and in the people they surround themselves with. They have great coping skills to deal with adversity. It's not just about being talented. Elite athletes must possess all of these traits to excel at this level. The average person does not have the mental fortitude that it takes to create such an elite athlete. I believe that, if given the right circumstances, with the right environment, and with the right support team, you can accomplish extraordinary heights in levels of achievement.

Nothing in sports is impossible. Humans have shown that they can produce unbelievable effects when put in the right environment. I personally believe that we all possess the mental capability to drive our bodies to heights never thought possible. Think of the story of the housewife whose child was trapped underneath a car. The woman, without hesitation, lifted the car up without any problems. It is my contention that, if one person can do this, we all can.

The key is that we have to figure out a way to unlock the secret to do this on a regular basis. It seems to me that each generation unlocks a millimeter of the knowledge needed to gain the entire knowledge necessary to do it all. But if you really think about it, once we get to that point, we'll all be the same, and once again, we'll be searching for more, better, greater.

All human beings move the same. When we are born, we go through the same infantile movements as everyone else in the world.

We continually progress from lying on our backs, to rolling over, to moving up on our forearms, to crawling until we have managed to stand upright, fighting off the effects of gravity. Crawling, for example, is important for neurological development along with muscular development. Some infants are not allowed to crawl as much as they should. These infants are left in cribs for long periods of time, put in jumpers, and others are left in car seats. Crawling promotes the alternating use of the arms and legs that help develop the neurological system. Each side of the body is forced to work to propel the body forward. This has been shown to increase the communication between the right and left sides of the brain. This cross-crawling motion develops both motor skills and learning. This doesn't allow for the proper repetitive neuromuscular development to take place. This can have a real affect on the development of walking, running, and sprinting in years to come.

Crawling is important in developing binocular vision. Binocular vision is the process of training the eyes to look off into the distance and back to the hands to properly judge distance, speed, and mobility. This is key in the development of the proprioceptive (knowing where you are without looking), vestibular (balance), and visual senses of an infant.

As we advance from our stumbling stage into the walking stage, the body progressively adapts to the stresses put upon it and uses the correct muscles and the correct motions to complete the smooth movement of walking.

We have been given everything needed for proper movement from the day we are born. It is up to us to mess that system up, which, as human beings, we do from approximately age five on. Children tend to imitate what they observe in their immediate environment. Wanting to be like the adults, children tend to mimic what we see. We watch mom, dad, aunt, or grandpa walking, standing, and sitting. Over time, those images of movement are recorded and repeated by the child, slowly creating variations in movement. Poor posture and lack of repetitive movement can further weaken certain muscles involved in proper movement. When this happens, the child will begin to compensate ever so slightly. These slight compensations can lead into full-blown compensation patterns that become hardwired into our nervous system.

As your body begins to compensate for certain weaknesses, your nervous system begins to modify your movement as a protective mechanism for you not to hurt yourself. Over time, this becomes the person's normal movement. Through general repetition, you begin to feel normal even though you are moving less than optimally.

Have you seen someone one who slouches forward at the shoulders or, worse, rotate at the shoulders when walking? at the shoulders when walking? They don't understand what you are talking about when you tell them to straighten up. They have no idea because their brain thinks that their poor posture is correct.

A mother came to my office with her daughter, who was experiencing lower back pain. As I was taking the history, I noticed that the mother was standing there with extremely rounded shoulders and with a forward head placement. I completed my consultation and exam with the daughter and was preparing for them to leave, when the mother said to me, "Doctor, when you're finished fixing her back, you have to help her with her poor posture." I told her that would be easy. I walked over to the mother and put one hand on her lower back and the other hand on her shoulders and gently pushed her upward, correcting her posture. I said she has learned this from you. The mother couldn't believe what I did because she thought that she had normal posture.

Athletics and sports are all about human movement. Athletic movement is taking the human body to the demands needed to produce movement, strength, explosion, power, and speed to accomplish the task at hand for the particular sport that you are engaged in. The more movement your child is exposed to early on, the better off they will be. Do your children a favor. Get them outdoors and moving. They can play anything they want, as long as they are running, jumping, throwing, catching, and everything else that comes with being a kid. The more kids are exposed to all types of movements and positions, the better off they will be in the future. Walking, running, jumping, twisting, and leaping have shown to develop much more than just your muscles. It develops so many things in your neurological system, as well as stimulating your endocrine, vascular, lymphatic, and sensory systems.

Times Have Changed

When I was a kid, you could roll out of bed and play whatever sport you wanted to without much training. If you had above-average talent, you would most likely move on to the next level because the competition wasn't as intense as it is today. It doesn't work that way anymore. The bar has been raised too high. The bar will continue to be pushed upward as time goes on, so it's a good idea for you to prepare appropriately.

If you feel that your son or daughter is an above-average athlete, he or she will probably need some help in developing their talents to be relevant to play at the next level. You, as the parent, will have to take it upon yourself to help them in attaining their goals. If possible, find someone who is knowledgeable in their sport and who has a developed an "eye" for improvement. An honest outside opinion can go a long way in the development of an elite athlete. You don't need to spend a fortune in hiring professional trainers, nutritionists, and others for their advancement. Someone who knows the sport and who has been there can help without you going broke.

The parent and the athlete must understand that, if the athlete possesses the right passion and determination, anything can be achieved.

Attitude has killed many athletes, even the athletes that have natural talent. There are tons of kids out there with an attitude of entitlement. An attitude that says, "Hey, I'm good, so I don't have to work." That attitude is the kiss of death.

Once you get to a certain level in sports, you will notice that everyone will have the same amount of talent. It's up to you to develop the level of the work ethic and consistency that is needed to perform at this level. It takes a lot of work to get to the big leagues! Even if you have all of the talent in the world, there is someone waiting for you at the next level to drop you down a peg or two. Let's say that you are interested in playing at a Division I school. Right now, as you read this book, do you know the numbers that the coaches are looking for? Do you know what 40-yard sprint speed is needed in your sport at your position? How about vertical jump, three-cone shuttle, and bench press?

Every college sport has their minimums. Swimming, soccer, track, basketball, lacrosse, baseball, field hockey, and wrestling — all of them have minimum requirements to compete at certain levels. If you're a baseball pitcher that throws at 75 miles per hour, you're not going to make it in a Division I university or to the major leagues. If you're a male swimmer and your time in the 50-meter freestyle is 25.0 seconds, you're not going to make it in a Division I school or the Olympic trials. If you're a wide receiver in football and run a 5.0 40-yard sprint, you're not going to make it in a Division I school or make it to the NFL. Are there exceptions to this? Of course, but very few. To get to the top level of any sport, you have to be able to perform minimum tests to show that you have the talent needed for that level of competition. If you don't have these required times needed for Division I, start looking at Division II or III sports. Why? In some sports, you're going to find that, if you don't have the talent to stay up with the competition on the team, it's going to be a rough four years. Pain, injury, and mental stress will overload you on a regular basis.

Playing at a Division II or Division III school is something that more kids need to realize earlier in their decision making process when coming out of high school. First of all, it's damn good competition, and second, it's not all that easy. People have become accustomed to talking about going to the "big" schools, not knowing how difficult it is to play at that level. Playing at Division II and III schools is not something you should be turning your nose up at. The level of play there is better than you think. I've had football players come into my office from Division III schools every bit as big as their Division I rivals. They just lacked the speed or certain skills needed to keep up at the upper-level schools.

Know Your Limits

When I go to the golf course, there are normally four sets of tee boxes. The tee box way in the back of the hole is normally called the "tips" or the championship tee. This tee box was designed for advanced golfers. The second tee box up from that one is called the members' tees. They were designed for the average golfer. This is where most golfers tee off from. The third tee box is called the "senior tee," designed for golfers who are over the age of 60. This gives them a chance of playing with the younger players because it shortens the course for them. Since most people become weaker as they get older, these tee boxes take age into consideration so that you can continue to play the game no matter how old you are. The fourth tee box is called the ladies' tees. This tee box was designed for women who are not as strong as the men. It allows the ladies to remain competitive.

When I go to a new course that I've never played at, and the length of the course is 7,400 yards, guess where I'm playing? I tee off at the members' tees because it matches my athletic ability. Playing from the "tips" can turn out to be a long day if your talent doesn't match the length of the course.

The same goes for the athlete thinking of going on to play in college. If your numbers aren't matching up to Division I, then do yourself a big favor and play at a level that you can compete at. If you're 5'8 and weigh 175 pounds, the chances of you playing Division I quarterback are slim and none. If you are a lineman who can only bench press 200 pounds, you will not be receiving any recruiting letters from Alabama or Notre Dame. The key is to get real about your present ability and fit it in where you will have a competitive chance of playing and having fun.

Training at the Higher Levels

Let's say your son or daughter has the potential of getting to the next level. That level may be high school varsity, college, or even the pros. Let me be the first to congratulate you. Obviously, they have exhibited sufficient talent that has been noticed by coaches, who have made mention to other coaches who have become interested. The work doesn't end here. It's just beginning.

Let me give you your first wake-up call. For many of you, if you feel that you are training hard now, don't take this too hard — you're not! You will find out that the next level is absolutely no joke when it comes to training. You will learn that training is year-round, and the coaches don't care what you think. Either work hard or get out. Sorry to put it so harshly, but that is the reality of Division I. Your cardio workouts and weight-lifting workouts are going to be much more intense than you've been accustomed to. For college, Division I sports are the big leagues, and you must be prepared, or it's going to be a very difficult situation for you.

In football, some Division I universities have been known to have 21 straight days of double sessions without any days off. That means you wake up and have to be at the facility at 6 a.m. for breakfast check, meetings, morning practice, lunch, weight lifting, meetings, second practice of the day, dinner, meetings, and then you can return to your room at about 10 p.m. that night. Then you do that all over again for the entire time your coach has outlined for summer camp.

Then the season starts. In many schools, all classes are to be taken by 1:00 p.m. because meetings start at 2:00, then practice, then lifting, then dinner, then meetings, and then you have to study… five days a week. One day, you have a game, and one day, the NCAA gives you off.

The same goes for every other sport. Whether its field hockey, soccer, swimming, tennis, or baseball, the intensity of this level of play in college is going to be way above what you are used to. Now is the time to develop a working mentality so that you are as prepared as much as possible.

Did I mention off-season? In football, for example, off-season starts as soon as you get back from the Christmas holiday. Most programs have running practices every morning at 5:30 a.m., then breakfast, and then you attend classes. After class, you return for weight lifting, and then you can go back to your class work. The time stress alone is something that can wash out even the most talented athlete.

How Are You Training?

Most American athletes don't know how to train properly. Most workouts that the majority of athletes go by are usually "hand-me-down" workouts from athletes before them. A lot of times, these workouts are from someone else that was doing them at another school or from another sport. In some cases, trainers at colleges or universities develop a "one-size-fits-all" program for all sports. That means that the same workout that the football team performs is the same one the girls' field hockey team performs. This is where a majority of problems begin.

For some athletes, they understand the importance of overall fitness and how it will help them in their sport. They understand that it takes an extraordinary amount of effort to prepare their bodies to get to the next level. The kids who get it are the ones who do well. It's the kids who think that they just show up and everything will work out who are the ones who end up failing and wondering why they failed later on down the road. Trust me, if you have an attitude centered around laziness, you will be washed out in a heartbeat.

I train young athletes in my office on a daily basis, and I can tell from experience that the kids with the passion to excel are the ones who make the highest gains in strength, speed, explosion, and recovery. We tell each and every parent and athlete that our type of training will be the hardest thing that they will ever do in their lives, but the results will be exponential. If you get it in your head now that you have to work harder than anyone on your team, it will begin to pay off for you in the future.

My Theory of Training in the U.S.

Most athletes train in the U.S. for whatever sport they are involved in. The traditional wisdom of sports training has always has been repetition. Play as much and as often as you can, and you will get better. Over time, this theory worked, but then coaches began to devise "drills" for each position so that they could develop more specialized skills. This broke down the various movements and skills to a point where they could be much more refined. Again, this worked, but was each athlete maximizing his or her talents? This type of training based its results on the team and not the individual. It is my opinion that each individual makes up the team. If you can get each individual to properly do his or her job, as a coach, you will have a much better team.

In the U.S., we continue to do this type of training without asking a few important questions. Wouldn't it be more important if we took each athlete and properly prepared him or her for the position that they are playing for? In other words, wouldn't it be more efficient if the athlete trained his or her body for the demands of a particular sport before they went out and did all of those drills? It seems to me that, if you develop the body to handle the demands of the sport, then you can plug in the skills needed for that sport. This way, the athlete's chance of injury will drop considerably, and his or her performance will be much better. If the athlete was trained to properly absorb the force needed to protect against injury, you can then prepare him or her to properly generate more forceful strength. This type of power can translate into shoring up the weak links in the chain that holds your team together.

So is it bad to find a personal trainer to help you develop? The answer is no. But find someone who isn't going to keep telling you what you want to hear. You have to be properly evaluated to make sure the trainer fully understands what is going on with your body. Before you are allowed to train at my facility, you are examined by me first so that I can identify any restrictions, compensation patterns, or injuries you may have. If any of these are identified, you will be treated to remove any types of damage or restrictions before you begin. If you don't, you run the risk of strengthening your weaknesses.

Once you find a trainer that you are comfortable with, commit to him or her. Follow their advice, work with them, and listen to them. It takes a commitment from both of you for you to succeed. Most trainers are well-intentioned people, with some knowing more than others. If you feel comfortable with the one you've chosen, then jump on the wagon and listen to them so that you can get the very best out of your workouts.

Identifying Athletic Weaknesses

The first and foremost thing that an athlete needs to understand is that they must be free of restrictions. The majority of athletes have some type of restriction or weakness. Restrictions are defined as any type of inhibitive movement within a muscle, muscle group, joint, or soft tissue of the body. These restrictions can be from old injuries such as sprains or strains, any type of tears, or other faulty patterns that have developed over a period of time. What happens if these are not recognized? The athlete will begin to compensate for those aberrant movements to protect from pain. The body will recruit a host of other muscles to do the work of the inhibited muscles, which leads to a faulty motor program and, eventually, a faulty movement pattern (compensation).

When this happens, the athlete cannot be as efficient as possible. For example, let's take two like-sized athletes playing dodge ball against one another. They're the same height, the same weight, and the same build. One athlete can move better side to side, has a better throwing motion, and can jump higher. The other athlete is a little slower from side to side, can throw but is not as strong, and his or her vertical leap isn't as good as the other person's. At the beginning, a coach may look at the inferior athlete and say to him- or herself that they're not good enough to play against this particular athlete. But, in essence, if you took the inferior athlete and removed all the restrictions and began developing them in ways of using their muscles in the ways they were intended to be used, that athlete could improve tremendously over a given period of time.

I've said this many times — there is no such thing as a bad athlete. There is only an athlete who needs to develop his or her bodily systems to a higher level.

There are many examples of athletes that start off as extremely good athletes when they are young and eventually begin to fizzle out as time goes on. This has to do with certain injuries that were overlooked and improper compensation patterns that began to develop. These patterns develop over a period of time, and it often begins slowing the athlete down and dulling his or her reaction time. There is also an eventual loss of strength. Over the years, I've had many parents enter my office describing to me how good their child was, and then all of a sudden, their skills began to deteriorate. I explain to the patient that, many times, this sudden, downhill pattern wasn't due to loss of skill but to bodily restrictions. These restrictions won't allow the athletes to perform at their normal levels. I have been able to correct these faulty patterns and improve the skills and athleticism of athletes just by removing restrictions. Once the faulty patterns and restrictions were identified, it allowed them to free up their body to move correctly. Improved speed, coordination, strength, and explosion were results of this correction.

I have developed an extensive examination for athletes to expose the restrictions, motion problems, and hidden injuries that are stopping them from excelling. This can consist of past damage, which produces scar tissue of the joints or muscles and shortening of the muscles over tension of the ligaments and tendons. Once identified, these restricted areas can be relieved, allowing for better range of motion, increased strength, speed, and athleticism. Every athlete's body is different — different restrictions, different body types, different metabolisms, and different sizes. That's why it is so important before you start training for an athlete to be examined properly to locate all restrictions in his or her body. In my office, there is no "one-size-fits-all" training. Each training session must be developed for the individual, pertaining to each individual restriction or weakness. In other words, I develop a training program for each individual to fail. Once they can begin to show that their body can handle the demands of these exercises, then their program is changed. Once again, that program is written so that they have a chance to fail. Each athlete must prove that they can hold position(s) properly before they can advance to the next level. That is why I say that each program is written in order for them to fail. This way, the only direction for them to advance is up.

If an athlete's muscles can properly absorb force, his or her chance for injury is drastically reduced. The athlete then is progressed to begin training to develop neurological speed, muscular strength, explosion, endurance, and recovery.

There is no mystery in developing an athlete. The athlete must be able to use his or her body in the way that it was intended. To do that, you must be free of restriction and taught how to use these muscles in the specific manner in which they were designed to be used. There are times when it takes more work to be able to produce this due to the fact that some of these areas have been shut off for a long time due to inactivity, bad posture, or other injuries. More importantly, it's up to the athlete to "want and demand" success before they begin to train to achieve the desired outcome.

Everyone knows of the athlete that just steps on the court or field and is instantly successful in whatever he or she does. For whatever reason, this person is free of restriction, free of faulty movement patterns, and can do anything with little effort. This happens mainly in the younger years, anywhere from age seven to 12. Some children advance physiologically faster than others, which give them an added advantage in athletics when they're younger. There comes a time in and around the 15-year-old mark where most athletes' physiologies begin leveling out. That is when you will notice the children that were behind in years past now developing skills to a higher level. All of sudden, the playing field begins to level out, and it's now where the hard work will begin to pay off. The child with a good work ethic will continue to advance; however, the child who chose to be lazy will now seem to be slowly left behind.

The marquee question is how do I develop my youngster to become a better athlete? First and foremost, it's up to them to make up their mind that they want to become better. Without the mind, the body will be left behind. Second, confront the weaknesses and the restrictions within their body. Once these are confronted and corrected, you will see an immediate change in the athlete at any age. What you have to understand is that, when your body is operating properly, meaning that all of your muscles are properly elongated, they are then able to hold proper position and can absorb force properly. From there, you need to learn the proper skills to perform a particular task in order to excel in your sport. In the U.S., we drill over and over and over to drive in muscle memory into our nervous system to be able to repeat movements. No one ever takes into account the exact muscle physiology needed for an athlete to perform that task. It's not about big muscles. It's about long, lean, explosive muscles that have the proper speed, endurance, and recoverability that make an elite athlete.

"No one wants to hear the labor pains. They just want to see the baby..." **Lou Brock**

Gym Rats vs. Athletes

Too many athletes are becoming "gym rats" rather than athletes. They are being told that it's important to become bigger, stronger, and faster. They're not told that they have to develop more athleticism, an ability to recover, and an ability to turn their muscles on and off on demand. And nowhere is anyone being taught to prevent injury.

If you ask anyone who is involved with sports such as football, the first question they are going to ask you is, "How much do you bench?" The bench press has been put up on a pedestal as the sacred cow of sports training. It is an important exercise, but it has gotten way overblown in training. At what point of the game do they blow the whistle and stop the game to bring out the bench press? You're right. They don't. What I'm trying to get across is that I'm not against weight lifting, and I'm not against bench pressing. What I am against is the notion of trying to think that kids need more strength than they do athletic training. Most programs put too much emphasis on lifting weights rather than spending time in developing youngsters' neurological systems.

In a roundabout way, weight lifting first began to prevent injury. Coaches began to realize that the bigger guys were out-performing the smaller guys. They told their athletes to lift weights to get stronger to prevent the beating that they were taking from the stronger competitors. A lot has changed. Athletes of today are bigger, faster, and stronger. But it seems that injuries are on the rise like never before.

Athletes are paying up to $8,000.00 per month to work out with trainers to prepare them for the NFL combine. Many NFL coaches are becoming more skeptical about this formal training because, in many cases, the player is being solely trained to pass the NFL combine test rather than preparing the athlete to compete at the level of the NFL.

As I've said many times before, many of the trainers and coaches go about their programs wrong. To prove my point, let me first ask you a question. What seems to be the most popular weight lifting exercise in the gym for male athletes? If you said the bench press, you are right. Now in your experience in athletics, how many chest muscles get blown out during the year in all sports? Now, if I asked you another question about injuries, how many hamstrings get injured across the board in all sports? If you answered a lot, you are right again. If that is the case, and it is, why aren't we concentrating our efforts on strengthening the glutes (buttock muscles) and the hamstrings (back of your legs)? When was the last time anyone asked you, "How much were you able to lift today for your hamstrings?" The hamstrings, glutes, and quads are the main muscles to develop power, explosion, and SPEED! We've already discussed how important speed is in sports, so why is it that most trainers and coaches don't have a specific program to develop these areas? The answer lies in the fact that many of these so-called experts are lacking serious physiological education.

Training for Your Sport

Years ago, I referred all of my athletes to personal strength trainers. These were top trainers, the best of the best. I found that most of the athletes got bigger, faster, and stronger. What I began to observe over time is that EVERYONE ended up becoming injured. I couldn't understand why every athlete whom I referred to these trainers ended up coming back to me as an injured athlete. It was at this point that I continued my quest to find a better way for my athletes.

I began to look around and noticed that it wasn't the trainers. What I found was that it was the training itself. I looked at the NFL injury reports and noticed that the injury rate has grown steadily each and every year. When I began to investigate what trainers really did, it dawned on me that most of them we're just doing the same thing. Most of the training exercises were based on information that had been passed down from one trainer to another without any science to back it up.

For every trainer that I came across, there was a different opinion on how to train an athlete, even though most of the training was the same. I contacted a sports research professor at the University of Oklahoma and asked him if there were any true random, controlled, or double-blind studies performed on athletic training. The answer was no. There have been studies done on random aspects of training, but nothing that truly quantified results. It is close to impossible to put a strict study regimen to this task. There will be an opinion on training for every grain of sand on the beach.

One day, I was introduced to Jay Schroeder, a trainer who should not be called a trainer. I call Mr. Schroeder a "human performance whiz kid." He is the only person that I have ever spoken to who cared about the ultimate performance of the athlete. Not only is he concerned about athletes, but more importantly he is just as concerned with all types of human performance. No matter a multi-million dollar athlete or a housewife looking to be more fit. What surprised the heck out of me when I first spoke to Schroeder was that the first thing out of his mouth was making sure that the athlete never got injured. He was the first person in the fitness world who ever told me that he centered his workout protocols around injury prevention.

This was a new concept for me, a trainer worried about making sure that the athlete developed with the central notion of keeping themselves injury-free. But then I learned that this wasn't just another trainer. This man knew how the human body worked better than many doctors that I know. He was educated in the physiology, neurology, anatomy, endocrine, lymphatic, and other systems of the body. He had a full grasp on how to make them work together for the benefit of the athlete. But there was one other thing. He wasn't just a trainer for elite athletes. He did as much study on housewives working at home as he did on hockey players playing on the ice.

I have learned as much as possible from this man in the area of athletic performance and athletic training. His background is completely different than any other trainer. He truly had his hand on the pulse of human performance. He works out of Gilbert, Arizona, and Minneapolis, Minnesota, and has developed a large following of athletes that range from world-class athletes to kids in middle school.

Jay is a very atypical man in the fact that he eats, sleeps, and drinks the pursuit of perfection for human performance. Did you notice that I didn't say that he is interested in how much you can lift? Schroeder is obsessed with perfection and creating the best athletes possible. There is no second-best for Jay and his athletes because he feels that each and every athlete only uses about 40 percent of their natural ability. Schroeder developed an axiom that he expels with frequent fervor —

"The will to prepare is more important than the will to succeed." I can tell you that when you really come to fully understand this concept, you will turn your athletic career around.

Schroeder's premise of working out is the use of the physical, emotional, intellectual, and spiritual aspects of your body to train. When you begin to understand how to bring everything that you've been given in your body to the training area, you will develop better results. According to Schroeder, you bring EVERYTHING with you — your emotions, intellect, spirit, and strength. Jay has been known not to take an athlete into his gym until he can raise his or her resting pulse by five to eight beats per minute BEFORE they walk into his gym.

He wants to make sure that you are ready to train, not just to go through the motions of working out. He will train you for a desired effect — improvement and nothing less. You will work harder than you ever thought imaginable. The results are exponential. I have seen his clients do incredible things in short periods of time. One of those that comes to mind is Adam Archuletta. Archuletta was an average (at best) defensive player out of the University of Arizona. After working with Schroeder, he became a top first-round draft pick in the NFL. The work that Archuletta went through was more than impressive, but more impressive was his will to succeed.

Schroeder, an expert in the physiology of sports training, has developed a protocol for sports training. He feels that most U.S. athletes spend their entire careers practicing their sport but never preparing their bodies to excel in their sport. This is an entirely new definition of sports training. Schroeder has developed a set of unique training protocols that are developed to strengthen one muscle group at a time. His belief is that, in order for any athlete to perform a certain movement, they must be able to properly hold position. A muscle must be able to go through its normal range of motion without any type of restriction in order to optimize that particular movement. If it can't do this properly, then the body will help by using other muscles in that area to assist. The problem with that is that those muscles aren't designed to take on this load, and after repetition of movement, these muscles begin to break down. This is where injury develops. You will begin to see overall performance begin to decline.

Eventually, the athlete may develop a serious injury in that area. Schroeder has shown through training hundreds, if not thousands of athletes, which he can develop strength, explosion, speed, endurance, and a better way to recover.

Schroder Training

I've studied with a lot of people who consider themselves experts in the field of sports training. There are very few who truly understand how to make players become better athletes more than Jay Schroder. When first meeting Mr. Schroder, I was impressed by the depth of knowledge that he possessed as compared to many other trainers that I've spoken to in the past.

Schroder has developed a training protocol that is designed for the athlete to fail. The reason for this is to expose all of the athlete's weaknesses so that they can be corrected. The more weaknesses that are exposed, the better off the athlete will be as far as developing increased performance. Most athletes don't want to confront their weaknesses, nor the depth of their inability to perform. This program has been designed to expose all weaknesses so that the athlete can identify and correct them in order to pursue optimum performance. Once exposed, the athlete can train and predict the peak of their improvement and elite performance.

The foundation of Schroeder's program is predicated on the following:

Extreme Maximal Velocity
Extreme Maximal Load
Extreme Maximal Volume

Mr. Schroeder has developed what he has called the "Deadly Seven" exercises based on this premise of high load, high velocity, and high volume. The athlete must be able to hold proper position for a five-minute period. This also develops the muscle to properly absorb force. When a muscle can absorb force correctly, the chances of injury are extremely remote. As they progress, the athlete can continue on to develop explosion and speed.

It's important to think about training in a different light. Do you want to train a lineman in football the same way you would train a field-goal kicker? The answer is yes and no. Every athlete has to develop the foundation of training the muscle to absorb force and to properly hold position. They can then begin to develop specialized movements. To develop properly, you have to meet the prerequisite in order to maximize an athlete's training potential. Schroeder's results with his athletes are nearly too unbelievable for most people to comprehend. His accomplishments with most athletes are way beyond the results being produced from the majority of the entire professional training profession.

The father of Jake Bequette of the University of Texas wrote this testimonial:

"They had the pro day at Arkansas yesterday (3/10/09). Jake ran 4.62 in the 40 at a body weight of 271. [He] dropped a tenth of a second in the 40, with an additional 11 pounds of body weight compared to last year. I thought this might be even more impressive — he did 4.02 in the 20-yard shuttle. He actually ran another one below 4.0, but [the officials] said that he missed one of the lines. He also increased his bench 90 pounds in the past 18 months."

Reflecting on Jake's humble beginnings, his father adds:

"He ran a 5:09 at 230 pounds when he met you in late 2006, and he couldn't bench his body weight. After Jake got the [Iso-extreme] positions down, that is when every result began to explode."

What I'm trying to get across to you is that there are people out there like Jay Schroeder who have taken sports training to a much higher level. It's not about lifting weights; in fact, the majority of Mr. Schroeder's training doesn't involve lifting weights. He has developed an entire protocol to develop athletic ability by turning on the correct muscles and then having them contract the way they were designed.

I can personally say that I've adapted Mr. Schroeder's protocols in my office for both athletes and non-athletes alike. I can honestly tell you a few facts concerning his theories.

- There's nothing easy about them.
- The results gained from performing Iso-extremes correctly are exponential.
- They will prepare any athlete for whatever sport they're involved in without injury.
- You will see improvements the likes of which you've never thought possible.

Interview with Jay Schroeder

I conducted this interview with Jay Schroeder this past year about his training philosophy. Personally, I was fascinated by the lengths of personal study that Schroeder has gone through to prepare himself to develop other humans to optimize their individual performance. Talking to numerous trainers over the years and after meeting Mr. Schroeder, it was apparent that this man has studied well beyond the average fitness trainer. Using his own body as his lab, he has developed an unprecedented way of training athletes to be able to perform way past what they thought possible. His unique outlook on human performance is why I chose him to interview and to explain to everyone his tenets of building a better athlete.

Conway: How did you come about developing your theories, protocols, and philosophy towards training athletes?

Schroeder: I was an athlete when I was younger. As I played sports, I found that I was injured on a regular basis. I couldn't figure out why this kept happening because I always did more than what was asked of me. I always pushed myself way beyond what was asked of me, so if they asked for 10, I did 20.

I was an average college football player, who, after having moments of brilliance, I would return to average the very next play. Then I got into a motorcycle accident that left me paralyzed from the chest down.

That's when I began to read and learned to read as much as I could on the subject of training. I read as much as I could on how to train for movement and performance. While lying in bed, I began to use this myself in my mind over and over, hour after hour, day after day. At one point was able to get up and walk again.

I noticed that, after doing all of this stuff in my head, I became faster, stronger, and fitter after being down and out for over a year and a half. That really opened my eyes to what real preparation training might be. If somebody can do it in their head and can't move at all, then what could someone who could move around accomplish?

Everything I read was Soviet and Eastern Bloc information. I took an immediate interest in it and began studying it in great detail. I was able to travel there twice and meet and work with various coaches and create long-term relationships. I began gathering information and testing it. As I continued to test various exercises, I decided to challenge them. As it turned out, many of my theories were correct, and it was at that point of researching and experimenting [that] I began to develop my own system.

I developed a tremendous respect for the Soviet coaches and trainers. I never really paid much more attention to the U.S. trainers or coaches because it was always the same with someone's little twist to it. It seemed that the U.S. always had the exact same problems.

What I learned in working with the Soviet coaches is that, if you want to evaluate something, don't look at a success case. Look at the failures and see why they failed. If they are within this system and they all failed the same way, then you have a true system. If you look at successful people, they are successful for a variety of reasons. Most of the time, it happened by chance. I was looking for a way to duplicate it so that every athlete who had aspirations of playing pro would now have the opportunity.

There was only one in thousands making it to the elite level, and I wanted to replicate that performance. So I found that the Soviets and the Eastern Bloc countries can do that type of replication.

When I lived in Russia, what I noticed really shook me up. The Russians were small. Their facilities were a wreck. There was no milk to be had. There was no meat to buy, no vegetables to be found. There, water had rust in it all the time, which was normal to them. The first time I took a shower, I shut the water off and began toweling off. I felt water on my foot and looked down and noticed that the drain from the urinal was next to the shower that drained right into the area that I was standing in.

There were dirt floors, weight lifting bars were bent, [and] the weights themselves were ragged. The Russians had this way of approaching everything they did. Every single person there was able to duplicate what the last person did. You would go down the line with 25 to 30 people doing a clean-and-jerk exercise with 120 kilos on the bar. Every single person would execute the move correctly. There would be a little bit of rest, then they would add weight and execute it again, every one of them.

They were fast when they ran. I would go and watch them run, and everyone was fast. Not like watching athletes here in the States with the disparity of speed with that size group. Everyone was running fast. Jumping — that was a whole other story.

This showed me that you could duplicate and replicate through training alone. I trusted what they had to say after seeing for myself.

Conway: As a parent speaking without any knowledge, what can parents do to help their children become better athletes?

Schroeder: There are two parts of this answer that will formulate to one answer. I was talking to Pat Casey (the first man to ever bench 600 pounds in the U.S.) on the phone, to ask him questions about his training and his opinion of his success. He said to me that people don't understand hard work and discipline. They think if they go and spend an hour and a half in the weight room [that] they worked hard. They have no conception of what it takes to put real work in.

I worked with Mark McCoy, whose wife was an East German sprinter when it was still East Germany. As we began to talk, I asked her a few questions about her success. She stopped me. She said, "You're probably going to ask me what drug regimen was I on." I told her no, that I wasn't going to ask that. She went on to say that she was never good enough because, to be on the drug regimen, you had to be in the top one percent of the sprinters. There was no money for anything less than that.

I asked her, "How do you get so good? How did you get so many people to get to that elite level?" She said it was easy. In Russia, "We don't take off for your birthday. We don't take off for Christmas. We don't take off for any holiday. We train seven days a week. We train as if it's the last day we'll ever train again in our lives. In America, you guys train instinctively." Which means, I don't feel so good today, so I'll back off today and come back tomorrow.

The answer to your parents is educate your kids to what real hard work really is. Teach them what discipline is. Go out and get a laborious job, working on a farm, shoveling hot asphalt on a hot summer day, something that is physical so that the kid can learn what hard work is. What it comes down to is that they don't fully understand what hard work is. When they play the game, they practice whatever the coach says, go to the weight room three days a week, and they think they're working hard. Unfortunately, that's not what cuts it.

Conway: How does your philosophy differ from the average trainer?

Schroeder: When you look at various programs, they all look similar because exercise is exercise. The way they differ is this — I approach every individual with extremely high expectations. You're a human being with capabilities of being as awesome as your brain will allow you to be. There is no genetic limitation. Genetics have no part in anything until you are at the upper half [of a] percent of the best in the world. Other than that, genetics is just an excuse.

I have extremely high expectations of the athlete that I'm training. My training programs are written accordingly. Each program that I personally write for each individual is based on the high expectations I have for them that day. This all leads to the overall high expectations that I have for them in their sport.

Conway: What do athletes need in order to develop the skills necessary to become a real athlete?

Schroeder: Let's go back to the Soviet system for a minute. Everybody who is going into track, soccer, [or] basketball, they knew the history of their sports. They knew the history of soccer from all around the world and understood the history of the great players from around the world before them.

Athletes need to study and understand the reason why the individuals perform a skill the way they perform it today. How all that came to be? When they do that, then they will create an interest in their own physiology in how muscles work, the order they work, and why they work in that order.

The best example would be Larry Bird versus Magic Johnson. Larry Bird couldn't jump, couldn't run. He was physically a dweeb. Magic Johnson dominated everyone he came against in that time. Yet they were both two of the greatest basketball players in NBA history.

How did that come about? Larry Bird understood that his brain put him in the positions he needed to be in to give him the opportunity to display his many talents on the court. Magic Johnson would just physically dominate you to create those situations.

You can be successful in a multitude of ways, but you have to understand which approach you're going to take and why you're going to take it. You can't determine that until you know the history of the sport, the history of the athlete, and how the performances and skills started as opposed to where they are when you are attempting to do them yourself.

Conway: If my child is in a sport now and I'm trying to get them the correct advice, how do I lead them to the correct way of training?

Schroeder: I think the best answer to that question is what I just went over. Study and determine what capabilities you have, the kind of person you are, the emotions you can display, the intellect that you are willing to put into it, and create a way of performance that can allow you to be successful at a high level many, many times in a row, rather than just once in awhile. That can only come about by study, not by playing.

The one thing that most parents don't understand is that, the earlier that you begin to specialize, the lower the level of performance you'll achieve and the shorter amount of time that you'll be able to demonstrate it. They don't want to prepare for the sport; they want to play the sport. That's where the accolades are, that's where the trophies are, that's where the pats on the back are — gold medals and scholarships at the end. The best in everything in all of the world are the people who prepared to get there. They just didn't arrive. They prepared for it through a lot of the things that we're talking about right now.

Conway: What mistakes can an athlete or parent avoid when they begin to train?

Schroeder: Thinking that strength is a cure-all to everything. Thinking that, if they are great in the weight room, they'll be great on the field. Spending too much time performing a skill or training for a skill with less than their best effort. To keep in mind that "Well, little Joey tried hard" is not considered a best effort.

Best effort is little Joey gave 100 percent intellectually, emotionally, psychologically, physiologically, and spiritually. It takes all of that to reach the truest high level of performance of elite performance. People just waste time by not working hard. "Well, I strength-trained today. I did six sets of three of 150 pounds, and last week, I could only do 140 pounds…" It's really no big deal because what speed did you display it at? What emotion was behind it? The way you practice and the way you train is the way you're going to perform on the field. So if you have a lack of intellectual participation in practice or your workout, when you get into a tough situation on the field or court, you're going to have a lack of intellectual participation, and your performance will suffer. If you don't raise the level of emotion while you train and then you are asked to raise the level of emotion on the playing field, you're not going to be able to, and your performance will falter. Those faltering can range from looking back to a minor injury to a major injury to a career-ending injury.

Conway: Can anyone go into a gym without any knowledge and better themselves?

Schroeder: No. That is what I was just trying to say. You can't just go to the weight room and just lift weights just the same as someone else and expect the same results. You don't know what the other athlete had going for him that allowed him to become an exceptional athlete. You don't know what negative he had to work around. You can't just walk in there and just do something. You have to study. You have to understand your mind, your body. You have to understand what the most successful people do in that skilled display.

Conway: So if my child is forced to work out in the gym with the coach for their sport, is there anything they can do to better themselves?

Schroeder: Yes. If they adhere to the principles of human movement that muscles only work properly when moved at maximum velocity, actually at 93 percent or more at maximum velocity. That if they train at anything other than a right angle, it's wrong. That if they put forth everything they have including emotion, intellect, psychology, physiology, and spirit into every rep, every set, and every exercise they do, then there is a lot to be gained. That's not what's taught in the weight room. What is taught in the weight room is lift more weight, or do it for more reps, or do it for three days in a row instead of one day in a row. They can overcome all that garbage if they participate with all of those parts of what makes up a human.

Conway: Do you feel the mental challenge in preparation in sports is more important than the physical challenge?

Schroeder: Obviously I do. I was able before my accident. I was a 4.9 40 (yard dash) guy. After my accident, I was a 4.3 40 (yard dash), and I didn't move. I only did it in my mind.

So, absolutely, the mental and emotional part overrides everything. That's the computer (the brain) that gives the command that tells the order in which to do it in, at what level it should be done, for how long it should be done, what velocity it should be done. The mental part is 99 percent of it.

Conway: You did this training through mental imagery, visualization, dreaming?

Schroeder: Yes, I used all of them. I pushed my mental limits even more so than my physical limits. I did this virtually 20 hours per day because I was confined to a bed and couldn't move. You know, if you lay in bed all day, you don't get tired (laugh). I just laid in my bed and just trained over and over in my mind. I was lifting weights. I was running all in my mind. When I came out of it, people would ask me, "Weren't you in an accident? How did you get so fast?" I'm not quite sure what I said, but it was real, and I was stronger and faster than I ever was.

Conway: So if someone doesn't have 20 hours a day to do what you did, in your opinion, what is the optimum time they can do so the brain will make those changes?

Schroeder: You can do it every night before they go to bed. They have six to ten hours available to them every single night. Every day, they have that available to them, and it doesn't take any other part of their day. By training, it leads to many, many other benefits including proper restoration, proper recovery, and organ function all by getting the proper sleep. There is no reason why they can't do it.

Conway: This is the last question. What most parents want to know is, what does it take for my child to become an elite athlete?

Schroeder: To understand that the will to prepare for success is more important than the will for success.

Chapter 9

Sports Injuries: New Paradigm of Injury Treatment

If your children play sports, there is a high degree of probability that they are going to experience an ache, pain, or an injury that may eventually sideline them. Although pain is a part of sports, it doesn't have to debilitate you. By understanding different types of injuries, along with how they occur, you can help your young athletes prevent injuries from occurring in the first place.

There are various types of injuries that occur in sports. You can't prevent all injuries; however, you can prepare yourself so that you can prevent the majority of them.

The most common injuries are:

- Sprains and strains
- Abrasions
- Blisters
- Concussions
- Fractures (broken bones)
- Dislocations
- Knee injuries
- Shoulder injuries

Injures can range from bruises, sprains, and muscle strains to muscle tears, broken bones, and concussions. Most of these injuries lead to inflammation, which is swelling, sending signals to the brain that are interpreted as pain. The stronger the message sent to the brain, the more pain that you will experience.

Other types of injuries are labeled as traumatic injuries. These types of injuries occur after some type of collision or impact. Sports such as American football, lacrosse, wrestling, soccer, rugby, basketball, hockey, and field hockey can produce high collision impacts that can lead to traumatic injuries. These injuries include fractured bones, concussions, ligament tears, cartilage tears, and any eye injuries.

Many injuries that occur during sports are due to overuse injuries. These types of injuries occur mainly as a result of over training or practicing. Overuse injuries are injuries that occur to a part of the body used on a repetitive basis. Runner's knee, for example, is an injury to the knee from a person running more mileage than their muscles can properly support. When the muscles around the knee shorten or weaken, they lose their ability to absorb force, which transfers the force into the knee. This will set you up for inflammation, pain, and injury.

Another example of an overuse injury is called tennis elbow. Tennis elbow is a form of repetitive stress to the outside of the elbow that comes about after hitting ball after ball without sufficient strength of the forearms to properly absorb the force. That force is then transferred to the outside of the elbow, which causes strain on the tendons. Inflammation occurs around the tendon, which sends a signal to the brain reporting damage that result in pain. The key is to train the muscles to absorb that impact of repetitive hitting so that you do not experience an injury. The same goes for runners. When the muscles of the legs are properly trained to absorb force from the feet pounding the streets over and over, a runner will be able to continue to run without injury.

All of these injuries eventually lead to pain.

Pain is a sensory signal sent to the brain indicating that there is damage in a given area. Pain is the body's way of telling you that there is damage in a certain area. Pain is something that you should pay attention to so that damage, short term or long term, doesn't set in. After the signal has been sent, the body normally goes into repair mode, sending in swelling that contains scar tissue. This is the body's attempt to help patch up the damaged tissue. If you continue to override the signal with a pain reliever and continue to use that area, you run the risk of further damage. That's why it is so essential to get to the cause of the pain rather than attempting to cover up the pain with a drug.

There is a difference between pain, tightness, soreness, aches, and feeling uncomfortable. For years, the saying has gone, "No pain, no gain." Well, that isn't true when it comes to real pain. Most seasoned athletes understand the difference between true PAIN from soreness and other sensations like pain, pulling, strain, and weakness. Pain is damage, and it needs to be attended to.

Lifting weights is a great example of pain without damage. After a strenuous day of lifting weights, many athletes feel a residual pain or tightness in their muscles. It's called a muscle ache and is a form of overexertion when you lift weights. Seasoned weight lifters understand this feeling and grow accustomed to it. Rookies in the gym who experience this feeling for the first time tend to think of it as an injury. It can be somewhat an intense muscle tightness feeling; however, you're not technically injured, and the discomfort will go away in a few days. You have taken the muscles past their normal physiology of what we call metabolic breakdown. That means you've used the muscle past all of its reserve fuels, and now the muscle needs to repair itself before it can perform that type of exercise again.

You can damage the soft tissue if you lift weights that are too heavy for you. When this happens, the load exceeds the ability of the muscle to produce enough force to contract, and the fibers break down at the tendon. The fascia disrupts, and an entire injury sequence begins, beginning with swelling, loss of motion, and eventually, pain.

Experienced athletes know how far they can push their bodies. Inexperienced athletes don't fully understand their limits. This comes with repetition and good old experience. You will begin to understand how far you can push yourself to produce improvements in your body as time goes on. Experience will teach you what real pain is and what metabolic breakdown is.

Fatigue can also produce a feeling of pain. Fatigue can occur from different sources. One is a neurological breakdown, where the muscle doesn't receive a full neurological (electrical) signal allowing it to carry on its normal activities. Fatigue can also occur from a decreased store of protein, carbohydrates, and water. Muscles need protein, water, and carbohydrates to carry on their normal metabolic functions.

Soreness is a sensation that some might perceive as pain. Again, soreness is usually the feeling that you will experience when you have pushed your body to extremes, and the nervous and muscular systems are attempting to repair. There is nothing wrong with soreness. When properly fueling your post-workouts with protein and water, the soreness can be kept to a minimum. Once you begin to work out, and the blood gets back into the muscles, you will also see how quickly the soreness will go away.

You can also suffer from mental fatigue. I explain this as one of those days where your body showed up for training, and you mind was left at home. Mental fatigue is normally described as repetitive, intense mental effort. Mental fatigue can be caused by continual mental effort and attention to a particular task, as well as high levels of stress or emotion. Stress and extreme, focused thinking can add to this condition, as well as repetitive high emotions. Basically, this is any type of repetitive, intense mental thinking for prolonged periods of time. This type of mental fatigue can lead to physical fatigue. Mistakes and other types of miscues can lead to errors in judgment in movements or position that can lead to injury.

Muscles are designed to do two things, move bones and absorb force. Whether you are walking, running, jumping, or throwing, your muscles are designed to absorb the force produced in movement. Like the shock absorbers on your car, muscles are designed to absorb that force before it gets to the ligaments, tendons, or joints. If that force ends up at a joint, it can produce inflammation in that area, causing pain and limited mobility. Some people turn immediately to taking anti-inflammatory medication. Sure, it works, but you are only treating a symptom. If you continue to constantly treat the symptom and not treat the underlying problem, you're heading for serious injury.

If your young athlete is experiencing ongoing pain, then you need to evaluate the "why."

- What does their posture look like? Is one hip higher than the other? Or is one shoulder higher than the other?
- Do they have poor technique in the sport?
- Are you in good physical condition?
- Do you feel grounded when you stand or walk?
- Have you lost strength, speed, or power over the last few months?

These questions can help you find out why you may have continued pain. If pain continues, you need to see a qualified doctor, who can help you find the imbalance or dysfunction that is causing your pain. You can be covering up an injury and not know it. Get to a qualified health care provider to have an exam.

Evolution of Sports Injury Treatment

For over 25 years in clinical practice, I've been fascinated with the treatment of sports injuries. For years, medical doctors treated athletes normally with medication and instructions of using ice and rest. As time went on, medical doctors began to refer their patients out to physical therapists when they repetitively noticed that medications didn't work. Chiropractors showed that with certain manipulations to the spine or extremities they could alleviate many sports injuries where medications couldn't. Chiropractors then began to use various physical modalities, combining them in their practices with chiropractic manipulation. There was a definite improvement with patient outcomes when combining manipulation and therapeutic modalities. Many of these treatments were helpful, but the speed of treatments never advanced as time passed.

There has been a great deal of controversy and skepticism concerning chiropractic manipulation or adjustments. I can tell you without any hesitation that a properly indicated and well-performed adjustment to the spine is safe and can be more effective than any drug being advised. The power of the manipulation goes way beyond the nonsense that certain medical doctors claim can hurt people. How many people have been killed by manipulations to the spine? According to my literature review, the estimated risk for serious complications from cervical manipulation is 6.39 per 10 million manipulations. For lumbar manipulation, it is 1 per 100 million manipulations (*Integrative Medicine 1998; 1: 61-66*).

How many have died because of medications or the wrong medical treatment? According to Vic Schayne, PhD, in his article, "Medical Treatment is the Third Leading Cause of Death," quoting Barbra Starfield, MD, "In spite of the rising health care costs that provide the illusion of improving health care, the American people do not enjoy good health, compared with their counterparts in the industrialized nations. Among thirteen countries including Japan, Sweden, France and Canada, the U.S. was ranked 12th, based on the measurement of 16 health indicators such as life expectancy, low-birth-weight averages, and infant mortality."

Even more significantly, the U.S. medical system has played a large role in undermining the health of Americans. According to several research studies conducted in the last decade, a total of 225,000 Americans per year have died as a result of their medical treatments:

- 12,000 deaths per year due to unnecessary surgery
- 7,000 deaths per year due to medication errors in hospitals
- 20,000 deaths per year due to other errors in hospitals
- 80,000 deaths per year due to infections in hospitals
- 106,000 deaths per year due to negative effects of drugs

New Thinking Brings About New Ways of Treatment, Rehabilitation, and Sports Performance Training...

Before you throw in the towel thinking that you've tried everything possible to relieve your pain, injury, discomfort, or disability... STOP! Don't do another thing until you've read the entire chapter of this book. I'm about to turn everything you know about sports injuries around 360 degrees. I'm then going to give you a blueprint on how the latest technology can have you feeling better, moving better, and overall getting you back in the game faster than you've ever thought possible.

In my office, I have turned away from conventional treatments for the sole fact that I've found successful alternative ways of relieving pain faster than most standard treatments. Searching for better ways to relieve pain and improve performance has been and will continue to be my main professional goal. I want to offer patients answers to injury and disability they never thought possible before.

My type of practice of sports injury rehab is changing faster than most doctors fully understand. Over the years, I've co-developed a treatment protocol that we have proved to be 95 percent faster in relieving pain as compared to the majority of conventional treatments. Because I decided to take a chance to step outside the box in a big way, the payoff for my patients has been exponential.

Let me give you a classic example of "traditional medicine" not fully understanding the new paradigm in healing. A fifteen-year-old football player was referred to me by his coach. This young man was injured in a football game, which led to a complete tear of his anterior crucaite ligament (ACL) in his knee. He had complete ACL reconstructive surgery, during which they took tissue from another part of his body to use as his new ligament in his knee. The surgery went well, and he was referred by his orthopedic surgeon for traditional rehab at a local rehabilitation center. He was scheduled to be treated at this rehab center for a minimum of six to seven months before he could return to training for football. After two weeks of therapy, his mother was not pleased with the way they were progressing and decided to bring him to my office.

I examined the young man and agreed to treat him. I explained to his mother that my way of treating was extremely "outside of the box," as compared to conventional rehab for this type of injury. She listened to my explanation of treatment and agreed to allow me to begin his rehab. The treatment was a combination of both the MyoFascial Disruption Technique (MFDT) and the use of the ARP Wave. The young man was a hard worker and progressed well over time. We did a small test at the end of the third week, by having the patient jog for a distance of ten yards ten times at 50 percent of his normal run. The key at this point was to observe the level of any compensation patterns in his gait. This would tell me what muscles were not fully contracting at this point and allowing for the proper absorption of force. He did extremely well reporting, no pain in his knee while running. I detected minor compensation patterns that assisted me with the continuation of his program. At the end of seven weeks, the patient was tested again by running 30 fifteen-yard sprints up to 100 percent of his normal run. The patient exhibited zero pain and zero evidence of any compensation patterns. The patient was then tested in lateral movement, oblique movement, and jumping off of boxes set at various heights. There was no evidence of pain and no evidence of any compensations patterns. The patient was released from active treatment following this evaluation.

Remember, Pain Is a Part of Life... Suffering is Optional.

If you open the phonebook or look on the Internet, it seems that every doctor advertising is a sports injury expert. The Yellow Pages seem to be filled with doctors claiming to be sports injury doctors. The problem is that most of these doctors only dabble with sports injuries. Most of them have general practices, and as a marketing ploy, they throw "sports medicine" into their ads. Now don't get me wrong, there are very qualified medical doctors out there doing good work in the sports injury field. The only problem is that most of them end up at the same conclusion — prescribing medication.

There is a great deal of disparity in this field. Many people think of orthopedic surgeons as the only sports medicine doctors there are. Orthopedic surgeons are excellent at setting bones and performing surgery; that's what they've been trained for. Their expertise is to make sure that, if they have to do surgery for a broken bone or repair torn tissue, they can correct that damage and make sure that you go into and out of the anesthesia without dying on the operating table.

Don't get me wrong. If you've injured yourself to the point where bones have been broken or crushed or arteries have been damaged or joints have been dislocated, then it is a good idea to contact an orthopedic surgeon. Orthopedic surgeons are trained to put things back together. Once they complete a surgery, though, they don't normally get involved with the therapy or rehabilitation portion of your recovery. In many cases, you will be referred to a physical therapist. A physical therapist is trained in the rehabilitation of various types of injuries, ranging from stroke victims to athletic injuries.

The profession of physical therapy believes that, by using different modalities, including ice, ultrasound, conventional electrical stimulation, and taping, your body will begin to heal. These modalities have been shown to aid the body to heal. Unfortunately, the latest research has shown that conventional electrical stimulation (interferential, high volt, low volt) is not as effective as it once was thought. Many insurance companies are now stopping payment for this service. In many cases throughout the U.S. and abroad, physical therapists haven't changed their modes of treatments that have been used for decades. This is not to say that physical therapy doesn't work; it does. But the fact remains that new technology has sped up the healing process, and patients can be out of therapy and back enjoying their lives much faster than what is presently being offered.

Years ago, I realized that how I was treating patients was a bit "vanilla" and that I had to change the way I went about things if I was going to treat athletes. If I was truly going to be the best, I had to find better and faster ways of relieving pain and strengthening for rehab. I realized how important it is to most athletes to get back on the field or court as fast as possible. I was also not only helping athletes but nonathletic patients as well. As rewarding is it to help a professional athlete get back on the field after a major injury, it's just as gratifying to help an elderly person regain his or her health as well.

I found that there were manual methods of therapy and rehab being used in Europe and other places outside the U.S. that were extremely effective in correcting pain and muscle/joint imbalances. Deciding to return to school, I studied with many different instructors, many from overseas.

Back to School

After building one of the largest chiropractic practices in the country, I decided that big wasn't necessarily better. I became more entrenched in managing a big practice, which was pulling me away from taking care of patients. I found myself in practice doing what I was taught to do. But it wasn't enough, and I began to become frustrated. I was frustrated in the sense that it was taking me too long to get the injured patients back to what they wanted to do. I knew deep down there were better ways of doing things, but at that point, I just didn't know what. At that point, I decided to return to school to develop a more advanced form of treatment to offer my patients. I enrolled in the post-graduate program at the University of Southern California Health Sciences, headed by Dr. Craig Leibenson.

Dr. Leibenson, an internationally recognized researcher, author, lecturer, consultant, and sports medicine specialist, developed a program based on the best available research from around the world. I was lucky in the sense that I picked the right program that was staffed by excellent instructors from many different schools of thought. This education provided me with the building blocks needed to expand my mind to begin to think about how the body can heal in a nonconservative manner. One of the top instructors of that program, Dr. Scott Chapman of Massachusetts, along with his wife, Dr. Carol DeFranca, were pivotal in teaching me the complicated internal mechanisms of the human neuromuscular system. Their knowledge could fill volumes of books.

Many of the treatments that I learned were based on a European manual neuromuscular treatment, including the research developed by Dr. Carl Levitt and Dr. Vladimir Yanda from the Czech Republic. These two world-class research doctors pioneered the use of functional medicine that is used throughout the world today.

I began using and implementing everything that I learned and started to attain amazing results for my patients. I then began treating a few professional athletes, and once again, I was getting better results than the team doctors and trainers. So I knew at that point that I had an understanding in treating complicated cases with good results. But that wasn't good enough. I knew deep down that, if I was going to continue to work with professional athletes, I had to find a way to achieve even faster results.

After studying these advance methods of treatment, I continued researching on my own and began to look into the scientific literature for any clues for treatments that would speed up the healing process. I came across information on a very different type of manual treatment that had been sitting there for years, and I began to experiment with some of it. I brought it up to two of my colleagues, Dr. Brad Hayes and Dr. Hugh Gimmel, who were very involved in active, random, and controlled research. We began clinically testing and researching different aspects of this treatment. Dr. Gimmel, who has been in the research aspect of our profession for most of his career, began to find more supporting literature for this type of treatment. Dr. Gimmel was able to link the important clinical information with the scientific literature for us to proceed with an active treatment. After testing this treatment on family, friends, colleagues, and then patients, we began to see repetitive, predictable patterns that produced results for patients suffering with pain across the world.

This is where I've decided to step outside of the box of conventional thinking in the health care field. I wanted to help develop a new paradigm of thinking in assisting the body to regain its health without the use of unnecessary medications and/or surgery.

Let's Go Over the Basics of Injury

Muscle has different functions, but let me explain muscles' two primary purposes. Muscles are designed to move bones. When you want to touch your shoulder with your hand, the muscle must first contract to move your hand from point A to point B. The second function is that muscles were designed to absorb force. That means that, just like a shock absorber on your car absorbing the force from the ground before it can transfer to the frame of your car, the muscles absorb force before it reaches the joint.

Before the muscles can do any of that in the first place, they must be able to receive a proper nerve (electrical) supply. When the neurological system isn't properly responding and doesn't send the proper signal to a muscle, the muscle slowly over time begins to shorten. When a muscle shortens, it loses its ability to absorb force.

When the muscles cannot properly absorb force - that force will continue on until it reaches the joint or other tissue including tendons, ligaments or cartilage which are not designed to absorb any appreciable amount of force. That tissue, ligament, tendon, or joint isn't designed to absorb force and will eventually create inflammation that leads to pain.

The key to stabilizing the joints of your body is having the muscles contracting as fast as they were designed to. When the muscle receives less of a neurological signal, the muscle can't work (contract) as fast as possible. A muscle that is properly elongated cannot get hurt. This is mainly because it can absorb the maximal amount of force, keeping the force away from the joints.

Ligaments and tendons are not designed to absorb force. When this force is transferred to this area, the ligaments and tendons can begin to break down. When this happens inflammation is produced. Inflammation produces the chemicals that cause messages sent to the brain that there is damage in the area. Pain is produced as a result of this action. The ligaments and tendons are your last mode of protection to save a joint from becoming compromised. If compromised, dislocation or fracture can occur. But let's take it one place further.

Let's say that your muscles can't absorb force over a long period of time. The force then transferred to the joint (or joints) will begin to cause ongoing trauma, and over time, the bone will begin to adapt to that force and trauma. Ever heard of degenerative joint disease... arthritis?

Degenerative joint disease is also known as osteoarthritis. It's basically a breakdown of the joint in the spine, knee, hip, ankle, and neck. There are other sites; however, these are the more popular areas of arthritic symptoms. It begins with force not being absorbed by the muscle and then the force is transferred into the joint. Over a long period of time with a repetitive amount of force being transferred into the joint, the joint begins to breakdown. The breakdown, sometimes mild and sometimes severe, over time can become a painful problem.

The predicament that arises is that mainstream medicine will prescribe a medication to relieve pain. The problem with that is that the medication only creates a chemical reaction to tell the brain to stop the pain or temporarily reduce the inflammation. They haven't attacked the "real" problem that is causing the pain to begin with. I'm all for pain relief, but the problem remains that, if you medicate the pain only, you'll never get to the underlying problem. Force being generated and put into the joint will only get worse if left uncorrected. On top of that, you have the added problem of the potential side effects of the medication.

Another Example of New Treatment Available

Here is another example of a post-surgical patient who was referred for standard physical therapy. A young man 17 years of age injured his shoulder while playing football. An MRI of his shoulder revealed a tear of the labrum of his shoulder. The labrum is the cartridge that surrounds the inside of the ball and socket joint of the shoulder. The young patient had surgery in a major metropolitan hospital with a renowned orthopedic sports doctor. After the surgery, the patient's parents, who were comfortable with my work, told the orthopedist that they wanted their son's rehab done in my office. The doctor agreed and sent a multiple-page rehab instruction sheet to me for review. His prescribed rehab was outlined for the patient to be in rehab for a minimum of six months or longer and that full range of motion wouldn't be expected until the fourth month. I explained to the parents that I wouldn't be following the doctor's instructions and that I would be doing my own rehab protocols. The parents agreed to let me do my rehab, and therapy began. At three weeks, the patient was able to have an active, full range of motion without any pain or restriction. Weakness was noted, with some slight compensation patterns as well. At the end of the seventh week of treatment, the patient was tested with weights and throwing. The patient reported no pain, no weakness, and no restriction of motion. He was released from active treatment and allowed to return to training for football.

Let's go over a new or acute injury — a sprained ankle.

Once you turn your ankle, you stretch the ligaments and tendons that support the ankle joint. Usually, swelling begins to appear in the joint, and the ankle itself becomes much larger.

231

What happens when your joints begin to swell?

When the body recognizes an injury, it releases chemicals that act on our smallest blood vessels. The action of these chemicals is to widen (vasodilate) these vessels, which attempts to increase the amount of blood flow into the area. But more than blood flow enters the damaged area. Other fluid-containing, infection-fighting cells, along with adhesive tissue (scar tissue), are released into the area to help in the healing.

The standard way of treating a sprained ankle is known as RICE. RICE is an acronym for rest, ice, compression, and elevation. This has been used for decades, but there is a much better way to relieve the pain and inflammation for a sprained ankle. I recently read an article in a professional periodical referring to RICE as the way to treat sprains. The problem is this type of treatment is outdated. I can't tell you how many athletes come into my office after receiving treatments with their doctor or therapist for weeks but continue to suffer with pain. For some, this is extremely detrimental due to the fact that many athletes don't have that kind of time to wait. It could literally mean the difference between a Division I scholarship or none.

New technology has been discovered and developed that has been in use for many years. It is amazing to me that most doctors have absolutely no clue that these treatments even exist. It is extremely difficult for people to change. Change is a difficult process, and for many, it never comes because it takes them out of their comfort zones. Believe me, I'm the biggest skeptic there is when it comes to new information about treatment. The difference with me is that I will look into it. You have to prove to me that there is merit to what you are proposing, because I will dismiss it if you cannot explain it properly in a limited amount of time.

Times Are Changing...

Times have changed, and with new technology, so has the treatment of injury to the human body. For years, it has been understood that, when someone becomes injured, you have to "rest" the area. The current literature, though, overwhelmingly shows that this is not good in many cases. Many studies have shown that active movement is much better in healing damaged tissue than the alternative of splinting, casting, or resting. In fact, studies show that joints under stress will heal faster than joints that are immobilized. There are major hospitals now actively exercising patients that are in intensive care. They've found that even really sick people can begin to move and will suffer less depression and get out of intensive care faster.

I take the position that, if the muscle cannot absorb force, then there is a neurological delay causing the problem. In order for the muscle to contract correctly, it needs to be supplied electrical energy from the nerve. If that nerve isn't functioning properly, then the electrical (neurological) message will not contract the muscle fast enough. This leads to the muscle not being able to absorb that force. The force then travels to the tissue (tendons, ligaments, bone and fascia), which isn't designed to absorb.

The first thing that I must determine through examination is if the body is sending the correct neurological signal to the muscle to absorb force. If the nervous system isn't doing its job, then we know at that level where the origin of the problem began. I have to identify all participants in this injury, including the muscles, fascia, ligaments, tendons, bone, and joints. Here is the major KEY to understand — where you are feeling pain isn't necessarily where the damage began. It's where the pain ended up. The damage was most likely produced in an area away from where the patient is experiencing the pain.

When pain or inflammation ends up at or around a joint, I know that most likely the damage didn't start there. There is a normal breakdown of the supporting muscle way before the joint exhibited pain. If we don't find the origin of the breakdown, you won't get to the source of the problem. This is why taking medication only covers up the pain without finding the exact nature and location of the injury.

To diagnose the injury properly, a doctor needs to find out where the origin of the problem began, not where it ended up. One more time — where you feel the pain is where the pain ended up, *not* where it originated from. I look at most sports injuries neurologically, not physiologically, because I believe that, in order for a muscle to fail, there is an extremely high likelihood that it was not receiving a proper nerve supply. If your muscles aren't turning on fast enough, then they lose their ability to absorb force. And the only reason why they can't turn on fast enough is because the nerve supply to that muscle is diminished.

Take a look at any three- or five-year-old when they move. They jump, squat, and roll effortlessly the way they were designed. When you are three to five years old, you move correctly. As you get older, you learn how to move incorrectly, developing compensation patterns mainly from mimicking your environment. When you develop from an early age, children tend to imitate the people close to them. Over time, they watch mom, dad, and siblings stand, slouch, sit, and walk. Youngsters want to be just like the grownups, and eventually, they mimic most of their movements. Change doesn't happen until the youngsters begin to watch mom and dad move improperly. At this age, they tend to imitate what they see, slowly weakening the smaller supporting muscles. Slowly, the posture begins to break down, which starts a compensation pattern. When the muscles break down, they can't absorb force properly, and slowly, aches and pains begin to develop.

As you develop and age, most movements and postures worsen, unless you make a conscious effort to properly work your muscles. As your movement patterns change, slowly over time, the muscles begin to shorten. When the muscles shorten, they can't properly stabilize the joints. This is where aches and pains begin to develop.

Show me a five-year-old with a back problem. You will be hard-pressed to find one with a bad back. How about finding me a ten-year-old with a back problem? The reason is that, at these ages, the body works correctly. The muscles contract quickly and repetitively, allowing for the muscles to support all of the major joints correctly. It's not until we stop using muscles correctly when the problems like back pain and other pains begin to develop over time. This is the main reason why it is so important to remove all restrictions before the athlete begins to train.

When beginning to train without removing bodily restrictions or properly lengthening shortened muscles, you will begin to strengthen your weaknesses.

Dr. Conway

A New Approach in Treating Injury and Strengthening Athletes

I believe in a very different approach in assisting the body to recover from injury or surgery. It starts with the examination. Once I've become satisfied that there are no types of serious medical conditions which need an immediate referral, I will begin with my examination.

Recent studies have shown that many orthopedic examinations can create a false positive result, causing a missed or improper diagnosis. I've turned away from this type of testing and began using a more functional way of testing years ago.

I take a comprehensive history of your problem. I will let you explain to me in detail how you were first injured, situations that possibly led up to the injury, and any other vital information you feel important for me to understand. I have developed a series of unique questions that will also help me pull more information out of you that will lead us in the right direction. My goal is to locate the exact area of pain in what I call the "pain generator". Once located, I can then begin to design a target-based treatment plan that will lead you to full recovery.

The Exam...

At my office, we start with a functional examination to see what muscles are working and what muscles are not. This is a series of movements performed by the patient that will allow me to better understand what muscles are turning on and turning off properly. This begins with just standing to evaluate your muscular posture without movement. Then, a major part of the exam is a walking exam to see exactly how the muscles and joints perform when put into motion. This is important because you can see the restrictions that lead to the exact areas that are causing pain.

This will allow me to put together a complete visual compensation pattern produced by the muscles that aren't working. This leads to examining the neurological system. The information gained by this exam will tell me if the muscles are getting the appropriate signal from the nervous system, which allows the muscle to contract fast enough. If a muscle can't contract fast enough, it isn't properly prepared to absorb force. Many neurologists have said that muscle function is an outward expression of the nervous system.

Special tests are performed for structural abnormalities that lead to muscular compensation patterns, which lead to weakness. These compensation patterns can lead to putting undue stress on a particular joint(s). Direct muscle testing will also be used to measure the amount of strength loss or other areas of damage leading to the painful site. Muscle inhibition or damage can lead to compensation patterns. Compensation patterns are a series of movements that the body programs to avoid pain and damage. This information provides me with indications that certain muscles are not functioning properly, allowing the body to "favor" the damage. This is where aberrant movement begins to develop. Aberrant movement is when a person begins to use muscles not designed for normal movement. It can result in a small, little glitch in movement or lead to an overwhelming limp.

Continuing, I will test for fascial disruptions, which are overlooked by almost every doctor and therapist in the field of sports injury treatment. This one area is responsible for more disability and discomfort than most people think. Fascia is a protective covering of tissue that covers everything inside the body. Once fascia becomes disrupted, it can become the major reason for pain, inflammation, and restriction of movement.

There is an axiom that I tell my students when I teach throughout the country. "He who treats at the point of pain is a fool." I say this because, many times, where the patient points to where the pain is, is not where the damage is coming from. It's where it ended up. The damage can refer the pain to other sites on the body. If only looking at the site of pain, you can miss the entire problem. Many doctors become blinded when treating a point of pain rather than searching the entire area for the true area of breakdown or damage.

New Thinking for New Treatment (MFDT)

Fascia is a supportive tissue that is located throughout the entire body. The easiest way I can describe it to you is for you to picture the transparent film or tissue on a raw chicken breast. That's fascia.

The fascial system is a complex network of fibrous tissues that envelops the body just beneath the skin all the way to the skeletal system. Fascia makes up 19.5 percent of the average male's body weight. It is a connective tissue web that surrounds every tissue in the body. It surrounds nerves, bones, arteries, and veins, as well as muscles. It covers the muscle, and it is intertwined within the muscle. It doesn't receive a direct blood supply, and it doesn't have an origin that attaches with the muscle.

Fascia has been called the packing material of the body. It interconnects all of the organs and envelopes the muscles and other soft tissues of the body. This interconnection also acts as a secondary communication system in the body. Fascia assists as a functional foundation for the muscular system. Fascia also assists in the structure and strength of the muscle. It helps in pumping the lymphatic system throughout the body. It provides a support system for nerves, blood, and lymph vessels as they interconnect the muscles.

We have found that fascia can become disrupted from its original position. Fascia once disrupted has been found to become one of the main pain generators to most soft tissue injuries. It can cause pain, disability, swelling, and loss of strength and motion. If left uncorrected, it can turn into long-term disability. This disruption will cause a dysfunction of the surrounding muscles, causing altered movement patterns. This can lead to other surrounding muscles picking up the slack of movement, causing them to break down as well.

There are several ways for fascia to become disrupted, and this can lead to several different types of injuries:

- Ankle sprains
- Rotator cuff injury
- Elbow tendonitis
- Carpal tunnel syndrome
- Achilles tendonitis

- Hamstring pulls
- Osgood-Schlatter's Disease
- Lower back pain
- Patellar tendonitis
- Headaches

- Groin strain
- A/C shoulder separation
- Lace bite (hockey)
- Heel spurs
- Wrist pain
- Turf toe

- Plantar fasciitis
- Shin splints
- IT band syndrome
- Finger sprains
- Bicep tendonitis
- High ankle sprain

Once the disrupted fascia has been properly identified and diagnosed, pain relief can be seen in as little as five minutes. When fascia distorts, wrinkles, twists, bends, or pulls away, it can create a tremendous amount of pain and loss of motion. We named this treatment the "MyoFascial Disruption Technique" (MFDT). I co-developed MFDT, along with Dr. Brad Hayes and Dr. Hugh Gimmel. We have taught this treatment to doctors all across the U.S., and presently, it has been instituted within the curriculum of the Anglo-European College of Chiropractic in Bournemouth, England.

New Treatment for Soft Tissue Injuries

Soft Tissue Injury: Any injury that involves the muscles, ligaments, tendons, and fascia.

As I mentioned before, I needed to find a better way to get athletes back on the field faster. Diving into the research on past treatments, I came across information on soft tissue treatments. One particular article fascinated me in its simplicity concerning fascia. The doctor's theory was that, when fascia becomes disturbed, it can lead to inflammation, pain, and loss of motion. That article led to me to other writings from practitioners that practiced over forty years ago. The various articles described in their own ways that the fascia was a major pain generator, and if corrected, pain relief was seconds away. I continued to dig for more information, but it became an arduous situation. I came across many different articles that discussed different ways of treating these injuries, but no one had really put it in one type of readable format.

I presented my information to Dr. Brad Hayes and Dr. Hugh Gimmel. Dr. Gimmel presently is a research professor for the Anglo-

European College of Chiropractic in Bournemouth, England. Dr. Hayes is a practicing doctor of chiropractic, whose expertise is in insurance fraud, coding, and educating doctors how to properly interact with insurance companies. Between the three of us, we began tearing through the research on this type of soft tissue treatment.

There was evidence that research pertaining to these soft tissue injuries dated back to the 1950s, concerning the healing of soft tissue damage without the use of modalities. Using his academic research experience, Dr. Gimmel painstakingly weaved his way through the maze of manual medicine/soft tissue research to put together the information needed for us to develop the MyoFascial Disruption Treatment (MFDT). Both myself and Dr. Hayes have performed most of the clinical trials in our daily practices. We see hundreds of patients per week and have been using this treatment successfully on our patients for 10 years.

We named it the MyoFascial (my-o-fas-shal) Disruption Technique (MFDT), and it is a system of manual treatment provided by the doctor to reinstate disrupted fascia in a given injured area of the body. Dr. Gimmel did the bulk of the academic research, and Dr. Hayes and I did most of the clinical studies. We came up with a treatment protocol based on the research and the clinical trials we performed. The results were so fast and effective that we all had a difficult time believing the results.

Since that time, Dr. Gimmel continues to actively research and test the MFDT treatment protocol. Dr. Gimmel also spearheaded the first peer-reviewed paper on MFDT with Dr. Hayes and myself. He is currently overseeing multiple studies at his place of employment at the Anglo-European College of Chiropractic in Bournemouth, England.

Here's how it started.

My first treatment involved a chronic sprained ankle. At the time, I was researching the different types of soft tissue treatments. I had met with a local medical doctor to explain to him about the types of treatments I was performing. We had a good meeting, and the next day, he decided to send me a patient who was having trouble with her ankle. She entered the office on crutches in an air cast. She reported that she had turned her right ankle on the steps at college, and since

239

that point, she had been unable to walk due to the pain. The incident occurred about three weeks prior. As she explained the details of the fall, she explained that her mother back home in New Jersey was sick, and she was unable to get back to see her because she couldn't use her right foot to drive. I sat with the patient and told her, "I have to be honest with you. I have a treatment that I feel will work well, but the problem is I've never performed it." I told her about my research and some test subjects but that I had never had a case like hers before. She said to me, "Doc, I'll try anything. I really need to get back to see my mother." So with that, we began treatment.

I began to treat her with the manual treatment in and around the ankle, and to my amazement, within five minutes, she was up and walking without any assistance. I continued to treat her, and after about 15 to 20 minutes, she was able to walk out of my office without any crutches or using the air cast. I was as thrilled as she was. She came back for a couple of follow-up treatments, and I helped her strengthen the area so she wouldn't do it again. What had happened was that the fascia around the tendons and ligaments attached to the bones of the ankle was disrupted — actually separated microscopically from the bone — producing the chronic pain and swelling. By attaching the fibers back to the bone, the pain immediately went away, the swelling dissipated, and the strength and range of motion came back.

When trauma occurs to a certain portion of the body, there is a high degree of certainty that the fascial component of that area will become disrupted or rearranged from its normal position. In the majority of cases, this can be the major source of pain. Once corrected, the patient can become pain-free in a very short period of time.

MyoFascial Disruption Technique (MFDT)

- New technique for soft tissue pain
- 95% faster than conventional treatment
- Effective for chronic and acute injuries
- Complete diagnostic analysis system to locate the underlying cause of pain
- State-of-the-art sports injury treatment

- Increase performance, increase range of motion, increase strength
- Apply MFDT to the following areas:
  o Spine
  o Extremities
  o Shoulder
  o Anywhere there is disrupted fascia

The sports world is looking for treatments that can return athletes safely to the playing field faster and more effectively than present-day treatment. By far, the most common sports injuries are of a sprain/strain nature. The conventional treatment across the country, if not the world, is ice, compression, electrical stimulation, and medication.

After treating hundreds of college and professional athletes, the biggest complaint I hear is that they feel that the "ice and stim" treatment isn't effective. The treatment tends to lessen the symptoms, but the athlete cannot continue to play without pain. MFDT is unique in the sense that we've been able to show clinical results that are 95 percent faster as compared to conventional treatment. Even chronic pain that an athlete (and nonathlete as well) has been suffering with will see almost immediate results after the first treatment.

Many times, diagnostic procedures including x-ray, MRI, and CT scans report negative findings, and the athlete continues to report pain. The problem is that many fascial disruptions cannot be picked up by these diagnostic images.

What MFDT Isn't...

MyoFascial Disruption Technique isn't

- Active release
- Muscle energy technique
- Rolfing
- Neuromuscular reeducation
- Massage
- Trigger point therapy

What It Is

MyoFascial Disruption Technique (MFDT) is a hands-on approach to treating soft tissue injuries. MFDT recognizes that most, if not all, soft tissue injuries are a result of a separation or a disruption of the fascia. The fascia can separate at the origin or insertion of a tendon or ligament. The fascia can separate within the muscle in a band-like separation. It can "wrinkle" like a shirt pulled out from your hamper. It can also "uncoil" in the extremities like a twisted slinky toy. Once these disruptions have been corrected, pain immediately resolves, range of motion is restored, and strength increases.

MFDT is not a "fly-by-night" treatment that alternative health practitioners are famous for. This is a scientifically based, clinically studied, and proven method of relieving pain and restriction resulting from disrupted fascia. A multi-clinic, multi-doctor case study of 15 cases has been submitted and accepted for publication and scrutiny to the *Journal of Manipulative Physiotherapeutics* (JMPT), which is a peer-reviewed journal on physical medicine. The technique is currently undergoing the second stage of the scientific process of scientific outcome measurement with extremely promising results.

Once disrupted fascia is corrected, not only does the pain decrease, but there is instant increase in range of motion and strength. On top of that, once the area has been corrected with the MFDT treatment, you don't have to worry about reoccurrence.

Here is what some athletes have said about the treatment:

"I had been suffering from severe pain in my hip and right leg for ten years. Throughout this time, I went to see doctors, physicians, sports physicians, and many other medical professionals. I had numerous x-rays, MRIs, and other tests, but no doctor or test could figure out the problem, let alone ease my pain and correct the problem. After seeing Dr. Conway, my pain was totally gone after three to four visits. I would simply say that Dr. Conway's treatments work! Dr. Conway and his treatments are amazing!"

- Jason Kalbach

"During the track season, I pulled my hamstring and was forced to miss the end of the season. After this, I had been rehabbing my hamstring for two and a half months. It seemed to be getting better but then remained where it was at, not allowing me to run like I used to. I then began to doubt if I would ever be able to run like I had been running before the injury. This is when I contacted Dr. Conway. After only one hour of his treatment, there was a noticeable difference in my hamstring. After the fourth treatment, I was able to sprint on my leg again like I used to. Thanks to Dr. Conway and his rehab staff, I am again able to compete at the level of competition that I desire. I have placed fifth at the Pennsylvania Indoor State Championships, seventh in Eastern States Championships, and twenty-sixth in the National Indoor Championships."

- Cody Schovitz

Here Is a List of Case Studies

A fifty-eight-year-old former college golfer entered the office with **chronic epicondylitis (golfer's elbow)**. Due to the chronic pain he was experiencing, he had to significantly reduce his playing time within the last ten years. After eight four-minute treatments, he was able to resume playing golf daily. **He won the senior state championship** two months after treatment concluded.

A thirty-eight-year-old female patient fell off a chair she was standing on and sprained her ankle. She arrived in a complete plastic leg boot given to her at the emergency room. She had ecchymosis (area of black and blue discoloring) and swelling along the lateral ankle spreading up into the lower leg. After a five-minute treatment, **she walked out of the office carrying the boot**. One visit later, the condition resolved, and she resumed all activities.

A twelve-year-old female patient had heal pain for four weeks duration. Treatment including medication, ultrasound, and electrical stimulation by other providers was ineffective. The previous diagnosis was a calcaneal spur. Treatment with MFDT in one four-minute treatment **reduced the heal pain by 75 percent**. A follow-up treatment completely resolved the patient's condition.

A fifteen-year-old gymnast entered the office with chronic hamstring pain and was unable to compete or practice. The patient and her father reported that she had been treated by a physical therapist for over five months. She was unable to pull her foot across the floor without sharp pain in her hamstring, unable to bend to touch her toes (normally, she could put her palms on the floor), and was unable to put her leg up on the table and stretch the hamstring without severe pain. **After one treatment, the patient got up and touched her toes without pain, and on the second visit, she was able to go into a complete split on the floor.** She needed follow-up treatment to increase the strength and endurance of the muscles to prevent future injury.

A seventeen-year-old male gymnast entered the office reporting pain and restriction of his left arm after participating in the rings. The patient reported that, when he pulled up in the rings, the pain stopped him from fully releasing his arms, and he had to stop due to the pain. MFDT treatment to the left upper arm, trapezius, and cervical area provided complete release of restriction and fully restored pain-free range of motion. After **two treatments total, the athlete was allowed to return to full competition.**

An eighteen-year-old college student on a scholarship as a member of a world-famous dance team entered the office reporting pain in the back of her leg. She reported **straining her hamstring muscle** and was unable to do the high kick the team is known for. She had seen numerous specialists who were unable to resolve her condition. She was concerned about losing her scholarship and losing a position that she had worked for years to get into. She drove five hours for two days of treatment (less than ten minutes each), and **her condition has completely resolved.**

A sixty-year-old female with **chronic bilateral knee pain** (2 years duration) entered the office reporting that the pain was making it increasingly difficult to get around. The patient was on long-term pain management involving daily intake of Percocet. An MRI of the knee showed mild-moderate degenerative joint disease. Arthroscopic surgery of the knee was performed with zero improvement. The orthopedic surgeon referred back to primary care physician for continued pain management due to the fact that he said she would not qualify for a total joint replacement, and it would have limited hope for improvement. The patient was also prescribed physical therapy, which provided no results. The patient lost 40 pounds, which didn't have any positive effect on the knee pain. After a brief examination, it was determined that she had medial and lateral myofascial band distortion that had progressed with associated shin splints bilaterally. Following treatment, the patient was scheduled for a second treatment seven days following. When the patient reported for her next visit, she reported that the pain in the left leg was completely gone, and the right leg was six days pain-free.

A fifteen-year-old baseball pitcher entered the office reporting pain every time he attempted to throw a baseball. The patient reported that the pain came on after about 10 to 15 minutes of throwing. His abduction (raising his arm upward from his side) was positive for pain at 100 degrees (180 degrees is normal), along with other positive orthopedic findings. He traced his index finger from his elbow to his upper trap as the pathway of pain. **After one visit, he had regained a full range of motion, along with negative orthopedic findings**. He was tested for strength loss and resumed pitching later that week without further incident.

The ARPWave

I came across a unit called the ARPWave that, quite honestly, I had a hard time believing in. I couldn't believe the results that the people of the company were describing. After working with an athlete who

245

was treated by this machine, I was quietly skeptical but interested in witnessing his results.

There is one thing that I hold near to my heart. I am one of the biggest skeptics you'll ever meet. The reason for this is that I truly protect my reputation for my patients' sake. If I recommend something, I want my patient to able to trust me enough that I won't steer them wrong. In the health care field, if I fell for every gadget and gizmo that came down the road, I wouldn't be in practice. My patients trust me for my opinion, and for that fact, I'm very apprehensive about lending my acceptance to anything that doesn't work. In the health care business, there is a new "elixir" born every minute. Most of them are totally bogus, but on the other hand, you have to keep your eyes open, or you can miss out on some exceptional developments.

I researched the ARPWave for about eight months to a year before committing to purchase it. Figuring that I had time to send it back if it didn't work, I decided I would test it on five of my more difficult patients. The patients that I used it on reported great results, and at that point, I was sold. I was looking for something to complement my other treatment (MFDT) that I performed with the athletes, and this seemed like the perfect fit.

The ARPWave was originally invented by Gary Thomas. Thomas was formerly trained as a pharmacist, however his real love was researching electricity and its effects on the human physiology. Thomas was also into bicycling and developed a need to better understand muscle potential while biking. He put together an EMG machine that would allow him to view the muscle response/potentials while he was peddling. This led him to discovering an alternate wave that he could use to relax the muscles.

ARP is an acronym for accelerated recovery performance, developed further by Denis Thompson and Jay Schroeder. Thompson began to develop this for athletes for muscle loosening but found that this machine went far beyond his original ideas. His research began to reveal multiple uses for the machine on a wide variety of injuries and diseases.

Denis Thompson began experimenting with the machine on himself, his family, and Jay Schroeder. Their combined experience in the physiology and kinesiology fields led them to probably one of the more effective machines on the market today. He found that he was able to help serious injuries where other forms of modality treatments couldn't get results. He got together with Jay Schroeder. Schroeder had been using and researching electrical stimulation in the Soviet Republic. He brought his knowledge and experience to ARP and has gone on to develop most of the treatment protocols for this machine.

As I began to use the machine, I learned two things. One, this machine has incredible potential for healing, especially when combined with the manual treatment of MFDT. Second, I knew that, to master this machine, it was going to take a lot of study to fully grasp the technical knowledge needed to use it to its full potential. I spent years studying with the founder of the ARPWave, Denis Thompson, and the developer of the protocols of the machine, Jay Schroeder. I also spent countless hours on weekends and nights studying the research of several scientists in the field of bio-electric healing, neurology, kinesiology, physiology, and bio-electric medicine. I was able to read the research of the Nobel Peace prize winner Bjorn Nordenström on bio-electric healing, as well as the research of Yaakov Kots from the former Soviet Republic, who was the original developer of "Russian stimulation." My goal was to fully understand how this machine worked and how it can be applied to patients to heal acute and chronic pain. What I found was information that was 360 degrees different than most modern day concepts on healing. The information that I came across was like what I found with MFDT, in that many of the concepts ran parallel together. And, by far, both were completely different philosophies as compared to modern conventional thinking.

Muscles contract and shorten as they fatigue, limiting their ability to absorb force, and, hence, are more prone to injury. When muscles shorten, this can have a profound effect on the fascial fibers that surround the muscle fibers. The combination of using both MFDT and the ARPWave has proved to be the fastest treatment that can be combined to rehabilitate most injuries. The ARP protocols condition muscles to absorb greater force by keeping them loose and elongated. The ARP protocols greatly accelerate recovery from all types of injuries by attacking the electrical origin of inflammation, thus

247

eliminating the production of scar tissue, calcification, and the shortening of muscle tissue. The ARPWave is the first machine of its kind to have the potential to virtually prevent most, if not all, injuries.

Modern day medicine is a science that feels that, after a correct diagnosis is made, a chemical such as a drug will be able to correct a problem. Medicine uses certain medications to treat various illnesses and injuries. When it comes to injury, just taking a pill only covers up the pain and doesn't allow you to correct the underlying problem. Another problem is that medicine works, but it is sometimes with a price. That price is called "side effects." There have been numerous reports of safe medications approved by our government only to be found out later to cause other catastrophic illnesses, resulting in a recall of that medication.

On the other hand, doctors like myself feel that, after a correct diagnosis, instead of prescribing medication, we should provide an alternative treatment to drugs and surgery. This is done by locating the physical breakdown that is causing the pain and then using manual methods of treatment along with bio-electrical protocols. After a proper diagnosis, instead of using medication, a doctor can use a new form of electrical therapy for the treatment of chronic pain and acute pain. The use of electric currents has been employed in healing damaged soft and hard tissue for years.

Electricity works on the positive (+) and negative (-) charges of your body in an attempt to create homeostasis (normal balance) within that damaged area. Bjorn Nordenström, MD, proved beyond a shadow of a doubt that he was able to shrink and eliminate certain cancer tumors with the use of electrical currents. Nordenström is a Swedish medical doctor who was past president of the Nobel Peace Prize Committee. He was able to do this by directing a small wire with electrical currents directly into the tumor itself. He proved this with many patients over a long period of time. Not only did their symptoms go away, but long-term follow-up showed no return of symptoms. Dr. Nordenström worked with many patients who were given very low odds for long-term survival. Dr. Nordenström's work was reviewed by top Yale University researchers, who reported that all of Dr. Nordenström's claims that he wrote about held up to scientific scrutiny.

The ARPWave is years ahead of its time and is changing the way we look at acute and chronic injury. Denis Thompson, the developer of the ARPWave, said, "The ARPWave can be instrumental in PREVENTING 70 to 80 percent of all sports injuries. It can also help prevent normal day-to-day injuries as well."

There are many electrical muscle stimulation units on the market that have claims of success, but none of them come close to matching the success provided by the ARPWave machine. Many insurance companies are beginning to deny payment for conventional electrical stimulation because if its lack of long-term success in treatment.

The Sacred Myth of Stretching – Shattered!

When you stretch, you stretch tendons and ligaments, not muscle tissue. Every doctor learned in physiology 101 that muscles either contract or relax. They don't stretch. Technically, ligaments and tendons don't stretch; they creep. This creeping movement takes weeks, and sometimes months, to make significant change. So if it is impossible to stretch muscles, then what are all the athletes doing when they stretch before an event? First of all, they put considerable stress on the ligaments, tendons, and fascia. Second, in many cases, a shortened muscle that is being stretched can create a neurological signal back to the brain warning it of impending damage. A signal is then sent back to the muscle, shortening the muscle as a response to the original message. A muscle that is shortened is more likely to become injured. When the ARPWave is placed on the muscle, within seconds it begins to lengthen. That is why the ARPWave can prevent most injuries before they happen.

The number one injury in athletics is that of tendons and ligaments (sprains). Repetitive ballistic stretching can cause fibers of the tendons and ligaments to weaken. This can also become a precursor to injury. The muscle almost never breaks down in the middle (belly) of the muscle. The injury is mainly at the joint, where the tendon of that muscle attaches. In many other cases, the ligaments that attach bone to bone become injured as well. Someone who consistently ballistically stretches begins to stretch (creep) the ligaments and tendons, setting themselves up for long-term weakness of the joint.

Now, if the muscle is completely relaxed during movement, it can do what it was designed to do — absorb force. If the muscle can't absorb force properly, the force continues to move (remember, once force begins in motion, it will remain in motion until it is stopped) to the next available area, the joint. This then produces the force for the ligaments, tendons, and fascia to absorb. But they weren't designed to absorb force, so the tissue breaks down, and injury occurs.

Neurological Muscle Injury

It is my belief that most, if not all, injuries are due to muscle inability to properly absorb force. This inability can be from a lack of or a decreased neurological signal provided from the central nervous system to the muscle, which inhibits the muscle from contracting correctly. This decrease in a nerve signal can be caused by an improperly aligned spinal column.

Muscles need an electrical supply from the nerve in order to contract properly. Contraction allows you to move the muscle. The faster the nerve impulse, the faster the contraction of a muscle, and the faster you can move the muscle. If the nerve signal is less than optimum over time, the muscle can begin to shorten. When the muscle shortens, it has less of a chance to properly absorb force and more of a chance to be injured. Another reason for the inability of a muscle to absorb force is that the muscles may have been trained predominantly in concentric contraction, not allowing full range of motion in eccentric contraction (concentric = shortening; eccentric: = lengthening). This is what happens when a person does repetitive heavy weight lifting. Many athletes get stronger, but how many are getting injured is the real question. The shorter a muscle is, the less force it can absorb. The longer and more supple a muscle is, the more force it can absorb. The ARP can instantly elongate a muscle, allowing it to absorb 10 times more force.

Where you are feeling the pain isn't necessarily where the damage is. It's where it ended up. That is what is so unique about the

ARPWave. The ARPWave can locate where the damage is coming from so that you can begin to heal the area properly. As an example, let's say you have shoulder pain. The shoulder is where the pain ended, but many times, the damage was caused somewhere else. The ARPWave will allow us to locate the area of damage, which is nine times out of 10 nowhere near the area where you are indicating the pain to be. Again, let me repeat this. The location or area that you feel the pain in is where the problem ended up, not where it originated. We use the ARP to find the muscle that failed and reeducate that muscle or group of muscles to properly hold position, thus eliminating the pain.

Case Studies

A sixteen-year-old female swimmer slipped and fell on the pool deck onto her elbow and reported pain, swelling, and lack of normal range of motion. She was unable to bend her arm at the elbow, reporting pain at about 15 degrees. The original diagnosis was bursitis. After searching with the ARPWave, the damage was found in the bicep area. After the first treatment, she was able to fully flex the arm at the elbow with no pain. The edema and pain was significantly reduced, and only one follow-up visit was needed. She returned to swimming without missing any time.

A male sixteen years of age injured his hamstring while wrestling. The patient reported that he was attempting to lift his opponent up off the mat when he felt a pop in the back of his legs. The examination revealed that the back of the thigh was swollen and discolored black and blue. He reported that just attempting to lift his leg up towards his waist caused immediate pain. With treatment using the ARPWave, the patient was able to lift his leg with much less pain after his first visit. The athlete began treatment on a Monday, and he was cleared to wrestle on Friday.

A forty-five-year-old presented with chronic pain in both knees. The patient reported that, over the past several years, the knees began to break down with pain and weakness. He reported that he would have sit and watch television at night with ice packs on due to the pain. "Doc, I'm at my wits end, and I think surgery is the only thing that will help me," he said. His doctor told him that surgery was the only way out, due to having a partial tear in his meniscus along with arthritis. Treatment began using the ARPWave on both knees, and within three weeks, the patient was back to working out again without any pain.

A fifteen-year-old basketball player injured his groin while playing basketball. The patient reported that he was stopping to position himself for a shot, and his leg slid on the wet floor. The patient reported that he felt a tearing sensation in his upper inside thigh. The examination revealed a moderate strain of the adductor muscles. Treatment began with the ARPWave, which stopped the pain in four treatments, and the patient then began to strengthen the weakened area. By the following week, he returned to playing basketball, having only missed one game. The patient went on to tell me that he had a friend at another school who had a similar injury two weeks before his. He relayed that his friend was nowhere near returning to practice because he still had pain.

A fifteen-year-old football player was hit and twisted his knee, completely tearing the anterior crucaite ligament (ACL) of his knee during a football game. He had complete ACL reconstruction surgery and was sent to rehab at a local rehabilitation center. They were told that he would be able to return to football in six months. Both he and his mother were unsatisfied with the way the rehab was going, so they discontinued his treatment there after three weeks and decided to come to my office. The patient entered with a moldable cast and was using crutches to walk around. We began treatment on a daily basis, and after three weeks, we tested the patient with a slow jog at 50 percent of his normal. Continued treatment was performed, and the patient was released to return to practice in four weeks.

Chapter 10

Nutrition 101
A Common Sense Approach

Nutrition can be very confusing for both parents and athletes. If you ask ten sports nutrition experts on what the proper nutrition should be for any athlete you will get ten different answers. Nutrition if strategized with common sense can be highly effective in helping your athlete optimize their performance.

Use common sense! We all know what foods are good for you. The rule of thumb is that if you eat good foods 85% of the time the other 15 % won't kill you. Kids are kids and no matter how perfect you think they are they are – when they are out by themselves they're probably going to eat some type of junk food. Don't stress out about it let them have a little fun.

This is where my 85/15% rule comes in. If you can get your athlete to eat 85% of their food with high quality calories such as lean protein, high quality carbohydrate like fruits and vegetables and fats than you feel good about their nutrition. If athletes are consuming 85% of their food from this high quality food then you won't have to worry about them when they go off their diet a little. Most kids will want to eat some form of junk food - get over it.

Educate them enough to get the good stuff in first. I've seen where some parents have gone overboard in trying to feed their kids perfect foods 100% of the time. I've seen those same kids go off the deep end when going out with their friends on their own. The barrage of television commercials of subpar food that are targeted at young adults is overwhelming. That's why education is the key to helping them keep their heads about them when they are on their own. They have to be responsible for themselves but they also have to let their hair down once and awhile as well.

Nutrition is about getting the right amount of calories in to maintain proper energy, optimize performance and promote proper recovery. Most people are confused about calories from different foods. Let's start off by defining what a calorie is. Calories are unit of measurement of energy given off of from the food that we eat. A calorie is a measure of heat. One calorie (technically called kilocalorie) is the amount of heat needed to raise the temperature by one gram of water by one degree Celsius. The more calories it takes to burn up a food the more energy it will produce in your body. Typically, the more dense the food the more calories are stored. Foods such as wings, or French fries are calorically more dense due to the amount of fat in them. An apple or a string bean is less dense because there is no fat and will burn much quicker.

To give you an idea of some representative numbers, your average male at 170 pounds has a daily maintenance energy need of about 2200 calories and a female of 135 lbs about 1900 calories. That number can change quite a bit depending on the size of the person and the amount of movement/exercise they do in a day.

There is a chart that floats around the nutrition circles that is based on metabolic changes of both men and women. The rule of thumb is 14-16 calories/lb current bodyweight for men and for 13-15 cal/lb for women. These are only estimates because this calculation is based upon a few things. First is resting metabolic rate, second is thermic affect of activity, third is thermic affect of food, and fourth is non-exercise activity.

Take 15 calories times you current body weight and it will give you - your maintance calorie total. So for example if you were a male and you weighed 200 lbs., you multiply the 200 times 15 and you will come up with about 3,000 calories per day. Please keep in mind that this is an ESTIMATE, you'll have to play with this to better understand your own body. It has a lot to do with your muscle type, the amount of exercise you get in a day, the general amount of movement you do in a day and some other genetic occurrences.

Let's say you want to lose or gain weight. The best starting point will safely be about 20% change from your ideal maintenance values. If you want to lose weight (for a male weighing 200 lbs.) subtract 20% from the initial 14-16 calories/lb. to begin your equation. Subtract 20% from the bottom side of the equation which is 14 minus 20% which will give you 11. Take the 11 multiply it by 200 which will give you 2200 calories. This will allow you to lose weight at a safe level with exercise. This is not an exact science but a guide to help you figure your way through the maze of nutrition.

Here are the top 5 Nutrients that your body needs on a daily basis in order to survive and maintain proper bodily functions:

1. Protein
2. Carbohydrates
3. Fats
4. Vitamins
5. Minerals

Not all calories are the same:

- Protein: 4 calories per gram (16.8 joules/gram)
- Carbohydrate: 4 calories per gram (16.8 joules/gram)
- Fat: 9 calories per gram (37.8 joules/gram)
- Alcohol: 7 calories per gram (29.4 joules/gram)

Note: these are average values and can vary very slightly (i.e. protein ranges from about 3.8 to 4.2 cal/gram depending on the specific type of protein).

In years past fat has gotten a bad reputation. In fact, fat is as essential as any protein or carbohydrate in assisting your body maintain proper health. Fats from processed foods can lead to cholesterol problems if abused – they include potato chips, French fries, fried chicken, or anything that is deep fried. The oils that are heated can create an unhealthy environment for the human cell which can lead to cell damage. These are mainly called trans fats (saturated fats).

Good fats include avocado, fish, oils such as virgin olive oil, flax oil, evening primrose oil, almonds, flax seeds, walnuts, sunflower seeds, and peanuts. Monounsaturated, polyunsaturated, and omega-3s provide many health benefits for your body. Be careful, as with any fat they are higher in calories and need to be eaten in moderation.

Athletes Nutrition

Now that you've chosen to become an athlete it's up to you to be disciplined and responsible for your nutrition. This is a part of being an athlete making sure that you are fueling your body in the way that you can perform at your best. You have to eat to compete. If you're filling up on junk food you're probably going to feel fatigue sometime during the game, event or practice. Recovery is as important as participating or the game itself – maybe more important. The proper nutrients provided in the food that you eat are directly responsible in helping your body repair itself so that you can go out and continue to perform.

Part of being a good athlete is being able to recover. Food can help you recover faster. If you are a junk food eater then you are possibly promoting inflammation. We commonly think of inflammation as a reaction to trauma or infection. Inflammation can build up within the body as a reaction of inflammation producing foods. These foods include high starches, potatoes, pasta, cakes, cookies, chips, breads etc. Foods high in saturated fats like fried foods and packaged foods can as well cause an inflammatory process.

Inflammation is a process that can cause a number of symptoms within of the body. When inflammation occurs, chemicals from the body's white blood cells are released to protect us from foreign substances. Sometimes, however, the white blood cells and their inflammatory chemicals cause damage to the body's tissues. This can produce aches, pains, stiffness and a general feeling of fatigue. After an intense workout your body is attempting to repair itself and if it has to deal with excess inflammation then the recovery process will be impeded.

You will end up in a endless loop - your body constantly fighting to get rid of the inflammation that you may be causing from eating.

You end up being the hamster in the wheel - running like crazy and not getting anywhere. Many low quality foods can cause inflammation and athletes don't need to deal with inflammation. Fried foods, high sugar, packaged foods like cake, chips and other snacks. On the other hand, fruits, vegetables along with lean proteins will assist in decreasing inflammation. It's up to you to help your body help itself.

Protein vs. Carb's

We've all heard about how important 'carb loading' is before a big game or meet. Nothing can be further from the truth. This began with marathon runners. The thought was that by eating a lot of carbohydrates (pasta, bread) the night before the event the runner could store sources of sugar for the run. What people forgot about was protein.

Protein is made up of amino acids that are the building blocks for protein synthesis. Without protein muscles can't repair themselves from the intense training or activity that the athlete performs in. Glycogen is the main fuel for exercise; research has shown that muscle protein is broken down in endurance and strength training. Research has also shown that there is between a 40 to 60 minute window for increased protein production if fueled properly. That means that within that time period it is important to supply the body with between 25 to 50 grams of protein. This window allows for this protein to become assimilated by the muscle faster than normal. There is data that shows room for carbohydrate consumption within this time period as well. Approximately 20 grams of carbohydrate will allow ample storage of sugar for the muscle to store for the next time the muscles are used in a strenuous fashion.

A lack of protein can lead to decreases in strength, endurance and damage to the muscle. It is important that athletes continue to ingest the proper amount of protein to recover properly.

It's easy to suggest to a runner or swimmer that they need more carbohydrates in their diets. It's just as easy to advise strength training athletes to increase their protein in their diets because of all of the weight lifting that they are doing. Most athletes who strength train are brought up with the notion that protein is the fuel needed for extra muscle growth. For the most part there is less convincing these athletes - it's the other athletes who need to be convinced. The aerobic athlete needs as much protein as anyone else. The carbs help but that recovery starts with your muscle. When muscle tissue breaks down so does the athlete. You need protein to help in the repair of your muscles so that you can aid in your overall recovery.

Working with athletes of all levels and skills and personally experiencing breakdown from inadequate protein ingestion I feel that you need to follow these protein suggestions. According to some research current recommendations for protein ingestion is 1.2 grams per kg of body weight per day for athletes such as body builders. For endurance athletes protein consumption was listed as 1.6 grams per kilogram of body weight. Anywhere between the 1.2 and the 1.6 grams of protein per kilogram of body weight is recommended for athletes who strenuously train and compete on a regular basis. This is much different than the current RDA recommendations of 0.8 gram of protein per kilogram of body weight.

At my office we tell all of our athletes that they need to ingest bare minimum of 100 grams of protein per day. If they are working with us and their workouts get intense then we take that up to 1 to 1.5 gram per pound of body weight per day. I recommend a multi-vitamin to be added each day. The reason for this it to make sure on the days that you don't eat as well as possible that you supplement your diet for the day. Think of it as an insurance policy. Certain athletes burn calories much faster than others and free radicals can form. By adding a solid multiple mineral and vitamin supplement you can offset this potential oxidation process that can lead to cellular damage.

I'm not a fan of taking a lot of supplements. As an athlete, I feel that if you are getting 60% protein, 25% carbs, 15% fats you're getting the adequate nutrition that you need. When you train or compete at 100% then you will turn the proper systems on in the body to assimilate the nutrients needed to perform at an optimum level. The key is to vary the foods that you eat. Make sure you are getting all different types of vegetables, fruits and make sure you mix your proteins between fish, turkey, chicken, steak and eggs. Don't forget nuts and seeds along with different cheeses will round out your daily requirements for nutrients needed to fuel your body.

Many athletes take tons of supplements without really understanding what they are taking. Yes, I believe there are certain supplements that can help athletes but they need to be taken with care. Most of these supplements that are ingested will be excreted in your urine. What begins to happen is that many of these athletes end up having the most expensive urine on their team.

The Importance of Protein

Every cell in the body contains protein. These cells that contain protein are in a continuous state of break down to support all of the tissues of your body. The body needs to replace these proteins to maintain proper balance.

In order for your muscles to recover properly you need to ingest amino acids. Amino acids are the building blocks of protein. Protein is what the muscles need to build or re-build when they've been damage or weakened.

When recovering from an injury it is extremely important that the muscles have the proper source of nutrition to rebuild. Protein has been scientifically shown to be the best nutritional source to facilitate healing.

When muscles are over used they begin to break down. Unlike carbohydrates and fats, proteins do not get stored in the body as a source of energy. That is why it is so important that you get the proper amount of protein in your daily diet.

Keep in mind that it is also important to ingest carbohydrates in the form of vegetables and fruits. Try to stay away from "whites"…bread, pasta, cakes, candies etc…

It also important that you take in adequate amounts of fat as well. The fat that you ingest should be the "good" fats such as extra virgin olive oil, fish oils, nuts, and seeds to name a few. The fact is: we all need fats; fats help nutrient absorption, nerve transmission, maintaining cell membrane integrity.

What is protein?

Protein is one of the basic building blocks of the human body, being about 16% of our total body weight. Muscle, hair, skin, and connective tissue are mainly made up of protein – however, protein plays a major role in **all** of the cells and most of the fluids in our bodies. In addition, many our bodies' important chemicals - enzymes, hormones, neurotransmitters, and even our DNA - are at least partially made up of protein. Although our bodies are good at "recycling" protein, we use up protein constantly, so it is important to continually replace it.

Proteins are made up of smaller units called amino acids. There are nine amino acids that our bodies cannot manufacture, so it is important to include all these amino acids in our diets. Animal proteins such as meat, eggs, and dairy products have all the amino acids, and many plants have some of them.

How much protein do we need?

Our protein needs depend on our age, size, and activity level. We recommend that you take one gram of protein for each pound that you weigh. This number that you come up with should be taken daily and spread out over all of your meals and snacks. It is recommended that you eat four to five times per day rather than three large meals per day. This will keep your blood sugar in a normal range and will be easier on your digestive system.

Shortcut: An ounce of meat or fish has approximately 7 grams of protein.

Foods High in Protein

The following examples are estimates. If you feel that you need to be more exact with your protein intake feel free to do more investigation on your own.

Beef
- Hamburger patty, 4 oz – 28 grams protein
- Steak, 6 oz – 42 grams

- Most cuts of beef – 7 grams of protein per ounce

Chicken
- Chicken breast, 3.5 oz - 30 grams protein
- Chicken thigh – 10 grams (for average size)
- Drumstick – 11 grams
- Wing – 6 grams
- Chicken meat, cooked, 4 oz – 35 grams

Fish
- Most fish filets or steaks are about 22 grams of protein for 3 ½ oz (100 grams) of cooked fish, or 6 grams per ounce
- Tuna, 6 oz can - 40 grams of protein

Pork
- Pork chop, average - 22 grams protein
- Pork loin or tenderloin, 4 oz – 29 grams
- Ham, 3 oz serving – 19 grams
- Ground pork, 1 oz raw – 5 grams; 3 oz cooked – 22 grams
- Bacon, 1 slice – 3 grams
- Canadian-style bacon (back bacon), slice – 5 – 6 grams

Eggs and Dairy
- Egg, large - 7 grams protein
- Milk, 1 cup - 8 grams
- Cottage cheese, ½ cup - 15 grams
- Yogurt, 1 cup – usually 8-12 grams, check label
- Soft cheeses (Mozzarella, Brie, Camembert) – 6 grams per oz
- Medium cheeses (Cheddar, Swiss) – 7 or 8 grams per oz
- Hard cheeses (Parmesan) – 10 grams per oz

Beans & Soy
- Tofu, ½ cup 20 grams protein
- Tofu, 1 oz, 2.3 grams
- Soy milk, 1 cup - 6 -10 grams

- Most beans (black, pinto, lentils, etc) about 7-10 grams protein per half cup of cooked beans
- Soy beans, ½ cup cooked – 14 grams protein
- Split peas, ½ cup cooked – 8 grams

Nuts and Seeds
- Peanut butter, 2 Tablespoons - 8 grams protein
- Almonds, ¼ cup – 8 grams
- Peanuts, ¼ cup – 9 grams
- Cashews, ¼ cup – 5 grams
- Pecans, ¼ cup – 2.5 grams
- Sunflower seeds, ¼ cup – 6 grams
- Pumpkin seeds, ¼ cup – 19 grams

Advanced Nutrition

This is probably one of the more complex areas of an athlete's life. Figuring out what to eat, when to eat, how to eat, and where to eat to get the correct nutrition to fuel your body for competition.

It doesn't have to be that difficult. If you take some common sense approach to understanding how your body works, you will find the perfect remedy to give yourself enough power and a chance to recover properly so you can compete. There are many specialized protocols or programs out there that promote advanced nutrition techniques. If you stay within the rationale of physics and biochemistry, your body will give you everything that you need as long as you're able to symbiotically work with the other laws of nature. Nutrition by itself is just one part of the equation of being an athlete – but it is a very important part of being an athlete.

The body is one dynamic living organism and it's not just one thing that makes it work properly. The right combination of rest, recovery strategies, and mental strategies which are needed to make the athlete optimize their performance – but it's it's the nutrition that pulls all fo these areas together.

Here is a trick that I use with a lot of athletes that has been proven time and time again to pick out the foods that are right for you to excel in sports.

I developed this after working with two different athletes; one a high-level professional athlete and the other was a high school track athlete. This track athlete came to me for an incidental injury that I was treating and the mother was asking me various questions about her daughter's performance. The mother went on to tell me that she wanted a special diet because the girl was about to enter the district championship meet in a week and a half. She wanted her on a special diet to give her more energy so she could place higher in her events. I asked the mother what she normally ate during the week and she told me that she ate anything she wanted, including chicken fingers, pizza, salads, ice cream.

I told her with a week and a half to go, leave her eating habits alone. If she's been doing well to this point there is no reason to change here this late in the season. If you change this type of diet this close to competition, the bodies will go through a fundamental shift that could affect her outcome. At this point in the competition stage you do not want to be making that change.

The mother was a little bit taken aback with me, but I explained to her that you have to use common sense in this case. It's too late to change what got her there, because obviously this food is not what's been running her down. We can show her in the future we can make her body work a lot more efficiently with better choices of food.

After the championship was over and the girl did well, we had her change her diet and we began training her for the future. I explained the basics of nutrition - getting good lean meats, high non-starch carbohydrates, and good quality fats in her diet. I did go on to explain the difference between the good fats, for example coming from avocados, as opposed to chicken wings. Carbohydrates in the case of fruits and vegetables eat as many. You want and as often as you want. As far as carbohydrates go - stay away from donuts, ice cream, the sugars, the cakes, the pies and you can have some pastas, rice, and things of that nature as long as you're trying to move as many vegetables and fruits as possible.

263

I gave them a thing to do which cost them approximately ninety-nine cents. I had them go out and buy a small notebook. I had her write down everything that she ate for breakfast, lunch, dinner and including snacks. I wanted her to keep that for 30 days and at the end of each day I asked her to write at the bottom one word: Poor, good, or excellent, and that represented how she felt at the end of each day. It didn't matter if it was directly related to food or just how she felt in general - to write that word at the bottom of the page.

At the end of 30 days I had the girl go back and circle all of the excellent days that she had. We repeated the same thing for the next 30 days. At the end of that second 30-day trial, she circled the excellent days. We were then able to pull out all of the appropriate foods corresponding to those days that showed repetitively over that two-month period. It seems that these foods - on a regular basis, gave this girl more energy and sustained her endurance for longer periods of time. I told them to build around that type of information and you will always know the best nutritional program that's best for her and not for others.

Hydration

Here is another part under nutrition that is misunderstood as well. Most athletes I see begin to hydrate when they get tired and thirsty - well too late to help then during intense competition.

- Humans can survive 4 times longer with water as compared to food
- Muscular Tissue is Approximately 75%
- The Average Person Needs Between 2 and 2.5 Liters of Water Per Day
- Endurance Athletes Need at 4 Hours at 70% VO2 Max – 11 to 15 Liters

It's important to know the facts about how important proper hydration is. During workouts or competition a 2 to 6 % loss of body fluid weight is not uncommon. To break this down a 200 pound athlete can lose 10 pounds in a 2 hour football practice. You just don't lose water; you lose important electrolytes that supply the muscles the nutrients needed to perform properly. Loss of calcium, potassium, magnesium and chloride are minerals that are lost.

What many people don't understand is that thirst isn't the main indicator of the need for fluid replacement. Obviously the more sun exposure and the higher the humidity the more fluids are needed. Studies have shown that colder volumes of fluid empty into the stomach quicker and are more readily absorbed by the small intestine. That is the key - quick absorption of the fluid into the body so it can replace what was lost.

You need to hydrate the day before you compete or workout. The key is to always supply your cells and tissues with enough water to allow your body to carry out its proper chemical reactions. This allows the body to help you use each and every system in your body without any problems. The time to hydrate is 24 hours before your competition or workouts. Attempting to hydrate when you are thirsty is too late. A 2% loss of one's body weight has been linked to a drop in blood volume. This causes the heart to work harder to move the blood causing an increase in your blood pressure. This can cause muscle cramps, fatigue, and dizziness.

50 ounces of water on a daily basis is necessary for proper hydration. If you are working out in hot humid weather exceeding 90 degrees and 90% humidity, you may want to double that intake to make sure you are properly hydrated. If the weather is above 85 degrees with high humidity it is a good idea to weigh yourself after each workout. This will let you know if you are dropping too much water weight after your exercise.

Dehydration

Dehydration is a state in which the body loses too much of is fluid reserve. It doesn't have enough water and electrolytes to maintain proper balance within the body. It is caused by a continual loss of fluid and not taking in enough to replace the fluids lost.

Symptoms of dehydration:

- Dark Yellow Urine
- Strong Smelling Urine

- Rapid Resting Heart Rate
- Muscle Cramping or Muscle Tightness
- Thirst
- Headache, Dizziness, Overall Discomfort
- Lethargy and Chills

Dehydration is a serious situation and can lead to more complications if not attended to properly. Symptoms such as body cramping, heart conditions, kidney complications, unconsciousness and in rare occasions, death. If your urine is grey or clear in color then it is a good sign that you are properly hydrated. If you continue to see bright yellow or yellow then there is a good chance that you are not getting adequate amounts of fluids.

Coffee, tea, soda, juice DO NOT COUNT as far as properly replacing your water. You need WATER....and you need it 24 hours before exercise or competition. Sports drinks such as Gatorade or PowerAde will help in replacing electrolytes and carbohydrates. But you need to drink 3 servings of water for every serving of one of these type of drinks.

Water or Sports Drinks

There has been a ton of controversy concerning what is better water or sports drinks such as Gatorade, PowerAde and Accelerade and others. These drinks were developed to replace electrolytes, carbohydrates and other nutrients when working out in strenuous or hot conditions. The loss of electrolytes can lead to fatigue or dehydration during strenuous exercise or competition.

There is no real direct evidence that sports drink help hydrate better than water during normal conditions in sports. The average person doesn't work out hard enough to worry about consuming large amounts of sports drinks. Sports drinks will help when the weather is humid and hot and the exercise or competition continues on for longer than expected. The carbohydrates along with some minerals can help the body recover a little better in extreme conditions. With some kids due to the sweet taste they will ingest more of the sports drink which leads to better hydration.

To properly prepare for competition or workouts begin to hydrate the day before. You will only need water to properly hydrate throughout the day. Pre-competition you should be drinking 2 to 3 hours before hand. Make sure you experiment with this so that you can time you bathroom urges. If the weather conditions are not optimum then drinking any of the sports drinks can help. The sports drinks will add some electrolytes along with carbohydrates needed in case you've lost more than normal salt or calcium intake (along with other electrolytes).

Rules you can work with:

1) Weigh yourself before and after exercise
2) More than a 2% loss of weight needs to be attended to
3) Drink 20 to 24 ounces of water for every 1 lb. lost
4) Drink 10 ounces every 30 minutes during exercise (as best time allows)
5) Maintain on 50 ounces of water per day
6) One sports drink to three water drinks (12-15 oz of water)

Sports drinks are good if used in the proper way. Don't think that drinking sports drinks a regular basis is good. The typical Gatorade has just about as much sugar in it as a coke. If working out in hot conditions it's good to supplement your body with a Gatorade or other sports drink. To drink them on a daily or hourly basis is not something that I would recommend. Get in the habit of drinking water to keep as hydrated as possible.

If the weather is hot or humid I feel that you need one bottle of sports drink for every two bottles of water. Other than that your daily consumption of water should be 50 ounces. I will say it again and again, it more important to hydrate yourself on a daily basis than trying to hydrate yourself once you start sweating. By getting in a daily routine of drinking water you will optimize your current workouts and recovery.

Energy Drinks

I was blown away when I was doing some work for a local hockey club when I walked into the locker room and witnessed case upon case of Red Bull stacked from floor to ceiling. I asked one of the players about it and he said, "that something we can't get along without, 'ey." Players drank this stuff incessantly before the game, in between periods, and sometimes even after the game. They wanted the feeling of "being on top of their game." After the shock wore off my face I asked my friend if he knew what they were doing to their bodies. He said the doctor on the team said it was harmless if you only drink it once in awhile.

Energy drinks are typically attractive to young people. Approximately 65% percent of its drinkers are between the ages of 13 and 35 years old, with males being approximately 65% of the market. (Mintel - Energy Drink Report 2006, 07.05.06)

A regular 12-ounce can of Coke or Pepsi has about 35 milligrams of caffeine, and a 6-ounce cup of brewed coffee has 80 to 150 milligrams of caffeine. Here is where lack of education can really harm individuals. Energy drinks such as Red Bull, Monster, 180, 5-Hour Energy and others are loaded with caffeine and other ingredients that have shown to have adverse affect with some people.

Based on an article written by Tara Parker-Pope of the New York Times, state that some energy drinks contain the caffeine equivalent of 14 cans of Coca-Cola, said Roland Griffiths, a professor of behavioral biology and one of the study authors. "Yet the caffeine amounts are often unlabeled, and few include warnings about the potential health risks of caffeine intoxication," he said.

Dr. Griffiths notes that caffeine intoxication is a recognized clinical syndrome included in the Diagnostic and Statistical Manual of Mental Disorders and the World Health Organization's International Classification of Diseases. It is marked by nervousness, anxiety, restlessness, insomnia, gastrointestinal upset, tremors, rapid heartbeats, restlessness and pacing, and in rare cases, even death.

Ms. Parker-Pope's article goes on to say, that in a 2007 survey of 496 college students, 51 percent reported consuming at least one energy drink during the last month. Of these energy drink users, 29 percent reported "weekly jolt and crash episodes," and 19 percent reported heart palpitations from drinking energy drinks, the report stated. This same survey found that 27 percent of the students said they mixed energy drinks and alcohol at least once in the past month.

Many people have come to confuse these drinks with electrolyte replacement drinks. Energy drinks do not provide electrolytes to help any athlete recover from strenuous exercise. Conversely, caffeine on the other hand is a known diuretic and the high amounts that are in these energy drinks can excrete water from the body to dilute high concentrations of sugar entering the blood stream, leading to dehydration.

According to Washington Interscholastic Nutrition Forum for coaches 2009:

- Energy drinks are fueled by caffeine and sugar
- Energy drinks are often not well labeled (5-500 mg caffeine)
- No research has been done to know how other "energy" ingredients react with caffeine or the effect they have on the liver and other organs
- Ingredients contained in energy drinks are not tested on kids so the effect of the interaction of ingredients is not known

Sports drinks provide electrolytes and a high concentration of carbohydrates which are beneficial for the athlete's body and performance. Energy drinks do not provide electrolytes, and have a higher likelihood of an energy "crash-and-burn" effect. Caffeine in energy drinks can excrete water from the body which can lead to dehydration. If the body is dehydrated by 1%, performance is decreased by up to 10%.

A 2006 study by Dr. Joel Stager of Indiana State University (Stager et al, *IJSN*; 2006) classifies chocolate milk as a recovery drink.

- In the study, nine male cyclists rode until their muscles were depleted of energy; they then rested four hours and biked again until exhaustion. During the rest period, different groups of cyclists drank low-fat chocolate milk, Gatorade or Endurox.

- During a second round of exercise, the cyclists who drank the chocolate milk were able to bike about 50% longer than those who drank Endurox; and about as long as those who drank the Gatorade.

Chocolate milk proved to be more effective than Endurox in allowing athletes to recover for their next performance period.

Listed from Wikipedia here is a comparison of caffeine in the various drinks:

Drink	mg/fl oz.
Coffee (Brewed)	7-16 (varies)
Coco-Cola Classic	2.875
Tea	5-6.33 (varies)
5-Hour Energy	40
Red Bull	9.64
Jolt Endurance Shots	75
Full Throttle	9
MP Max One Blast	59.15
NOS	16.24
Rip It	12.25

At this point there are no restrictions on energy drinks. Many other countries have taken action against these drinks. Deaths recently linked to energy drinks, has caused some countries to restrict and or completely ban the use of these popular beverages. Countries that have banned energy drinks include Norway, Turkey, France and Norway to name a few.

Chapter 11

Steroids, Drugs & Alcohol

F ew athletes and parents understand the topic of steroids. Everyone thought they were an expert in the area of steroids but they had little or no background of the subject. Most people have no clue about what steroids are or what they can do to you. Steroids or performance enhancing drugs are designed to boost your metabolic system, mainly the muscles, to help you gain strength, endurance and recovery.

Steroids are a medication that were designed to help patients suffering from various illnesses ranging from Arthritis, Sarcoidosis, Psoriasis, Herniated Spinal Discs, Eye conditions, and many other conditions.

Steroids were invented in the 1930s to treat a condition by the name of hypogonadism. This was a condition of young males who didn't produce enough testosterone. The steroid used showed success in treating this condition and used today. Various steroids are used for many different type of illnesses including herniated disc disease, Sarcoidosis, Muscular Dystrophies and others. They found that this compound increased the size of muscular tissue. This became the drug used by certain athletes to help their performance. Over time they found that as they continued to use it they experienced strength gains, muscle mass increase and were able to recover faster. As time evolved, this drug was developed to help suffering patients from various disease states. It began to be experimented with athletes to enhance athletic performance. It became illegal not by prescription but illegal without a doctor's note.

According to Steroid.com a physician named Dr. John Ziegler in 1954 attended the World Weightlifting Championships in Vienna, Austria, as the team's doctor. The Soviets dominated the competition that year, easily breaking several world records and winning gold medals in legions of weight classes. Ziegler invited the Soviet's team doctor to a bar and the doctor told him that that his lifters had used testosterone injections as part of their training programs. Americans returned from the World Championships that year and immediately began their efforts to defeat the Soviets using pharmaceutical enhancement. When they returned to the United States, the team doctor began administering straight testosterone to his weightlifters. He also got involved with Ciba, the large pharmaceutical firm and attempted to synthesize a substance with strength enhancing effects comparable or better than testosterone s. In 1956, <u>Methandrostenolone</u> was created, and given the name "Dianabol". What happened was people who began taking it saw immediate results in their physiques. The theory of "if an inch is good - than a mile will be better" came to be the norm. Athletes began to experiment by taking more and more. With trial and error they found the precise way of increasing muscle, strength, speed and recovery.

Steroids have been abused throughout the years - which is why they have such serious potential harmful side effects. Most of these chemicals are taken way past their prescription instructions.

Using steroids is a complex balance of chemistry usage. Most kids getting into the use of these illegal drugs have no idea of what or how to use them. They also have no idea where they are coming from as far as their production goes.

Enter Prohormones…..

Prohormone is a hormone precursor. Normally having minimal hormonal effect by itself the conversion from prohormone to hormone requires many different enzymes to be affective. At one point they were legal so many of the athletes began to use them because they were not on the banned list.

When the game of baseball was going downhill - enter Mark McGuire and Sammy Sosa the two long ball hitters, who saved the game of baseball. Both of these guys had a daily slug fest single-handedly brought the fans back to the ball park saving the game of baseball. Prior to this, the game of baseball was dead. A previous strike sent fans running from the sport while football began taking over as America's past time. As the race between these two players heated up a sports reporter discovered a bottle of Androstendione (known as Andro) in his locker. Androstendione is a prohormone but was instantly linked to steroids.

The hypocritical part of this is that everyone in baseball knew players were taking some type of performance enhancing drugs. The players knew it, the managers knew it, the union knew it, the owners knew it and no one said a word because they needed the inflated stats to bring the people back in to the ball parks. The NFL had taken over as America's game and they needed help getting people back in the stands. But now, everyone in baseball management is turning on the players like no one knew anything.

The FDA has moved to halt all sales of Androstendione as a dietary supplement and listed it as a muscle enhancer. The new definition under the FDA is that anabolic steroid means any drug or hormonal substance, chemically and pharmacological related to testosterone other than estrogens, proteins, corticosteroids, and dehydroepiandrostrerone. (United States Congressional records)

Why would anyone want to take them? For most athletes it is the completive edge - for others it is an egotistical vanity that allows the person to become bigger and bigger. But the facts remain the same – steroid abuse in on the rise.

I personally polled young athletes in my office with ages ranging from 14 to 21. I asked them if they knew that by taking steroids it would improve their overall performance in sports and given the chance to take steroid knowing that they were illegal would you take them?

74% Yes   26% No

Quite honestly I was taken aback by their answers. But it seemed to me that the overall feeling was that they didn't feel that the steroids could hurt them. It's my two cent opinion that because they can't see the damage they don't think there is a possible risk. In other words, if you come upon a patient suffering with cancer you can see the terrible effects this disease can have on the body. With steroids, the kids only see the other kids getting bigger, stronger and faster. In their mind they can't see the harm so therefore it's worth the risk.

Once limited to body building fanatics and professional athletes the use of steroids have trickled down to our youth. Young athletes at the age of 12 to 14 are beginning to use steroids to help them compete at a higher more competitive level in sports. This is a disturbing problem because of increased abuse over the years, and the ready availability of steroids and steroid-related products. People are surprised to find out that there are "knock off" steroids being sold to your kids. The profits in these illegal drugs are so high that people have been known to make it themselves or purchase it from tainted sources in Mexico and other places.

The National Institute on Drug Abuse (NIDA) estimates that more than a half million 8th - 10th grade students are using these dangerous drugs - and increasing numbers of high school seniors don't believe steroids are risky. Another study indicated that 1,084,000 Americans, or 0.5 percent of the adult population, said that they had used anabolic steroids.

Steroid use is far from declining. Among 12th graders surveyed in 2000, 2.5% reported using steroids at least once in their lives, while in 2004 the number was 3.4%. Anabolic steroids are produced synthetically and mimic the affect of naturally occurring male testosterone in the body. Testosterone is part of the endocrine system of the body that is secreted by the testes in males and the ovaries in females - and to a lesser degree from the adrenal glands.

The adult male produces conservatively forty to sixty times more testosterone as compared to his female counterpart. Females however are much more sensitive to the hormone.

These drugs are androgenic (promotion masculine characteristics) and anabolic (tissue building) steroids.

- Anabolic Effects:
    o Increased Muscle Mass

- o Increased Strength
- o Increased Bone Density and Bone Strength
- Androgenic Effects:
  - o Development of the Sex Organs
  - o Deeping of the Voice
  - o Growth of Beard and Body Hair

The problem when it comes down to our youth using these drugs is abuse. When a medical doctor prescribes a drug he/she has been properly educated in the use, dosage and side effects of the drug. The prescription is used for a specific response to a specific diagnosis. Kids just pick and stick and inject what they think is good for them. Where did they get their education from? They get it from the person selling them the drug. The drugs they are using are: Deca-Durabolin, Durabolin, Equipoise, Winstrol, Anadrol, Oxandrin, Dianabol, Depo-Testosterone, Equipoise and others. Street names vary but here are a few that you may hear or see in your kids conversations. Common names go as roids, gym candy, Arnolds, pumpers, stackers, weight trainers, sauce or juice.

Are there any long term health risks on using these drugs? There isn't enough peer-reviewed literature to state that steroids can cause death or long term injury. The evidence presently is anecdotal and on both sides of the issue there is no definitive proof that death or other harm can come from the use of steroids. Keep in mind that the current studies only point to healthy adult males. There is no evidence or studies linked to children - either male or female - use of steroids.

Popular <u>Steroids</u> – Parents, get to know the names of these drugs because I feel the more you know the better off you are in preventing your child from getting involved in the use of them.

- <u>Anadrol 50 (oxymetholone)</u>
- <u>Anadur (nandrolone hexylphenylpropionate)</u>
- <u>Anavar (oxandrolone)</u>
- <u>AndroGel (transdermal testosterone)</u>
- <u>Arimidex (anastrozole)</u>
- <u>Aromasin (exemestane)</u>
- <u>Clenbuterol</u>

- Clomid (clomiphene citrate)
- Cytomel (liothyronine sodium)
- Deca Durabolin (nandrolone decanoate)
- Dianabol / D-bol (methandrostenolone)
- Dynabolan (nandrolone undecanoate)
- Ephedrine Hydrochloride
- EPO (erythropoietin)
- Equipoise (boldenone undecylenate)
- Finaplix (trenbolone acetate)
- Halotestin (fluoxymesterone)
- Human Growth Hormone HGH (somatotropin)
- Insulin
- Letrozole (femara)
- Masteron (drostanolone propionate)
- Nilevar (norethandrolone)
- Nolvadex (tamoxifen citrate)
- Omnadren
- Primobolan (methenolone acetate)
- Testosterone Enanthate
- Sten
- Sustanon 250
- Teslac (testolactone)
- Testosterone CHP
- Testosterone Cypionate
- Testosterone Propionate
- Testosterone Suspension
- Testoviron
- Trenbolone Enanthate (Trenbolone Base + Enanthate Ester)
- Tri Trenabol
- Winstrol (stanozolol)
- Pituitary Growth Hormone (pGH)
- The Clear
- The Cream

Raising Elite Athletes*

Parents Learn What Is Going On

Learn as much as you can about what your kids are doing. It's worth the time to make sure you know what they are involved in and who they are involved with. The family unit as we once knew is has changed. You need to understand that the country that you grew up in has changed in more ways than you think. Teenagers and children younger than teenagers are subjected to drugs and alcohol at an unprecedented rate.

According to Carmen Ambrosino in his book, "The Parent Handbook on Drug and Alcohol Abuse," the statistics on teenage are rising.

- The age of experimentation has gone from 17 to 11 years of age, and the average drug user is experimenting with or using multiple drugs.
- One out of every 18 (6th) graders in the U.S. experiments with marijuana, yet, one in every 6 seventh (7th) graders admits to experimenting with marijuana.
- Oxycotin, a prescription narcotic, is on the increase nationally among 10th, 11th, and 12th graders.
- Inhalant use among 8th graders has increased nationally.
- Use of Ecstasy (MDMA), a club drug, increased nationally among 10th – 12th graders.
- There is an increase in the use of anabolic steroids among 8th – 10th graders, primarily among boys.
- Alcohol kills 61/2 times more teenagers than all other illicit drugs.

Besides the type of drugs that we are all used to hearing about there are other drugs that you should be aware of. These drugs are known as Performance Enhancing Drugs, (PED's) and it is estimated that over 1 million teenagers in the U.S. have used steroids and other substances to improve their performance. PED's are more popular than you think. In a local situation when a high school hired a new football coach the use of PED's so that they could get his attention. The pressure that he brought to the school about winning at all costs

277

pushed many of the teenage players into seeking out ways of increasing their performance.

A study conducted by the Blue Cross Blue Shield Association, 81 percent of teens surveyed indicated they had never had a conversation with their parents about PED's. Performance Enhancing Drugs (PED) are listed as any substance taken to perform better athletically. Usually a term given to the use of anabolic steroids as well as human growth hormone (HGH) these drugs have been linked to many professional athletes. Unfortunately now the uses of PED's are being used by athletes in high school.

More and more young athletes that the pressures to win can sometime be overwhelming and the stress leads them to look for answers to help. Sometimes those answers end up being chemicals to lend a helping hand. The media and others have pushed the idea that not making it to the Olympics, Division I or making the pros is considered failure. This ultra competitive environment in our present day society has led to the use of anabolic steroids and other performance enhancing drugs.

Even as far down as middle school this "win at all costs mentality" has created a wide open market for the use of PED's. No matter how much the President talks about the problem the thrill of victory and the deception of size is much too alluring for some young athletes. Like many of our entitled thinking society the easy way out makes much more sense to them at that time.

Are there 'gateway' drugs that lead athletes towards the use of PED's? There is no concrete evidence to support that question however some people think that many of the supplements can lead a kid to drugs. At any health food center or pharmacy kids of any age can go in and purchase various products that claim to make you larger and stronger.

A new rage in our society is the use of Energy Drinks. The basis for the drink is caffeine which is a known stimulant. Caffeine has been linked to high blood pressure, insomnia, ulcers, heart disease, osteoporosis and infertility. The constant repetitive use of these drinks can lead to changes in the body including dehydration. For every action in the body there is a equal and opposite reaction. High doses of caffeine can alter the normal physiology of the body.

Health store supplements have shown in the past to provide adverse affects on certain athletes. Many of the supplements contain Androstendione, Ephedra and Caffeine. Ephedra also called Ma Huang in Chinese. It is a known stimulant that constricts blood vessels and has been shown to increase the heart rate along with blood pressure. Ephedra was banned in 2004 due the on-going controversy liked to various side effects including death. Be careful, look at the product ingredients listed on the side of the package. Since Ephedra was banned a substitute of bitter orange (synephrine or citrus aurantium) is being used in many "Ephedra free" products. Another product that was banned back in t 2005 was a substance known as Androstendione. This product was made famous by Mark McGuire when he was accused of taking anabolic steroids. At the time the chemical Androstendione was legal in Major League Baseball but has been subsequently termed illegal.

Other product promoting increase muscles size and increased performances are termed legal at this point are as follow:

- Creatinine
- Glutamine
- Natural Testosterone Boosters
- Anabolic Flavanoids
- Amino Acids and BCAA (branched chain amino acids)
- NO (Nitric Oxide)
- HGH (growth hormone)
- HMB

Getting It Straight From The Source

To give you a better perspective on the subject I've posed questions to a multi-year user of anabolic steroids. This person is an ex-power lifter, that we will call Tim, to protect his name because he has stopped using for years and is raising his own family today. He felt it was important to tell us the facts on what it's like using steroids and the world of steroid users from the inside out.

Conway: How many different types of steroids are there that a kid can get their hands on?

Tim: There are two types, oral and injectable. Oral steroids are consisting of Dianabol, Anadrol, and Winstrol. The injectables are testosterone, Sustanon, Winstrol, Equipose, Deca-Durabolin, Tren, and HGH (human growth hormone). These are the basic types but they consist of different types and milligrams.

Conway: What are the prices of steroids and how much do they run per month?

Tim: Price really varies by type and milligrams. The better the type and higher the milligrams the more you pay. Your oral steroids are usually the cheaper of the two. Oral steroids can run between $1.00 to $10.00 per pill. Injectables are more expensive. All of the injectables come in bottles or ampoules. An average 10 injection bottle costs anywhere from $75.00 to $150.00. When you get into the amps depending on what it is - that can cost between $15.00 to $30.00 for one. When it comes to average cost you don't figure it out by month, you figure it out by cycle. A cycle is usually three months long and it has a pyramid effect. During your cycle you increase to your high a month and a half before you wean down to end it. Not to mention oral and injectable steroids are sometimes used together during this time. A beginner's cycle can average between $300.00 to $500.00 if done right.

Conway: Where do people get steroids?

Tim: There are a few different ways to get them. The internet is where you can get the biggest variety of them. Then the obvious one is at the gym where you train. Now a days you can get them at night clubs, but honestly if you knew the right people you can get them anywhere.

Conway: How does a parent realize that their child is taking steroids......What should they look for?

Tim: Besides the newfound obsession of working out constantly, the first sign that I would say is the drastic change of attitude or personality. You may begin to see subtle changes in their personality such as talking back more than normal, anger without reason, depression or anxiety, increased anger or violence towards their siblings, obvious signs for fast muscle growth or quick breakouts of acne.

Here is another problem that most people don't fully understand. Steroids are fat soluble so that it stays in your body fat for long periods of time. There have been some sources stating that the drug can last up to two years. It has been shown to cause long term depression in kids and has been linked to suicide.

Conway: What do steroids do for an athlete?

Tim: Two main benefits that steroids offer athletes are overall strength and endurance. When using steroids an athlete's power is quite different than when he or she was clean (clean meaning not presently using steroids). The athlete can train harder and for an extended period of time. The recovery time for your muscles is also much quicker. So for many athletes steroids allow for their muscles to gain in mass and strength in a short time. It will allow for the athlete to recover much faster allowing them to work even harder in the gym. It will take a lot of the pain way from lifting or sports - allowing them to continue to practice at high levels.

Conway: Are the effects on males the same as females?

Tim: The effects are quite similar however there are a few differences. Some of the similarities are the attitude change, size and acne. Both women and men will get bigger and stronger. Yet women experience more negative changes to their appearance. For instance women experience a decrease in breast size as well as a deepening of their voice. Their facial features change which tends to give a less feminine appearance. The voice will deepen to the point it will sound like a man speaking.

Conway: What are your negative experiences from using steroids?

Tim: There are many negative experiences I have endured from the use of steroids. The mental issues that I dealt with consumed me on a daily basis. I wanted to be the biggest and strongest person in the gym. I weighed 215 pounds and bench pressing over 400 pounds. But this wasn't good enough. In my mind I was still too small. I had to do more. I knew the steroids could make me even stronger than that. This mental state caused me to push the limits when it came to steroids. Lifting and my appearance consumed my life. I would obsess over lifting and getting bigger all day long.

This abuse almost cost me my family and friends. I fell into a depression because I didn't want to quit. This led me to the abuse of alcohol. Needless to say that didn't help. This only led to more anger and further depression. My girlfriend, daughter, and friends had enough. I almost lost everything that was important to me. I had some medical issues such as frequent bloody noses and dizzy spells. I decided to see a doctor. I didn't realize how far gone I was mentally and physically. After numerous tests the doctor found my liver enzymes were off. My blood pressure was elevated and my cholesterol was high. I looked like a body builder on the outside but I was a mess on the inside. I just thank God that I was able to salvage the relationships I had. It almost ruined my life.

Conway: What are all of the things that you've witnessed observing others taking steroids?

Tim: I've seen a lot of interesting things along the way. Guys in the gym would snap out on others around them for no reason - showing rage at the smallest things. At one point they would be talking to you normally and a few minutes later they would flip out and start screaming out of control.

I've seen guys finish a crazy set of dead lifting with bloody noses from their blood pressure being so high. The problem is that it wouldn't even phase them and they would continue without even thinking about it.

I've seen a guy push himself so hard that his tricep popped out of the elbow insertion from how damaged the ligaments and tendons became. Another lifter was squatting and both of his quads tore off the bone and he had to be carried out via an ambulance.

Guys will walk around with their bodies covered in acne from head to toe. You would be amazed at how easily some of these guys would flip and start a fight, even with their own lifting partner over a simple comment. This is just some of the interesting stuff I have seen.

Conway: Can you explain how an experienced person goes through their month using different performance enhancing chemicals?

Tim: The first thing you have to do is make sure your cycle has been set up with all the steroids you are going to stack together. Next, you get a calendar and mark the days with what steroids you will be taking and the milligrams. I used to mix insulin with one of the steroid compounds to accelerate the steroid in my system. With this, you have to be extremely careful because if you screw up it can cost you dearly.

One of the most important things is that you have all the end of cycle substances you will need in order to keep the muscle you put on. This is your Clomid and HCG. This calendar is the guide to your cycle. You must also keep track of your workouts and your weight. You are looking to see your progress throughout your cycle. Another important thing is your protein and carb intake. The goal is to keep the muscle lean and tight.

To get a accelerated effect to my steroid use I would add a specific amount of insulin into a mixture. It would drastically increase the effectiveness of the drug. You have to be really careful when using this combination because it can have some serious side effects.

Conway: How can I tell if someone on my child's team is taking steroids? What are the signs?

Tim: One of the first things to look for is a change in size. Many people when abusing steroids will begin to take on a large physique fast. So one day you see them and then you see them in about two weeks or so and you noticed that they've really gotten larger. Not seeing someone every day makes the size difference more pronounced.

Then comes the attitude change. The kid may go from a normal everyday athlete to a completely out of hand competitor that is overly aggressive. This aggressiveness will show as snapping at a normal question, talking back on a regular basis, abusing or tormenting siblings, fighting in school or other discipline actions in school.

Also look for how their attitude changes towards the other athletes and or coaches. You may begin to see them talking bad about someone just out of the blue. A week ago he was ok with them and now he is talking them down.

Conway: What about all of the supplements on the market being sold in health and food stores, do they do anything?

Tim: Taking the right supplements with the right diet and workout can help. But the thing is anymore there is a fine line between the two. You might find something at the health food store and then it's gone because the FDA found some type of anabolic pre-cursor in it.

Some other supplements are just a joke. They claim all this success with building muscle and after you spend hundreds of dollars you find out that it didn't work. They give a child the wrong impression because they put a body builder who has been taking illegal steroids (roidhead) on the label who swears by this product and insists this product is what makes them look the way they do. The problem is that they don't take the supplement....they take illegal steroids.

Conway: What are all of the things that kids don't know about steroids but no one ever tells them?

Tim: The problem is that most of the kids' educations is going to come from someone in the gym. That person as well was educated by someone else in the gym. Don't get me wrong there are some people (like me) who know what they are doing. Most people don't know what they are doing and that's where it gets dangerous.

To use them properly you have to cycle properly. That means there are specific days that you use and then you come off of them for a period of time. If you just "dabble" at this you can make mistakes and it can potentially hurt you.

No one ever tells you what you need to do to come off of a cycle the right way so your body doesn't go through shock. People don't realize how bad it screws with the endocrine system.

Kids don't understand the long term effects and the problems you will have when you are older. They aren't thinking about how down the road they may have to deal with depression, mood swings, and some physical problems. Everything that seems too good to be true is. On the outside you may look healthy and big, but on the inside you're a mess. Anyone that has used them usually finds out the hard way.

Alcohol

A major problem facing out teens today is the use of alcohol at such an early age. Children are being exposed to alcohol at earlier ages and parent need to know this fact. Athletes need to know how alcohol can disrupt your athletic performance and career. Most kids polled think that using alcohol is not a drug and that its just a recreational way of having fun without getting hurt. You need to know the facts if you are using or have used in the past.

According to Dr. Gary Wadler, a New York University School of Medicine professor and lead author of the book "Drugs and the Athlete," the detrimental effects of alcohol on performance are extremely well documented and include impairment of the following:

- Balance and steadiness
- Reaction time
- Fine and complex motor skills
- Information processing
- Boisterousness, unsteadiness, slurred speech
- Nausea, vomiting, marked unsteadiness, drowsiness

"Additionally, alcohol may impair temperature regulation during prolonged exercise in the cold, and in the heat, its diuretic effect may lead to dehydration," says Wadler. "Poorly appreciated is the fact that athletes who socially consume excessive alcohol the evening after a practice or a game may subsequently have an impairment of athletic skills for as long as 14 hours." Hangovers, the residual or "day-after" effect of alcoholic consumption, can result in symptoms of headaches, nausea, diarrhea, fatigue, dehydration, and body aches that can diminish athletic performance.

What are the long term adverse effects of alcohol?

The chronic abuse of alcohol may cause numerous adverse health effects which include:

- Chronic alteration of brain and nerve function
- Weakening of heart muscle
- Testicular shrinkage and male breast enlargement
- Impotency
- Elevated triglycerides
- Fat deposits in the liver
- Cirrhosis and liver failure
- Blood-clotting abnormalities
- Pancreatitis
- Vitamin deficiencies
- Chronic skin alterations
- Death

How is the degree of alcohol use categorized?

The Fourth Edition of the Diagnostic and Statistical Manual of Mental Disorders (DSM-IV) published by the American Psychiatric Association divides alcohol use disorders into "Alcohol Dependence" and "Alcohol Abuse." Alcohol dependence is indicated by evidence of tolerance and/or symptoms of withdrawal such as delirium tremens (DTs) or alcohol withdrawal seizures upon cessation of drinking. Alcohol abuse is characterized by recurrent performance problems at school or on the job that result either from the after-effects of drinking alcohol or from actual intoxication. In addition, patients with alcohol abuse disorders may use alcohol in dangerous circumstances -- e.g., while driving - and may miss work or school, neglect child care, or household responsibilities because of alcohol use.

Interview With A Drug & Alcohol Rehabilitation Expert

To help Parents better understand the problems facing out families with drugs and alcohol I've interviewed Mr. Carmon Ambrosino CEO of the Wyoming Valley Alcohol and Drug Services.

Mr. Ambrosino in known throughout the country for his ground breaking work in the field of Alcohol and Drug rehabilitation. Employed by Wyoming Valley Alcohol and Drug Services, Inc .since June 1, 1973, and became Chief Executive Officer in 1974. Presented over 2,600 presentations on chemical dependency during 34-year career was selected as community delegate for 1997 Presidential Summit, Philadelphia, for contributions and service to community.

Mr. Ambrosino is the author of an award-winning role-play presentation entitled, "A Family in Conflict", which has been presented to over 250 groups in Pennsylvania and New York and was awarded a National MARKIE Award for excellence in alcoholism communication. Former board member of National Certification Reciprocity Consortium (N.C.R.C.) representing Pennsylvania and Chairman of the Mid-Atlantic Region of N.C.R.C.

Mr. Ambrosino developed innovative forty-five (45) hour graduate course for educators on early detection, identification of high risk behavior children, intervention/confrontation techniques, co-dependency, ACOA, etc. Program has been approved for federal and state grants due to significant impact – Wilkes University, Wilkes-Barre, Pennsylvania.

Conway: Why do you think certain athletes take drugs?

Ambrosino: I believe that it boils down to seven areas that I talk about when teach seminars to parents, coaches, teachers and others.

1) We live in a culture that people feel a pressure or we need to win at whatever the costs. So winning is the bottom line so they are looking for the competitive edge.
2) Sometimes they lose and there are negative feelings and emotions tied or attached to that loss and they may view their own individual performance as being responsible for the team's loss. It becomes a reaction to the loss which kids clearly need

to understand that it's not about the wins and losses it about leaving everything you had out on the field.

3) The culture we're in just believes that drugs and alcohol is the cool thing to do. Years ago the peer influence was completely opposite in that it wasn't cool to do drugs. If you were doing drugs you were view as odd, weird or different. Now the view is cool amongst your peers which get is roots in the lyrics of songs, the movie themes, T. V. themes, just the general sociological culture that has glamorized drug use.

4) Often times the student athletes are coming from families that either condone the use of drugs and alcohol or they don't discourage the use through strong don't use messages. We find out that when there is a good healthy attitude that comes from families not condoning the use of drugs and alcohol we see research that show that drug use is lower in kids that come from families who don't condone the use of drugs or alcohol — and send a strong don't use message.

5) They emulate professional athletes. When you look at the number of athletes who get the headlines who are doing the drugs or alcohol there is an emulation by the younger athletes. Just as sometimes young girls chase bad boys student athletes more that often look for poor role modeling. They emulate the attributes of professional athletes.

6) The advertising claims whether it be for energy drinks, supplements or performance enhancing drugs these advertising claims are drawing the kids to them. When the kids see the ads with guys with big muscles they become enthralled. Student athletes are vulnerable, impressionable, they are easily led, they're here and now oriented so they don't see the macro picture they only see the micro picture. This is going to give me bigger muscles it's going to make me lean and make me compete better and besides everyone else is doing it so I had better start to make sure I can stay ahead.

7) Often time when an student-athlete begins to start using performance enhancing drugs has a lot to do with the people who they are hanging out with. We're attracted to peer groups

that if I'm a baseball card collector odds are many of my friends are collectors as well. A golfer – the chances that many of their friends will also be golfers. So we find out that their associations are often times with are with other student-athletes so that athletes that I delt with and when I talk to them about their peers probably some 90% of cases they always relate the story that they used together with other athletes on teams.

Those are the top seven (I'm sure there is more) that I after 37 years of working with drug related athletes have to hear about. I believe that coaches, parents and kids need to hear about the pitfalls as to where the lures are at.

Conway: Do you see a difference of drug abuse in 2010 as compared to 15 years ago?

Ambrosino: Yes, I see more honor roll students, more student athletes, more middle and higher economic children, and we also see more psychological and psychiatric implications of use because the chemicals are technological more powerful and for kids who use them are getting sick quicker. Heroin for example, is 65 to 90 % pure. 15 years ago you would never had heroin products on the street. The new technology from both the pharmaceutical labs and the street labs are making it much worse. The psych units are filled with kids that just shouldn't be.

Conway: Can an athlete become addicted to steroids?

Ambrosino: Yes. There are three areas that get athletes in trouble using steroids. Cycling, Stacking and Pyramiding.

Cycling is a process of the athlete taking multiple doses of steroids over a specific period of time. They then stop for a period of time and start again. The resistance, if you will, by taking multiple doses for months and then all of a sudden they stop and start again creates a physiological change.

Stacking is where they combine several types of steroids. An example would be where they take two or more anabolic steroids and mix an oral and injectable type of steroid and sometimes they throw in veterinary drugs like PCP into the stacking process.

Pyramiding they slowly escalate their use they reach a peek amount and then they taper off the dose so that they go up-down, up-down, up-down.

There are three types of ways of using steroids are what I see that gets athletes in trouble. Research is pointing out that there are some physiological linkages by the mere fact that many of the athletes that try to stop using the drugs aren't able to get off of them. So we have detoxified athletes who claimed that they couldn't physically get off of them. Psychologically as we know; irritability, aggression, potential for violence. There are withdrawal symptoms I might add as well from steroids which also gives rise to the physiological addiction. They include mood swings, restlessness, steroid cravings similar to other chemicals, and depression. We've seen depression up to one year after the use stopping the use of steroids.

People just don't get this – that most of these type of chemicals that are being used can stay in your system from two months up to eighteen months.

Conway: What effects can marijuana have on an athlete?

Ambrosino: I believe that marijuana is the most misunderstood drug on the market. Marijuana makes you dumber. People don't understand that effect the concentration, your memory, your thinking, judgment, your critical thinking processes are all effected. It produces a 'clouding effect' and you technically not able to differentiate between depth perception. It increases your high risk behavior. You also can develop a condition called "Anti-Motivational Syndrome" with the athletes becoming very lethargic, impaired concentration, impaired memory and inability to complete tasks that require find motor coordination and low levels of energy and loss of enthusiasm. When you look at marijuana a single joint will stay in the system up to seven to ten days. If you are using regularly it can stay in your body up to thirty days or longer. It compounds the effect of other chemicals as well. That's why this whole movement to legalize medical marijuana is something that I absolutely oppose. It sends a message that a category one drug, a schedule one drug, in the controlled substances act which is in the same classification as Heroin, LSD 25, Ecstasy. We're going to take a schedule one drug and move it to legalization for medicinal purposes - Heroin causes constipation - so why don't we start using Heroin as a substitute for Imodium?

Conway: Do you see a rise in designer drugs?

Ambrosino: That's an interesting question. There are some drugs that will rise while other less popular drugs will fall by the way side. I think that at any time when you talk about a concoction of chemicals being pulled together – and some of the steroidal drugs that we both know are listed as designer in nature. They're fashionable and years ago there were chemicals such as Chattanooga Toot Toot (Cocaine), Zoom (PCP), but now a days we don't see as many but once in awhile some kid will come in and talk about a new designer drug that is on the streets. Some of the steroid drugs have brought on the designer label because they are concoction of drugs.

Conway: Alcohol is the number one drug in the world how much of a problem is it with our youth today with underage drinking?

Ambrosino: It's been our number one problem and will continue to be out number one problem. It's a drug that they legitimize and validate. It doesn't have a drug classification in their minds. Young people don't even consider it even close to a drug. It's depressant – and if alcohol was manufactured for the first time today you would need a prescription from a medical doctor for it. That powerful that unpredictable but when I quiz young people they laugh when I link a drug with alcohol. They don't see the effects of it and think that the legal drinking age should be ten. It's the number one problem with kids and families.

I spoke to a group of parents the other night and told them that "your worst fear is the same fear I have. The loss of my child or my grandchildren, there is no greater pain in the world. But if I ask you

291

how you could lose your child you would probably tell me foreign wars, or from terrorism. I'm here to tell you that the top three killers for United States youth from age 16 to 21 are car accidents, murders and suicides. These top three killers of America's youth between the ages of 16 to 21 and the use of drugs and alcohol are responsible for 75% of death of those three classifications. So your kids are dying in the American communities and streets."

We're looking for weapons of mass destruction in the wrong place. They're drugs and alcohol there right here in the U.S. they're not in Iraq or other middle eastern country. Drugs and alcohol first destroy the individual, then the family, then the community, the state, the nation and then the world. We're losing our kids to this type of destruction not to other forms of terrorism.

Conway: Do you see young teens as alcoholics that come in for treatment?

Ambrosino: Yes. The earliest that we've ever diagnosed was a child that was 9 years old. They came from parents who were both alcoholics. We had to hire a special coordinator for adolescent therapy because we were getting so many referrals of kids under 18. We needed a way to control and monitor their treatment.

There are three legitimate schools as it pertains to the etiology or causes of alcoholism. The first school is the Physiological school which basically says that if you were born of parents who used drugs and alcohol the odds are that there is a 75% odds that the next generation will have some degree of addiction. If there are six kids, two to three of those six may well have a problem with addiction. They will have a metabolism or chemistry that predisposes them with regard to the genetics of addiction.

The second school of etiology is the Psychological. This school states that if kids have the following character defects: a very low self esteem, very easily overwhelmed, they have an inability to handle stress in their lives, they poor coping skills along with poor problem solving skills. If they possess these character defects its just a matter of time where they will be introduced to someone who will say, "here why don't you try this, this will make you feel better." These kid of kids wake up with a kind of hopelessness and will in due time pick up one of those chemicals out there.

The third school is the Sociological/Cultural and the School of Learned Behaviors. This takes in the religion, the ethnic background, environment in where they grew up plays a significant role in learned behaviors of the use of drugs and alcohol.

Conway: What do parents have to know to better help their son/daughter in sports (or in life)?

Ambrosino: The kids today are faced with a lot of unprecedented challenges that they've never been faced with before. The culture has changed the social moirés and what was once unacceptable is not acceptable. Parents need to know about the "Three P's"

The Three P's

If their kids hang around with unhealthy playmates they will be introduced to unhealthy playpens, and they will use unhealthy play things. I don't care how strong the child is. If they hang around with unhealthy playmates, they will be going to the unhealthy playpens of life and will pick unhealthy play things.

Your kids are very vulnerable, impressionable, they are pleasure seekers, they are followers, they are easily swayed or influenced, and the strongest research indicates that the stronger the family units the less apt your child will be influenced to make unhealthy choices.

The family unit research talks about them in two units - the risk factors and the protective factors. One parents need to know what the risk factors are out there that are facing their children. The protective factor is what they need to do to insulate and make their child more resilient so that they can handle any stressful situation. Moreover to deal with life's problems and feel good about whom they are as human beings.

Chapter 12

Recruiting

Attention: Parents of an upper level athletes who are being looked at to play Division I athletics - pay attention to this!

There are 20,000 high schools in the U.S. There are 120 Division I schools in the U.S. which means less than 1%, actually, 0.8% of all the athletes will be offered a Division I scholarship out of high school.

If you're thinking about the possibility of your son or daughter going pro then look again at the math. Let's just talk football for a second. There are 120 Division I football teams that have approximately 100 players on each team. When you look at all of those teams on any given Saturday afternoon, Notre Dame, USC, Alabama, LSU, Pitt, Texas, less than 3% of those players will make it to the NFL. Out of all of those players that make it those players will only last on average 3 years in the NFL.

According to Bill Pennington of the New York Times, "Excluding the glamour sports of football and basketball, the average N.C.A.A. athletic scholarship is nowhere near a full ride, amounting to $8,707. In sports like baseball or track and field, the number is routinely as Iowa's $2,000. Even when football and basketball are included, the average is $10,409. Tuition and room and board for N.C.A.A. institutions often cost between $20,000 and $50,000 a year."

Many parents are very surprised when they find out that they are only being offered a portion of the full tuition limits for the school. Women tend to receive more money than men but total money allotted is top heavy towards the men vs. the women.

The Business of Division I Sports...

Football brings in more money to the university that you think. College football generates $6 billion dollars annually. There was a 25% increase in football revenues in the last four years alone. According to Forbes magazine University of Alabama's football program had $54 million in revenue with an estimated $32 million profit. What many people don't know is that most football programs fund many of the other sports programs within the colleges and universities. At Alabama, 77% of the athletic department, bankrolls nonrevenue sports likes swimming and softball. This football popularity helps the overall presence of the school - scholastically and academically. When the football program develops more popularity it trickles down throughout the school including increased alumni donations and increase freshman applications.

Division I athletics revolve around one thing - money. The quicker you learn this, the better off you'll be. No matter what is told to you about traditions, the pageantry and the history of the schools - modern day division I sports revolves around money. It is a business and your son or daughter will be treated as such.

As your son or daughter progresses with their sports in high school slow interest will begin to develop with colleges and universities - as long as your athlete shows above average talent. That interest will usually start with the form of letters from colleges and universities. These letters will start trickling in when they are in 10th or 11th grade. The letter will outline the schools interest in the athlete and how their school will be the right fit for them to continue their studies. I like to call these 'fish' letters. Like a professional fishermen, they throw out large nets to capture all the fish swimming by at that time. As they pull their nets onboard they can separate the fish they don't want and throw the rest back in the water.

The same goes for the athletes being recruited. They send out these letters just to cover their back ends so just in case the athlete becomes someone of interest, they've made their contact and now have their foot in the door. Get ready if your son or daughter is talented - the letters will come and they will come often.

David Sills, a seventh grader who gave a verbal commitment to the University of Southern California (USC). Sills is a 13 year old quarterback playing at Red Lion Christian Academy in Pennsylvania. This is a bit unusual for football due to the physical demands of the game. In basketball it has been going on for years and there is no end in sight. In football – this doesn't happen much at all. The sad part of this is the fact that this is a verbal commitment. This commitment can be taken away by the university. This is where the parents need to be really protective of their child. We would all love to see our kids become the next Lebron James but that is an extremely remote circumstance. This is a BUSINESS and in business people can get hurt.

No matter what the coach's say about your child, no matter how much they praise you for raising such a talented athlete, no matter how much you hear - take it with as a complement and move on. The harsh reality of sports is that once you've signed the dotted line most coaches won't remember your name until you begin to produce on the field. The praise, the pat's on the back, the warm and fuzzy discussions will all disappear once you sign. They own you and the sooner you understand that the easier it will be for you. They're paying for your education, your books, your meals and your shelter. Don't think that the coaches are going to start coddling you just because they show up. You are going to work, and work hard.

We as parents love to hear good things about our kids. But you MUST consider the source - the recruiter is there to tell you what you want to hear. They are in direct competition with other schools and they are trying to get any edge possible to sign your son or daughter to their school. If you're an elite athlete the schools will find you - trust me. But if you're not the next Labron James then the process is a little different. Keep in mind at the higher end of the recruiting process the person that is sitting in front of you telling you how good your child is employed by someone else. If they don't generate the players that will produce more wins for the university they will be looking for another job in the very near future.

The Process

Contacts from colleges usually begin in the form of a letter. The letter will introduce the school and its program to you as well as their interest in your performance. As interest continues with your son or daughter contact will be by phone, email, letters and now texting along with other social media outlets are now being used to make sure they are staying out in front of the race to secure you child.

-   If you're not talking to the head coach then you're talking to one of the assistant coaches. Many times the head coach will send out one of their assistant coaches to speak with the family. Their job is to create an environment that shows you that your son or daughter is the only person on planet earth that they are interested in and they are the ones who want to be their friend.
-   It's a high pressure job because if they don't produce they can be fired. Think of your own job, if you aren't getting your job done at work there is a good chance they will find someone to replace you.

Same holds true for some of the assistant coaches. If they don't produce winners then their job will be on the line. If the assistant can't produce good players by first recruiting it makes the head coach look bad. If that happens then the head coach will instantly fire that coach for another coach who will get the job done....making the head coach look good.

It's a trickle-down theory.

"Everyone's Job In College Sports Is To Make The Head Coach Look Good."

Dr. Malcolm Conway

The assistant coaches, the secretaries, the trainers and doctors and even the person responsible for selling tickets are to make the head coach look good.

The head coach is more like an executive and as an executive's job is to make sure that others around him are getting their job done correctly. If everyone does their job properly then they should have a great chance of having winning team. So guess where the athlete fits in? Just like the people above, the athletes job is to make the head coach look good and for that they will give him a free education, room and board.

Let's take another look at the college recruiting process. There are many kids that fall through the recruiting cracks in the wall. Hopefully your high school coach helps in the process in getting your name out to all of the right schools. A good coach will gather your game highlights on video and put together a DVD to send out to as many schools as possible. From here, if coaches are really attempting to help you out, they will pick up the phone and make some phone calls on your behalf to sell you to the their program. Unless you are a bona fide superstar, the rest is marketing. You have to be seen and you need someone who they respect in your corner pushing for you.

In football for example, the major division I schools have 'war rooms' similar to what you may see on the NFL draft rooms on T.V. The higher ranked schools go after the higher ranked players. For example, the present top 10 schools like Alabama, Florida, LSU, Texas, USC, etc., will begin searching all of the top All State players from each state. They figure out what they need as far as player positions needed on their team and then see what players are available to fill that need. The lesser ranked schools will recruit based on video, scouting reports and personal contacts. Due to the heavy demands of the college coaching staffs, video is one of the more important ways of evaluation that is used.

In many cases you're going to have to take it upon yourself to get the word out. Letters of introduction, video and attending camps are some of the ways of getting your name listed with the coaches. There are online sites that will allow you to upload your film to one site. This allows the coach to go to this site to see your film. I feel this is a much easier and a more direct way of getting your film seen. The up side is that this use of the web minimizes the chance of someone losing your video in the mail or misplacing it. You give the coach the direct link to your site and he or she is instantly viewing your video.

There are only so many openings per team per year and many times the recruiting process comes down to mathematics. There are times that your sons or daughters may want to play at a particular school and it may be the year that your child's position doesn't mathematically fit the program. This particular year the college may have too many players at one position. In other words, if your son was a running back wanting to go to Ohio State the position may be filled with 3 or 4 other players.

If you are fortunate to receive a visit from a coach be prepared for the meeting. Have questions that you want answered ready to go before the coach comes to your house. The coach will be putting on his very best personality. He or she is there to tell you how wonderful your child is and how much they want you at their school. I'm not going to tell you that they are going to downright lie to you but I will say that many a story has been stretched. Just understand that it's a business and treat it as such.

Coaches that come to recruit your son or daughter will be putting on their best smiles, personalities, and come with their best prepared lines of bull crap that could make a U.S. Senator blush. They're there for one reason and one reason only – the success of their program. Your son or daughter is just part of the puzzle that gets them closer to that goal. As a part of that program you, along with the other recruited players, help them win which in time will help them advance their careers. I hate to put this so bluntly but it's the reality of college sports.

I'm not saying that all coaches are dirty scoundrels. Most of the coaches are good people but they are in a business, and as such, a parent and athlete must come to grips with this early. When it comes down to 'brass tacks,' they don't care about you unless you can improve their program. Let me say that one more time...**THEY DON'T CARE ABOUT YOU UNLESS YOU CAN IMPROVE THEIR PROGRAM.**

As a fan, you are a part of the business - you want a winner no matter how they go about it. Now it's a lot different because you are now directly behind the scenes with your child on the team and now you'll get to see how the business really works. Understand that it's a big difference from being a fan of a school to becoming a parent of an athlete playing for a school. This will probably be your first wake up call to the business of college sports.

Please Understand The Following:

College sports are built around money and if the teams don't win there will be less money coming back to the school. If there is no money there is no program. If the head coach continues to lose for long periods of time and the money starts dropping off – the coach will be looking for a new job. In some cases if the sport continues to lose and the money doesn't justify the expense they will drop the sport entirely. Syracuse University dropped a very successful women's swimming program in order to provide scholarships to a new women's hockey team.

How Do I Know If My Son/Daughter Is Getting Recruited?

You'll probably receive a letter in the mail from a college or university congratulating you on a great season. The school will lightly tell you that they have an interest in you but no real commitment on their end will be offered. The school will go on to explain how great their program and traditions are and how they feel you may be a real asset in their program. This is good but make sure you keep it all in perspective. This is one out of thousands of letters sent out by the school to capture your attention. I like to call them 'fish' letters. Just like a commercial fisherman throwing out a huge net into the sea they will then pull the net later on no matter what is in there. When they are ready they will only pull out the fish that they want and throw the rest back into the water. Well the same holds true for this example. They want to make sure that they make some kind of

300

contact with you just in case you turn out to be the next superstar coming out of high school.

BE CAREFUL: Many people get lulled to sleep thinking that because some big schools sent you letters you stop talking to the smaller schools. This can be a deadly mistake. The big schools will run faster than your 40 time and before you know it you're scrambling to find a school that wants you. **DON'T BURN YOUR BRIDGES!!!**

Once the letters start they'll keep coming week after week. The majority are 'canned' letters from the school sports program. If you receive a hand written letter and I mean a real hand written letter that shows genuine interest on their part. Keep in mind....you are still miles away from scholarship signing. If the hand written letters continue along with phone calls and in person meetings than you have a better than average chance that school will offer you a scholarship.

You may be asked to have an 'unofficial' visit to the school which is a visit to the campus at your expense. It may be to football or basketball game or just a general visit to the campus. You are still far away in the process at this point so keep everything in perspective. If schools are serious about you then they will offer you an 'official' visit to their campus at their expense. This is a great sign; in fact this is a sign to show you that they are serious about having you play for them.

The home visit especially by the head coach shows that there is serious consideration for you to attend that school. They may even offer you a scholarship right there in your house. If you are ready to commit then by all means do so, but if you are not, then don't say a work until you feel what is best for you. Stay true to yourself through this entire process and don't get caught up in the hype. Let your heart guide your though this process. Don't rely on emotion or a hard sell put on by the coach.

What Questions Do I Ask?

You have the right to ask any questions you want. Don't be rude but don't be sacred either. Before you sit down with any coach take some time and think off all the questions you want to have answered. When you do meet with the coach you will have questions on paper ready to go. In the light of college coaches changing jobs more than ever you have to ask the right questions so that you feel you will be going to the right school. Like anything else in life it all comes down to how much leverage you have.

If you are a football player and run a 4.2 40 and are the #1 recruit in the nation then you can be a lot more forward in your questions. Why, because they are drooling at the prospect of you catapulting their program up several notches.

It is always the right thing to do is always be professional. Don 't be afraid and don't be rude but get a heartfelt feeling to make sure you want to spend the next four years with this coach.

- Why are you interested in my son/daughter?
- What is your philosophy on playing freshmen?
- How many freshmen have played over the past three years?
- How many players are at my position?
- How many players are you looking at to bring in at my position?
- What do you expect from my son or daughter?
- Does your school violate the hours allotted by the NCAA for practice or meetings?
- What happens if my son/daughter gets hurt?

Now, if you're not that high up on the recruiting board then it pays to scale down the questions so you don't look over bearing. The old saying is that you can attract more bees with honey holds true here.

- Do you have any junior college transfers coming in?
- What players at my position can I learn from the most? (this will tell you how many kids are at your position without asking)
- In helping your program what do I have to do to succeed at your school?
- Are there many players on the non-travel squad at my position?

So here is how it works. The recruiter is going to tell you how great everything is in each question you pose to him. You have to get a heartfelt feeling if he/she is first, telling the truth and second he has enough character for you to attend his/her school

Pro's & Con's Of Choosing A School

Take out a piece of paper and draw a line down the center of the page and on the left top of the paper write PRO's and on the right side of the top of the paper write CON's.

- Quality of Education
- Graduation Rate
- Climate
- Facilities
- Trainers/Doctors
- Coaching Staff
- Location (how far from home)
- Playing Time
- Food Quality
- Dorm Quality
- Social Life
- Other Players
- Expense
- Campus Life
- Surrounding Town Life

Becoming Pro-Active

The first thing I feel that is important is securing video on yourself playing in games. Colleges what to see different things on film such as:

- Your Game Speed As Opposed To Timed Speed
- How Well You Play Defense
- What You Do When You Are Not In The Play (do just stand there?)
- How Do You Perform in Bad Weather

Parents: If you are taking the film make sure you do the best job possible. If your video camera is moving all over or shaking to where you can't see the game then throw it out and hire a professional. Do not follow your son/daughter only most coaches want to see the entire field of play.

Shoot from the highest point possible without distorting the video. Coaches want to see as much as the play as possible.

Remember that you should keep it to 5 minutes and under and whatever you do - <u>DO NOT</u> <u>NARRATE OR PLAY MUSIC WITH IT – NO FANCY GRAPHICS - NO VOICE OVERS</u>

Many times coaches will give you a copy of your game highlights that the schools takes for the team. This is probably the best way to send video out. If your school will make up a high quality highlight tape use it. If not you'll have to make your own. Remember coaches have to watch a ton of videos and the last thing they need is music, silly graphics or poor narration. They know what they are looking for so let them have it and don't add to it or your tape will end up in the garbage. If possible put your son/daughter vitals at the front of the tape including their height, weight, and playing number.

The latest way is to upload your video to the internet. If you are technically sound you can create your own web site. There are internet services that for a moderate fee you can load your video on to their site and then just tell the coach the web link to go to see for themselves.

I personally like this one the best because DVD's can get lost in the mail or misplaced on a coaches desk. The internet services will allow you to continue to add and update new film as the season progresses. This seems to be the most efficient way to keep the work on the coaches side as minimal as possible. It's very easy to drop the link in a letter as a reminder or if you are speaking to the coach on the phone.

Sending The Introductory Letter

An introductory letter is a letter to introduce yourself to the football staff. This is a way to let them know that you have an interest in their program and a way to introduce your video. Keep the letter short and to the point. It should included an opening paragraph explain your interest in their school and program. With today's computers you can put a picture of yourself on the letter with your name, address, sport, position, height, weight, and the particulars to your sport. For example, football, list your beat 40 meter sprint time, bench press, squat, vertical jump along with any pertinent stats that you amassed over the years. List they type of course work you are taking i.e., college prep, current GPA and class rank. List academic awards along with sports awards, organizations, extracurricular clubs, and don't be afraid to tell them about the other sports that you play. Letters of recommendation from other coaches, high school teachers, administrators or community leaders also goes a long way. DON'T include letters from Mom, Dad, sister, brother, aunt, uncle or other family members.

Depending on how early you send this you can send a copy of your transcripts as well. If they are interested they will want to get the ball rolling. They know if there interest is high on your they are going to act fast to get you to commit to them.

Here is how it works - if they are REALLY interested in you they will do what it takes for you to sign with them as soon as possible. If you are the type of athlete that they either don't know much about, or someone else was on their recruiting board before you it will take some time will play out.

Watch What You Ask For....You May Just Get It!

Tons of parents are proud of their little ones as they excel on the field or court. As each athlete continues to show improvement eventually scholarship talk begins. A common misunderstanding among most parents is the true definition of the word scholarship. Most parents don't realize that there are very few "full rides" in most college sports.

Let's take a look at baseball as an example. There are roughly a combined 400 schools between division I and division II that offer scholarships. In the 'Equivalency Sports' such as baseball the coach is instructed to divide up the allotted scholarships for their team. They get 12 scholarships for a roster of 30 in division I (only 9 for division II) so the coach has to make decisions on how to spend his/her money.

So you may be offered a half a scholarship with more scholarship money available based on your performance in the future. Another words, you produce then we'll give you more money.

In basketball it's about the same but a little different. Basketball is considered a 'head count' sport which means it can offer 'full ride' scholarships. In men's basketball there are an available 329 scholarships in division I and 290 scholarships available in division II. The numbers are about the same for women's basketball as well.

Gymnastics is about the same as baseball. The NCAA allows each division 1 gymnastics program 6.3 scholarships for men and 12 for women. In division 2 the ratio is 5.4 scholarships for men and 6 for women.

Field Hockey again is the same as well. They are allotted 12 scholarships and the coach can divide the scholarships to extend what they can offer to attract the players needed for their program. There are 77 division 1 and 26 division 2 colleges that offer field hockey scholarships. That's a total of 1,087.9 scholarships available in the NCAA.

Here is another problem that you've never probably thought about. In soccer, because it is a worldwide sport and universities recruit from all over the world. It's not good enough to be the best 'all conference' soccer player in your town because soccer across the world as if this writing is much better than U.S. Soccer. The NCAA allows each division 1 soccer program 9.9 scholarships for Men and 12 for Women. In division 2 the ratio is 9 for men and 9.9 for women. You can see that these scholarships are very watered down due to the simple fact of the numbers. By looking worldwide for recruits the scholarship money dries up pretty quickly.

Ok, so let's say that you secure a scholarship and it's off to college. Now the fun begins....right? Some athletes start at the Division I level but are overwhelmed by the total commitment that is necessary to survive in a scholarship program. The days are long, the stress is high and the commitment is daily. Even your days off are stressful because you have to check in the next day at a certain time usually early in the morning. So get ready for a very discipline lifestyle. The 16-hour days of practice, training, meetings, classes and mandatory study halls, which leave room for nothing else, not even a social life. This can be too much on some people and the stress is just too much. They end up leaving the program, giving up the scholarship to pay out of pocket for peace of mind.

This is not to scare you....more importantly to prepare you. <u>You ain't going to a country club</u> - you're going to pay back your part of the $120,000.00 education that was given to you as a scholarship. Once the honeymoon period wears off (the time right after you sign you letter of commitment to a school), prepare yourself for the worst. A lot of kids think that all of the hard work that they put in during high school will be over once they get to college. Than can't be further from the truth. Once you get to college the hard work just begins. Believe me, it's going to be a big adjustment and if you prepare yourself properly it can take a lot of stress off of you. Go in with a good attitude, do what you're told and work hard and you will have a great college experience.

The college sports environment is not for everyone. I can't tell you how many kids left my office so happy knowing that they received a college scholarship. They would never believe anyone if someone told them that in a year from now they would end up quitting because they couldn't take it anymore. Some athletes that I know gave it up because the training was too intense and others gave it up because they have been doing that sport since they were eight years or so, and find out they've just had enough. They've been doing the same thing since they were pre-teens and in their mind - enough is enough and they quit. They find out that there is another side of life in college including new friends, social life, clubs and other new interests.

Over the years parents have been known to sacrifice weekends, take time from their job, and miss vacations all in order to help their child become a better player. This includes specialty camps, travel teams, specialized training and other sport tournaments. Now that the athlete has decides to stop playing, it can be difficult for the parent to comprehend. Most parents do understand but still there are others become upset, because for many, a part of their life as ended abruptly. This can be difficult for some parents to handle.

In the recruiting process coaches are out scouring the country for fill the needs to their teams. Coaches need athletes that can handle the required demands of their sport both physically and mentally for this level of play. As I'm mentioned coaches are looking for people who can handle the rigors of their programs. They don't care about your disapproval of their workouts or meetings. They have an agenda set and you will fulfill that agenda or you will be finding your way out the door.

The work and the hours are more than demanding. Some athletes at the Division I level become overwhelmed by the total commitment that is necessary. The 16-hour days of practice, training, meetings, classes and mandatory study halls, which leave room for nothing else, not even a social life. You will give up your social life because most of your time will be centered on your sport, your studies and sleep. This can be too much on some athletes with the stress becoming just too much to handle. They end up transferring or outright leaving the program, giving up the scholarship to pay out of pocket for peace of mind.

Once you get on the field it's time to produce. If you don't produce rest assured that there is an athlete behind you that is waiting to fill your position in a New York minute. If you are unable to produce at your position you will become the lead topic of discussion at the coaches meetings. The head coach was the best athletes on the field and if you can't produce they will find someone else who can produce. In the modern day of sports it is not out of the ordinary for athletes to lose their scholarships. Some scholarships are given year to year and if they feel that you can't produce they will take their scholarship back. It isn't out of the spectrum of college athletes where coaches who don't like certain players will begin to badger, prod and demean them while working them out until they quit on their own. They do this to open up a scholarship for another player they think will make a bigger impact for their program.

The mentality in big time sports is that no one is immune to losing their job. Since the head coach and the assistant coaches know that they can be fired at any time they pass that mentality down to the athletes. Everyone in the system knows that if losses mount up a drop off in attendance will begin. This leads to a loss of revenue for the school and when that happens -heads will roll. Once a substantial amount of revenue begins to drop – the head coach is gone. You can see how it trickles down hill. Don't think that you and your child are immune to this…you're not! Learn it now and understand the harsh realities of college sports and you'll be much better off.

Since the colleges and universities found out how lucrative sports have become the pressure is really on for the coaches to win. It's simple – the more wins the more money comes back to the university. For many, big time college programs, the pressure on the head coach are lethal. It's win at all costs or find a new job - and that type of pressure can take the human element out of the game. Some head coaches are so isolated from the human segment of sports that if they do know your name in the first couple of years you'll be lucky. So don't be surprised when you show up on campus and the coach forgets who you are.

Most head coaches have to oversee several areas within their program. It's a tough job being responsible for the offence, defense, special teams, strength training, strategy, meetings, film study, practice and transportation. That's just a few of the pieces of the puzzle that the head coach has to be responsible for. They must rely on many of their assistant coaches to delegate that work out. Not to mention dealing with the off field problems that come up with athletes including robbery, pregnancy, drugs, alcohol and other violations of team rules. At this level, don't think that your son or daughter is going away to a special camp where the coaches really want to get to know them – this won't happen. The coaches have one thing on their mind - they want your kid to perform by whatever way possible. It's all about winning and if your child can't help their program they will find someone else who can.

I'm not here to scare or shock you - I'm here to open up your eyes. The school is about to give you thousands of dollars worth of education, meals, clothes, books and travel. I just want you to know - 'there's no such thing as a free lunch'. It can be a great experience and if you're not prepared it can be a miserable experience. My goal is to prepare you the best way I know so that you don't go into this segment of your sports life blind. The college sports experience sometimes isn't fair but if you prepare yourself properly the payoff can be one of the best experiences of your life.

Recruiting By the Numbers

Another area that most people won't tell you about in the recruiting process is the little subject called "grades". You are applying to institutions of higher learning and the whole idea is to gain acceptance into a school that is going to educate you.

You are first and foremost are a <u>STUDENT ATHLETE</u>! Most people these days think that the kids are athletes then students. Your there to learn more about the world around you in a physical, chemical, musical, educational, liberal, conservative, spiritual and intellectual way. College is a process to help develop your mind to think in many diverse ways. It will help you escape ignorance and construct a foundation of ideas that you can use as you continue your journey in life. Upper level studies will develop and expand your critical thinking and reasoning. If used properly, it can set you up for the rest of your life in ways you've never thought possible.

On the other hand if you're not properly prepared or you just go through the motions then it can be a complete waste of time. As a scholarship athlete don't take for granted the education that is being given to you as a part of your playing for the school. Understand that there are thousands of kids out there busting their butts trying to hold down low paying jobs in order to pay for their education. There are a lot of athletes who waste their time thinking that they don't need an education because they are going pro. That type of thinking is foolish for many reasons. One reason is that by educating yourself you can better prepare yourself for the harsh realities of life. Second, let's say you do make it to the pro's are you going to be properly educated in dealing with your finances, investments and purchases or are you going to continue to rely on others to tell you what to do? Third, the chance of the majority of all players making it to the professional ranks is extremely low. In fact, in the United States alone there is approximately three hundred million people and only 17,000 professional athletes. Now if we were in Vegas and betting if you will make it to the pro's the odds would be 24,550 to 1. Your chances of winning an Olympic medal is 655,000 to 1, chances of winning a Hollywood Oscar 12,200 to 1, and chances of being killed by a shark are 300,000,000 to 1.

But anyway you look at it, college recruiters are looking at your high school grades. They want to know if you are going to be an asset to their program. You don't have to be a straight A student although it would help more that you think. You need to be a good solid student enough to show that you are trying to make a difference. College coaches want athletes how can help their program.

Make sure that you do the work that is needed to get the grades necessary to open up coaches' eyes. Good grades will definitely start the ball rolling to get you closer to the school that you are interested in. There is an exception in that if you are a phenom in your sport and are running a 4.2 40 yard dash and your grades are bad somehow, someway, they will find a way to get you in. It's funny how some kid's grades get better as they get faster on the field. I'm being a bit sarcastic here and there are times when there have been athletes who have unbelievable stats on the field but can cut it in the class room. This is when they will persuade you to enter into a junior college to get your grades up for two years and then reapply.

On the other end....if you're good, but not outrageously good, and your grades are bad the schools will immediately begin to back off. Once they see that your grades are below average they will be looking for other recruits. Coaches want people who are going to contribute to their program. Athletes that come in with good grades help their program overall. Athletes with good grades help balance out the program for the athletes who aren't so good in the classroom. So one of the first questions coaches will ask is for your grades. So don't think that you can get away with doing nothing before entering college. And beyond anything else....DO NOT let your grades go down after your senior year even though you've committed to a school because it can come back and haunt you. If your grades drop low enough the school has the right to de-commit from the original agreement.

There may come a time when the school that you really want to attend is deciding between you and another player. If all of the 'on-field' qualities are the same between you and the other athlete it may very well come down to your grades. I know of coaches who had a difficult time deciding on a couple of players and when it came down to the last part of their decision it was who had the better grades. So don't think that grades aren't important - they are.

Good Character

More and more colleges and universities are looking for people of good character. They want to know that they don't have to bring you to their school and baby sit you for the next four years. They want to know that you have something to offer them and their team without the feeling of you sucking them dry.

"Character: A Decision One Makes When No One Else Is Looking….."

When they look at your game film they want to see your talent. But what a lot of people don't know is that they are looking at the film to see what you do when the play doesn't involve you. They want to see what you do when the play is away from you. Do you hustle to help out downfield or down court, do you just stand around waiting, do you give up too early, are you always around the ball, and do you play at 100% all of the time and for the entire game? Do you have "court or field" presence? Do you know where to go at all times?

Also be careful of you off field antics. Nothing can kill a scholarship faster than a criminal record. Underage drinking or other types of teen age crimes can set you back with the school that may be interested in you. It's these little intangibles that are really important in making up a coach's mind in whom they are going to choose.

Don't Get Greedy

There may come a time when several schools may be interested in speaking to you about playing at their school. Depending on how interested they are many of the coaches will attempt to come to one of your games to see you play. Treat each school with respect and humility as the process goes on. If they are showing you that they are going out of their way to bring you into their school - listen up because it may be a chance of a life time.

Here's why...there are 20,000 high schools in the United States. In football for example, there are 120 Division I schools offering full scholarships to those students graduating from high school. That means only 0.8 % of all graduating seniors will be offered a Division I scholarship.

The numbers are very thin so be prepared to compete for that scholarship money.

Here's a quick story...

A mother came into my office all excited telling me that a large Division I school had come to meet with her and her son for football. They had been sending letters and talking to them on and off and finally offered him a full scholarship his junior year if he gave a verbal agreement. The mother told me that she was holding off because she figured there would be bigger and better schools coming after her son. Well they turned down the school offering the scholarship and waited to hear from all of these other schools. Time went by and nothing happened. None of the other schools were interested and never contacted either the son or the mother. Running out of time she called the original college recruiter who she wouldn't return phone calls to a few months before. Now the shoe was on the other foot - they wouldn't return her calls and the once full scholarship went down the tubes. The athlete fell out of favor with this school and decided not to offer him anything at all. They found someone else of equal or greater talent and decided to go with him. The player finally enrolled in a school that he and his mother had to take out school loans out to finance his education and to play football at a Division III school.

Another parent and son came to my office for a sports injury. While I was treating him the father began to proudly tell me that his son was being recruited by a Division I school for football. He told me what a great guy the recruiter was and how he felt that his son would be a starter right off the bat for their team. I tried to tell him that they needed to be very careful of what the recruiting coach tells you because it has been my experience that many will lie to your face. The father was quite upset with me telling me that the recruiter was a great guy and would never do that. The father told me that they were looking at another player from another state but he assured me that his son was going to be there choice. Time went on and the phone calls became less and less until it was getting tough even to call the coach to see what the status was.

As signing day came - signing day went and no scholarship was offered. As in many instances they played one athlete against the other to protect themselves in case something went wrong with one recruit they still had the other recruit. The bad part of this story was that I was right and the kid ended up at a junior college to play football because no other college was interested in him.

What I'm saying here is that many times the grass isn't greener on the other side of the fence. If the offer is on the table really take a serious look at it and find some smart people who you trust to discuss it with so you don't go losing a potential offer.

Things You Need To Know About The NCAA

The NCAA is a matrix of rules and regulations organized to attempt to keep the honor of college sports. In their quest to attempt to keep the playing field level they have grown into a sizable collection of judicial oversight.

If you are going to accept money from an NCAA institution then you will have to abide by the rules set forth by them. It has gotten so complicated that most universities employ a specialist known as the compliance director. Their sole job is to keep current on all of the rules and regulations so that their team doesn't violate of the regulations. I can tell you from experience that there are many 'compliant specialists' who are not up on the current rules. Many a ball has been dropped by schools that have adversely affected the student athlete.

There are three major divisions in college sports with football having four levels of competition.

Division I is the highest level of college competition. There are 120 division I programs broken up into several divisions. Division IAA is a separate division for football which are teams allowed to offer scholarships but not as many as Division I. There is also a Division IAA Non-Scholarship. These schools can't afford to offer full scholarships however they still compete against Division IAA and Division I schools.

Division II has some scholarships to offer however the competition at this level is a drop off from the Division I schools. Over the past several years however the level of competition at Division II schools has greatly risen.

Division III schools do not offer scholarship money at all. These are smaller schools that have a football program that competes against other schools in the Division III conferences.

NAIA – National Association of Intercollegiate Athletics is a separate governing body separate from the NCAA. These schools are usually smaller schools, private or affiliated with religious denominations.

NJCAA – National Junior College Athletic Association are groups of two year colleges located throughout the country. Some junior colleges do offer scholarship money for the athlete. More and more Division I and Division II schools are looking to JUCO'S for athletes to fill their roster spots

NCAA – National College Athletic Association; According to the NCAA website; Our purpose is to govern competition in a fair, safe, equitable and sportsmanlike manner, and to integrate intercollegiate athletics into higher education so that the educational experience of the student-athlete is paramount.

An active member is a four-year college or university or a two-year upper-level collegiate institution accredited by the appropriate regional accrediting agency and duly elected to active membership under the provisions of the Association bylaws. Active members have the right to compete in NCAA championships, to vote on legislation and other issues before the Association, and to enjoy other privileges of membership designated in the constitution and bylaws of the Association.

There are some definitions and terms you need to know during the recruiting process.

Recruiting: Is being contacted by a representative of a college or university for the purpose of persuade you to enroll and play for that school in a given sport.

Contact: A face-to-face encounter between the athlete, athletes parents or legal guardians and the member of the schools staff for the intention of discussing playing for that school.

Official Visit: You will be allowed five official visits paid for by the school to determine if you are comfortable with that school. The school will can pay all of your expenses along with your parents. However, most schools have you visit alone both to keep expenses down and for you to mingle with the other athletes.

Contact Period: There is a set period of time set by the NCAA that allows for the visitation of recruiters to attend your game and/or speak to you.

Quiet Period: Again a time period set up by the NCAA that you may visit the school but the recruiters cannot make contact with you in person.

Walk-On: A student who attempts to make or join the team without any scholarship offered by the school. This is a person who thinks that they can request to come on the team with a possibility of earning a scholarship sometime in the future.

Preferred Walk-On: A student who was contacted (or recruited) by the school to play at that school without the offer of a scholarship. This is a person who thinks that they can request to come on the team with a possibility of earning a scholarship sometime in the future.

Grey Shirt: You are allowed five years to play a particular sport in college. In this case the freshman enrolls in the second semester rather than the first semester to gain an extra year of eligibility. By waiting until the second semester the player will be playing his fifth year in his sixth year at the school.

Red Shirt: You are allowed five years to play your sport. This is a year that you sit out of competition so that you can gain experience along with strength, speed, maturity to fit in when the team needs you.

Making Sure That You Are Eligible...

First of all make sure that you are eligible to go on to college. Make sure that your grades are within the range of the school you want to attend. Parents and students need to check out the following for correct eligibility:

www.NCAA.org
www.Clearinghouse.net

Unfortunately, don't trust your high school counselor for this information because many of them don't keep up on this. You are potentially receiving a lot of money from a college or university so do some work to make sure you get this competed properly. Make sure that your grades and courses are all up to date as well as your SAT/ACT's have been completed. You must meet certain core requirements in order to become eligible to move on to college. There are no negations with these requirements so make sure you know what they are and have been completed.

Some high school coaches are good at getting your name out to colleges. Over time some coaches have developed solid reputations with college coaches and can get a kid into school with just a quick phone call. Some coaches are terrible at it. Some are not as aggressive and others are downright lazy. If you suspect your coach not being able to get you name out you better take a pro active approach in sending your information out to college coaches. There are coaches who never played at a high end division football program. They may not have the eye that it takes to see that a certain player can make it at that level. There are a lot of coaches that have no idea on how to develop a Division I player. That is why you need to be proactive on your part to make sure your name gets out there.

On the other hand you may have a coach who will say anything just to keep everyone happy. They will tell your parents that you will be going to a certain Division I school just so they don't have to deal with questions and the nagging that some overzealous parents can be.

In some these cases it is wise to attend a certain college summer camp. You may need more exposure for the college coaches to see your talents. Beware though, many of these have become more of a money making venture for the coaches than actual recruiting camp. I will tell you that if you can stand out in a crowd you will get noticed. If you can afford it then it may be a good thing...but be careful.

If you are an elite athlete the schools will more than likely find you. If you are putting up the numbers or the times that are above the norms these schools will come after you. If you are good but not to that next elite stage than I highly suggest that you take it upon yourself to become proactive in the recruiting process. If you're a parent and your child is on the bubble, the more involved you become in the process, the better. Either way, if you want a shot at getting to play in college you have to make some noise.

Parents remember, before you start - you are here to work on your son or daughters scholarship - not yours. You may be as proud as a peacock but keep it sensible or your are going to make some vital mistakes that can end up costing you and your child dearly. Overbearing parents will get pushed to the bottom of the pile if you frustrate the coaches. It's good to make some noise but don't go overboard.

Here are my Do's and Don'ts That will help you simplify this stressful time period

Do's

- Keep All Expectations Under Control
- No matter who you talk to (college recruiters) treat them with respect the same way you want to be treated

- Put your video on line to make it easier for the coaches to see your highlights.
- Talk to as many colleges or universities as possible.
- Don't choose a school just for athletics…make sure they have a major you enjoy.
- Keep all recruiters at arm's length. They all talk a mean game so keep it in perspective.
- Prepare questions before hand prior to speaking with the recruiter – No Question is Stupid!!!
- Feel free to talk to recruiters on the phone.
- Make sure that your son/daughter looks at a school that they would love to attend even if the sport falls apart
- Encourage your son/daughter to look at a lot of schools to get a good feeling to where they want to attend
- It's never too early to start looking at colleges or universities.
- Accompany your son/daughter on as many trips as possible…. yep it's your right.
- Keep a calendar for all of the specific deadlines to follow
- You will get plenty of letters from plenty of schools….It doesn't mean a thing until you begin conversations with the schools.

Don'ts

- Get pushed around by a forward recruiter.
- Make sure your son/daughter is comfortable with the school…they have to be there for four years.
- Don't get hung up on names. Too many people get hung up on the school's name without thinking about the program.
- Don't think that you've been offered a scholarship that you can begin to take it easy.
- Don't worry about making the 'perfect' choice. It will all come together.
- Don't think there is loyalty in sports….coaches change jobs faster than they change their underwear.
- Don't let money be your sole focus of your search.

- Don't take recruiters word for anything - Research….Research
….Research for yourself.
- Parents; don't assume that your kid has everything under control. Watch, help and assist. This is a trying time for a lot of athletes and they need help dealing with the stress of their decision.

Check List

Keep it simple

Create the best highlight video possible.

Create an online site to showcase your video.

You will receive lots of letters from schools – keep them together .

Create a filing system so things don't get out of hand.

Choose about 10 schools to start on where you would like to attend.

Keep notes on your phone conversations with recruiters.

Ask the kids not playing questions about the program….they'll tell you the inside story.

Print out the emails that they send you and keep them in your records.

Save all text messages that recruiters send you…print them out if you can.

Check out the current program to see if your position fits in well and you have a chance to play.

As time goes on and it's getting closer narrow your schools down to 4 or 5.

Continue to narrow down your selections based on what you feel is right for you.

Design a Pro's and Con's page of every school so you can see what is best for you.

The Dark Side

There are many 'horror' stories pertaining to young recruits and the college or university that they intended to matriculate to.

Take the case of Daniel Smith who orally committed to the University of Hawaii who allegedly told Mr. Smith not to talk to any other schools because they were going to offer him a scholarship. Mr. Smith reports that he had to promise that he wouldn't entertain offers from other schools.

Coach June Jones who was the head coach at the time when Daniel was being recruited took a job with Southern Methodist University. Coach Jones took the defensive line coach with him to Southern Methodist so the man who was doing the recruiting for Daniel was now gone. The move by Jones left Smith standing with only a verbal commitment and possibly left him out in the cold without a scholarship from the new coaches Daniel and his parents are perusing legal recourse on this matter. This was written up by Andy Staples from SI.com and is being watched closely by many sports lawyers around the country.

Here is a story more close to my family. My son who was a walk-on at Syracuse University as a punter was asked to leave after the introduction of a new coach.

My son walked on to Syracuse University while Coach Greg Robinson was the head coach. He went through the initial physical challenges with ten other players attempting to make the team. My son and one other athlete made the team and were asked to join the team for spring workouts leading to the spring football game. The year went on he went through summer two-a-day sessions which lead into the regular football season. My son didn't start because he was playing behind Rob Long who is a nationally ranked punter. As time progressed, the head coach, Greg Robinson was let go by the university and a new head coach was hired. Except for one coach, all of the coaches under Coach Robinson were let go. This is somewhat natural because most coaches like to surround themselves with people who they know and are comfortable with.

The new head coach, Doug Marrone, came from the New Orleans Saints to bring the football program back to prominence. Coach Marrone was the offensive coordinator for the Saints whose supposed life's passion was to become the head coach at Syracuse University.

In January, my son began to practice with the team for the mandatory running and weight lifting session to prepare for spring football practice. After about two weeks into the running and weight lifting sessions my son and two other players were told that they had to leave the team. They were told that they violated team rules for taking a college course during the times that the coach scheduled the workouts. My son went to speak to the coach about this situation telling him that his course load was approved by the coaches last year. The one course that he selected was only offered at a particular time and it was part of his major and the coaches said it was okay. Coach Marrone said that he didn't care and that the old coaches aren't here now.

My son called me asking if it was possible for him to drop this course and pick it back up in the summer so that he could stay on the team. I agreed and allowed him to do this even though this was against my better judgment. My son had worked extremely hard attempting to make the team and I felt I owed it to him to help him continue with his dream. He dropped the course and told his coaches and was subsequently was allowed back on the team.

Another week passes and coach Marrone hires a new special team's coach Bob Casullo. Casullo came to Syracuse from the Tampa Bay Buccaneers in the NFL. Coach Casullo comes in like a rabid drill sergeant in a failing platoon. He meets with the players on the special teams and tells them he doesn't know them all but he is going to do his best to get rid of them. As you can understand, most of the players were sitting there in shock. They couldn't figure out why without seeing anyone kick or punt on the field yet that he wanted to get rid of them the first day he started. Obviously, as you will read, it was a pre-planned system to clear out players to open up new scholarship opportunities.

As a part of the head coach's philosophy of getting the team "tough" all players were to be running outside. The problem with that was that the temperature in January at Syracuse, New York, at that time of year was about 10 degrees with a wind chill of five to ten below. In the coach's infinite wisdom, the players were only allowed to go out to the field in gym shorts and jerseys - that's it! But, ok, that's football....get tough or get out. While at practice, with 20 mile an hour plus winds, the new coach Casullo had most of the kickers and punters practice while he evaluated them. Oh, by the way, did I tell you that the coaches were all bundled up in heavy hoodies, coats, gloves and long pants. It's amazing how tough the coaches can be on others but not themselves.

Practice continued while all kickers attempted to kick into winds that would have made any professional kicker pack it in for the day. Two days later a group of the players from the special teams were told to show up for a 6 a.m. meeting with the new Coach Casullo. Casullo walks into the room, while the players sat waiting to find out what Casullo had planned for the day. In football it is normal to have a meetings and today should have been no different than any other day. Casullo walks to the front of the meeting room and states in a matter of fact voice "your services are no longer needed here - so clean out your lockers." With each player stunned with what was said, one young man asked the coach, "coach you're making a decision on me only after one day of kicking?" Casullo then put his head down and walked out of the room without uttering another word. That was it...nothing more, nothing less. The players had nothing else to do but to go and clean out their lockers.

My son was one of the casualties from this mess even after he dropped a course to be able to stay on the team. He made the best of it and decided to transfer to another Division I program to play football.

Am I writing this to wine and cry - absolutely not. I understand the dynamics of Division I football and many times it isn't pretty. I'm trying to give you a real life example of how Division I programs operate. It's not about anything but winning - which is good or bad depending on how you sit on this issue. I'm not here to say it's right or wrong - I'm trying to point the fact out that it is what it is. What I want you to understand is that Division I football and other Division I sports, are about the coaches, the winning, and not the players! It's about the money, the administration and the coaches.

The program at Syracuse is not an atypical football program. There are many Division I programs throughout the nation just as abrasive or worse. The goal of this writing is to prepare you for the little things that no one else is going to tell you.

It was apparent when Coach Robinson was head coach at Syracuse it was a more laid back environment. There was discipline with Robinson but nowhere near, the intensity brought to the university program as coach Marrone did. Many times this type of discipline is needed to turn a program around. You need to know the different type of coaching styles at the higher level of sports so it never comes as a shock to you. I personally have don't have any problem with heavy discipline. I have a problem with coaches who can't treat their athletes as men and women. There is a big difference between handing out heavy discipline and being ignorant because you've gained a temporary whiff of power.

Commitment doesn't mean anything in this the modern era of sports. In the modern world of college football a "commitment" simply means "the school I currently think I might attend…maybe." This holds true to the schools and the potential players themselves. Commitment is a word that has been diluted to the point that by my way of understanding it means I think, I may or it's possible. Schools will de-commitment on a player if they get a better deal as well as a player will de-commit from a school when they get a better deal as well.

In football, there is a National Signing Day which always lands on the first Wednesday of the month of February. That was designed to be the 'drop dead' date for a recruit to commit to a school but there have been many instances where players pushed that back. Up until this first Wednesday a player can commit to a particular school which used to mean that the player was off of the market. What it means in today's rules is that the coaching staffs at rival schools start to recruit that player even harder to get them to go to their school.

Nothing is more reprehensible than the situation with Louis Holmes, a defensive end, who signed with the University of Arizona in 2006. Holmes was walking towards his press conference when Pete Carroll was on his cell phone trying to get Homes to come to USC. Here is a kid who is on the way to speak to the media with a coach doing whatever he could to change his mind to come to his school.

Father and Son Recruiting....

Here is a great story right from the coach's mouth. This is a story written by Terri Bowden, son of Bobby Bowden head coach of Florida State University concerning recruiting.

"It was the last week of recruiting, and the No. 1 defensive player in the state of Florida was named Martavius Houston. He was a defensive back from Boyd Anderson High School in Fort Lauderdale, and he had the choice of going to any school in the country. However, by this final week he had narrowed his decision down to two schools. He was either going to go to Auburn and play for me or he was going to go to Florida State and play for my ol' man, Bobby Bowden (I'm sure you've heard of him).

Per NCAA rules, the head coach is allowed only one official home visit. I strategically looked at the calendar for the best chance for me to go into his home and hopefully close the deal. I decided to have my home visit from 6 to 7:30 p.m. Thursday night. He had a basketball game Friday night, which would keep him busy, and he had no more official school visits left for the final weekend. I made up my mind that Thursday night was do-or-die time with this recruit.

I booked the flight to Fort Lauderdale and rented a nice Lincoln Town Car in order to impress him when I drove up. As I met him and his mother on the front porch, I immediately hugged his mom and told her how much I loved her and turned to Martavius and said, "Son, you're going to win a Heisman Trophy at Auburn University."

I followed them into the house and proceeded to sing his praises – nonstop – for an hour and a half. I said, "Son, you are the No. 1 recruit on my list, the best player I've ever seen, I'm going to make you my star, I'm going to make you my captain, and you're going to win two Heisman trophies at Auburn. Only Archie Griffin at Ohio State has ever done that." The more I talked, the bigger his eyes got, and the more he started leaning off the front of that chair. As most coaches will tell you, when you get a "leaner" you need to seal the deal right then and there. I wanted to stick my cell phone in his face and say, "you call that Bobby Bowden right now and tell him you don't want to go to FSU, that you want to be an Auburn Tiger."

However, high school coaches do a great job of prepping these young men by telling them not to get pressured into making a decision in front of the head coach but instead to wait until they can be alone with their family and loved ones so they can make a rational decision. So although he didn't verbally commit right there, I believed I had done the best selling job ever – I knew I had him.

As we walked back out onto the front porch, before I said goodbye, I turned to his mom one last time, hugged her neck and reminded her how much I loved her. Then, with all the sincerity I could muster, I looked that young man directly in the eyes and said, "I have never told anybody this before, but you're gonna win three Heisman trophies at Auburn. You'd win four, but you're gonna be in the NFL by then."

As I turned to leave, a long black, stretch limousine pulled up in front of the house. A little, short driver with one of those driver's caps and half-jackets on got out, walked all the way around the back of the limousine and opened the back door next to the curb.

Out stepped my ol' man.

He had scheduled his official visit for 7:30 p.m. on the same night.

As he waddled up that sidewalk wearing that silly-looking safari hat and those red/yellow/green sunglasses that he always wears, my eyes got as big as saucers and my jaw dropped.

My ol' man stepped up on the porch, said hello to that mama, shook Martavius' hand, turned to me, patted me on the head (in front of both of them) and said, "Terry, when you get home, your mama wants you to call her."

That's all he said!

You talk about dirty recruiting – it doesn't get any dirtier. Nobody has ever been "who's your daddy-ed" worse than that.

*I mean, who do **you** want to play for – BOBBY – or terry?*

I'm sure every coach out there has his war stories to tell. I just thought you'd like to hear mine.

Incidentally, Martavius Houston had a great career at Auburn University.

Revolving Door of Coaching

On the other hand many coaches are looking out to feather their nest.

Just because you get recruited doesn't mean that it's over. Also, just because you sign a contract it doesn't necessarily mean the pressures are over either. Keep in mind coaches change jobs like most people change clothes. There are numerous stories of coaches recruiting certain players only to leave the school that same year for another job.

Coaches will sit in the living rooms of the players homes telling them that they are a vital part of the universities program and won't be leaving any time soon. Well, you have to define…any time soon. It that means in the next five minutes well then okay, they're not lying.

Coaches are notorious for wanting their own recruits. It's part ego, its part planning and moreover it job protection. They want complete control over the entire process. They want to be able to say that it's because of their choices that built the program. They don't want others saying that well it wasn't their recruits it was the other coaches before them if they have a winning season.

Brian Kelly ex head coach of the University of Cincinnati, left Cincinnati for the University of Notre Dame even though he left his team high and dry for the bowl game that the team earned. Kelly who took over for Charlie Weis, who took over the job of Ty Willingham, will coach the 2010 team. Willingham who was pushed out by the university was doing a good job but Notre Dame's people in the know thought they were getting a steal when they landed Weis after a winning season with the New England Patriots. Obviously that didn't work out.

Lane Kiffen left Tennessee for Southern Cal where many of the recruits were called by Kiffens coaching staff and were persuading recruits to change their minds from going to Tennessee and to follow Kiffen to USC.

Just keep in mind that just because you've signed on the line everything is over. It's just beginning and you have to realize it's a 'every man for himself' attitude in this environment.

Early Recruiting

Believe this or not, but there are some kids being recruited as early as the seventh and eighth grades. There have been many kids....did you hear that KIDS, who have been approached by coaches, agents and companies. Many of these kids have been in basketball but it's starting to be filtering into other sports.

The wisdom that comes with the higher ups at the NCAA sometimes boggles the mind. They say that they are there to protect the amateur status of all athletes. The NCAA has now decreed that seventh graders are now available as college/university prospects.

For those of us who aren't up on this on a regular basis the rule was changed from a prospect in ninth grade to seventh grade. This is for basketball only – okay, wow that makes me feel better! C'mon, seventh grade? When you can't control the feeding frenzy going on with high school players what is going to start with the middle schoolers? Will Mom and Dad get that money for the house five years early? Will the 'gear' start rolling in with Nike, Addias, and Underarmour begin stacking up in the closets at home?

What can kids possible know about what universities have to offer them in a form of education at that age? Most kids get most of their backgrounds of colleges or universities based on what they see on TV. The see the teams winning, they see the fan fare of the crowds but they aren't seeing what is going on inside the class room. Oh, believe me, I get it....it's all about the money. But this move that is now a few years old is more of the fact that backs up my premise of Division I sports revolve around one thing...MONEY!

"On this team, we are all united in a common goal: to keep my job." Lou Holtz

Summary & Frequently Asked Questions (FAQ)

T hank you for taking the time to read this book and let me offer my congratulations for getting through book without throwing it out of the window. I'm sure there is some information in the book that may upset some people. My sole intention is to open the eyes of all parents and athletes so that they can prepare for a great athletic career. I hope you found the information informative enough to help you through the maze of sports information catered to athletes.

My basic premise of the book is that there is no such thing as a bad athlete. It is my opinion that kids grow up different and have more or less opportunities to develop differently than one another. Some are more physiologically more advanced than others. Some were exposed to movement earlier in their life than others. Don't despair if your child seems to be a little bit behind their peer group. With hard work and passion they can develop into an elite athlete.

A strong dose of passion can take an average athlete much further than a lazy talented athlete any day of the week. It's all about attitude. Help your young athlete develop an attitude of winning and everything else will follow. *Successful athletes do the things that the unsuccessful athletes don't want to do.*

Take one step at a time with your young athlete. Keep it all in perspective as far as their talents go. If they are good when they are young that is great just keep them going and over time if they are truly talented it will show. Don't get fooled if your local area isn't all that talented that makes your child look like a real pro. Be careful, many parents get sucked into this and when they leave town to compete it becomes a real eye opener when their child is getting "schooled" by the other players.

If your son or daughter is an elite athlete then take the time to find them the appropriate help to develop them to the next level. Support them, help them and above all listen to them when they need someone to talk to. They may seem to be self driven but even the most independent athletes need someone to listen to them when things aren't going their way.

If you young athlete is average that is okay – most athletes are average. Support them to have as much fun as possible. Make sure they work hard and develop a strong work ethic and you will see it will pay off in their future endeavors.

Raising athletes is a challenge - not that raising any child isn't. The travel, the meetings, practices and games are very time consuming. I take my hat off to you for taking the time for your child to participate in sports. It means a lot to them having your support. Do your best to be there at their games. It means more that you think.

Over all there is no magic bullet in raising an athlete. It takes work, time, some patience and common sense. When you time comes to look back on this time in your life you will see that it was the most exciting time of your parenting life. One of the most important thing that you can do to you young athlete is to instill a persistent work ethic. Teach them that it takes hard work that never ends. If they can establish this early on they will see much success on the athletic field.

Learn to keep you mind wide open to your available training or coaching. If you can find someone who can help develop your young athlete even though it is a bit uncommon as compared to what everyone else is doing – go for it. Always keep in mind is that results will tell you if it's working or not. Are they getting faster, stronger and are they able to recover properly. More importantly, are they getting injured? If so, something is not working. No one is truly injury prone. Everyone can improve no matter how uncoordinated they are.

Parents please lighten up a little about your athlete's talent or performance. When it comes to your young athletes please ask the question to yourself, "am I doing this for me or am I doing this for them?" Make sure that the athlete is doing for themselves and not you. There is way too much stress in our society as it is they don't need you to pile on more. They need a safe harbor to dock their boat when they come home at the end of the day. They deal with as many stressors as you do during the day so they need a safe place to come home to. It's up to you to help create that supportive environment.

Curtail your temper at games. Coaches, referees and other parents are human and have feelings. Sports don't instantly give you the right to start telling everyone off when things don't go your way.

The chances of your child going on to a Division I school are very slim. It happens but just because your child shows aptitude doesn't mean they are going to receive a scholarship. It is extremely difficult for the majority of athletes to earn a full scholarship. The talent level at the Division I level is extremely high so take it in stride as you're your son or daughter progresses.

If you're going to coach your child make sure that you are separating the duties between parent and coach. On the field you're a coach and off the field you're a parent. Keep it simple from the start and you will have a much more enjoyable experience with your team and your child.

For the most part most coaches are doing the best they can be. Just like everyone else, there are good coaches and bad coaches. Either way, let them coach. Don't try to sabotage them if you don't feel they are doing the right thing. If you feel they are doing something that can harm an athlete then by all means open up your mouth and protest. Just don't do that because they didn't play your child or they didn't run the play you thought was better.

Keep your eyes open with your kids about drugs, alcohol and steroids. Observe the obvious when they are home and if you feel that there begin to show major deviations in their normal routine start investigating. There is plenty of information on the internet for you to educate yourself to the substances that are being used today by young adults.

If your son or daughter does get a call or a visit from a college recruiter takes it one day at a time. Take a pro-active approach to make sure you ask the questions you want and don't be afraid. You're sending your young athlete to a college for four years so ask what ever question you want. Make sure that you understand that most of what come out of recruiters mouths are soft sells to make you feel comfortable with them in an attempt to bond with you. They're not bad people there just people doing their job. Just understand that college sports are a business and with most business transactions you must cover all of your bases before you sign on the dotted line.

Question & Answers:

We've asked several parents of athletes to write in and ask us your questions on how best to help your son or daughter be the best they can be. Here are a few of the questions and answers on this subject.

Is it wise to play multiple sports?

Yes...I feel that the more sports you play the more rounded you will become both as an athlete and a person. Playing multiple sports develops multiple coordinating systems within the body allowing the body to adapt to more challenges. It also stimulates the brain to react in different ways allowing for a more complete nervous system.

There may come a time when specializing in one sport may be important. If you feel that you have a REAL chance at a college scholarship or that you feel that you have a chance of becoming a professional at an earlier age then by all means specialize. It's different for everyone however on the whole for the average, above average athlete, play as many sports as you can.

Is It Important To Attend Specialized Camps?

In certain aspects the answer is yes. Certain sports or certain locations you won't get exposed to the right people who make decisions on college scholarships. Again, this is for the athlete who feels that they have a legitimate shot of a college scholarship.

Also understand that many camps across the country are nothing but money makers. Don't think that you are going to attend a camp and the coaches are going to keep your picture by their night stand when you leave. The only way that will happen is if you can run as fast as the wind, jump higher than the mountains and have strength to lift a truck. Anything short of that, they will tell you, "thank you for your money and hope to see you next year."

Football camps have now shown to be BIG money makers for the coaches. The problem with many of them is that there are so many kids attending that the type of instruction needed is lost.

Baseball camps, field hockey camps and others are camps you may need to get to in order to be seen. But don't go unless you are ready to perform. Just as well as you can be spotted as a potential scholarship candidate you can just as easily be scratched off the list with a poor performance.

With sports such as tennis, golf, swimming are mainly individual and many times going to these camps are mainly for technique training only. These aren't they type of camps that coaches come out to see if they can find athletes for their program. In tennis for example, if you're not in the top 100 of the junior ranking most if not all Division I schools won't come out and watch. So do your homework before you outlay a lot of money for something you may be able to get accomplished with your local coach.

How Do I Know If My Child Is An Elite Athlete?

The first indication is that your son or daughter will show extreme talent up and beyond the other kids on the field. They will dominate most of all of their play when paired up against their competition. You will see that at each level that they get involved in that they become the "go to" person on the field. As they progress in age, they will progress in talent, and it will become apparent that they have much more talent compared to all other athletes on the field.

Should I Look Into Private Schools To Specialize In A Given Sport?

You should only think about this only if you don't feel that you are not getting the proper exposure at your present school. There are advantages in attending certain schools that have both an academic curriculum to help you develop the proper study skills needed for college. Some schools also specialize in certain sports and develop winning programs that attract colleges looking for personally to fill their rosters. You have to look at the entire situation to make sure that this move it the right one for you...both athletically and academically.

How Can I Really Get Involved With My Child Sports?

The biggest thing you can do for your child is to be there for them. Be there when things are going bad to have an open ear to listen. Sometimes they just want to vent...be there and listen.

Be there when things are good and celebrate with them their accomplishments. Support for your child really goes much further than you know.

How Do I Know If My Child Is an Elite Athlete?

You'll know. When you see your son or daughter day after day or week after week DOMINATE their competition it will dawn on you that you have something special. I will warn you though, some kids can develop faster than others and when they get into high school the playing field begins to level out. If your child continues to dominate their competition at this level then you'll know by the amount of phone calls that will begin. Elite athletes stick out like a sore thumb...and you'll notice because your son or daughter is making it look too easy as compared to their competition.

If My Son or Daughter Isn't All That Good In Sports What Should I Do?

If they really love the sport then continue to encourage them to play. Not everyone will turn out to become a superstar in sports. Be realistic about their talent and help them develop a work ethic that will help them improve. I've seen average and some below average athletes develop a strong work ethic that propelled them to playing where otherwise they wouldn't even have made the team. Remember its sports – it's not the end of the world. We would all love to be the next Michael Jordan but that isn't a reality. We all have talent and many times its in areas other than sports.

How Do You Prevent Burnout?

First we have to define the word burnout. It's a slang word used primarily to describe over work or over utilization of an athlete. Burnout can come from a variety of sources including playing too many sports, not properly organizing your daily affairs, not training properly, not sleeping properly, not eating or hydrating properly, and not taking time away from your primary sport.

According to Jay Schroeder world class human performance physiologist that by not training at 100% you don't properly turn on all of the systems of your body that can have a physiological response to fatigue to the body. Any time you drop below training of 90% you will tend to develop a burn out feeling. By always training your body at 100% your body will know exactly how to recover as long as you are fueling it properly with proper nutrition and hydration.

Sleep, or lack thereof, can be one of your worst enemies. It's the body's way of repairing and preparing for the next workout or event. Athletes have to take sleep as serious as they take their training.

Organization: if you constantly fly by the seat of your pants attempting to juggle school, practice, games and your social life there will be a brick wall waiting for you to crash. By preparing your time and having the discipline to say no when you don't have the time you will stop the stress that can lead to burnout.

Taking time for yourself to be a kid. Academics are very important, sports are somewhat important (looking at the grand scheme of things) and social time just to 'mess around' with your fiends is just as important. Take some time for yourself and have some fun.

My daughter has practice at 6:00 a.m. what is the best thing for her to do as far as eating and drinking?

It's not the time to break out into the Denny's Grand Slam breakfast. Too much fat and carb's at once can weight them down like a ship's anchor.

The first thing you can do is make sure she is getting enough water the night before. Sometimes during heavy practices (especially swimming) the athlete doesn't realize that they lose so many fluids.

So in the evening well before bed have them drink about 25 ounces of water.

In the morning light meals consisting of protein will help including peanut butter on celery or peanut butter on slices of apple. Small amounts of Gatorade (or similar) will allow some sugar into the body. Fruit is always a good choice along with some nuts of their choice, unsalted are best. Afterwards make sure they get some carbs' like bagels or whole wheat bread along with protein to help rebuild the muscle that was torn down.

Is Creatine important to give my child to help them build muscle?

In my opinion - No. I have yet to see any credible studies that have shown that Creatine increases muscle mass or increases athletic performance. Over long periods of time I've seen it retain water which gives the impression of larger muscles - but not actual muscle growth. There is some evidence that for sprinters, swimmers, and runners that it can help assist the body in stabilizing oxygen for very short periods of time.

What do I need to know about college scholarship?

The first thing you need to know is that your son or daughter has to be good enough for a university to decide to pay for their education. They have to be good enough for that level of competition. Next, if your coach isn't a pro-active coach in getting tapes or contacts to colleges or universities you need to take it upon yourself to become proactive. The time to do it is in your son or daughters junior year of high school. Every school has an interest in a player who can help their program - but don't waste their time if your kid can't perform at that level. Be realistic in the fact that your son or daughter may only have the talent or the size for a lesser division college or university.

A letter written by your child to the assistant coach who is responsible for recruiting in your area is important. The key is to introduce yourself, explain that you are interested in their school and helping their program. Send tapes if you have them and keep them brief - nothing more than five minutes. You can also use an internet service or YouTube to showcase your son or daughter. With the advent of the internet this has become more popular for parents and coaches. This will get your kid on the radar and if they are interested they will call - it's that simple.

What Should I know about the recruiting process?

The first thing you must know it that you must be real with yourself and real about your son or daughters talent level. Know that if that your child is truly an elite athlete the schools will contact you. Keep in mind that most recruiters are there to recruit for their program not your child. It is a business and you need to treat it as such because if you don't there may be a great deal of disappointment down the road.

Don't believe everything that comes out of the recruiter's mouth. He or she is competing against other schools and some of them will say anything you want to hear in order to get you to sign with their school. There are more broken promises during the recruiting process than goes on in Washington, D.C. Know in advance what you want out of the program and the school before you talk to any recruiting coach.

If your child is on the bubble then you have to take a pro-active approach to the colleges to get your name in front of the coaches. This includes summer camps, sending letters of interest, sending video, creating a web site, using an existing web recruiting site and even a phone call will help. Don't be over bearing, don't be rude, but be upfront and find out what is needed to get your foot in the door.

Are Supplements Necessary?

If you are eating a well rounded diet than I feel that you don't need supplementation. Although most young kids don't eat all that well and in this case I would recommend a multiple vitamin. I would make sure that your young athlete gets adequate protein and water. Other supplements that have shown to be of benefit athletes are fish oils that help with the removal of inflammation, Vit D, has shown to boost overall immune system,

What Do You Feel Are The Important Highlights of Helping My Son or Daughter Become an Elite Athlete?

Mind – working on the mental aspect of your game
Hard work – there is no substitute for hard work
Water – no less than 50 oz. per day
Protein – 1 gram of protein per pound of body weight
Sleep – important for recovery – 7 to 8 hours per night
Attitude – a good attitude will help you achieve your goals

About The Author

D r. Malcolm Conway is an internationally recognized sports injury specialist, author, wine maker, performance coach and speaker. He has been the owner of the Conway Clinic for over 26 years specializing in acute and chronic sports injuries offering state-of-the-art sports injury treatment. Dr. Conway has treated some of the highest paid athletes in sports and continues to work full time in his office located in Northeastern Pennsylvania. Dr. Conway has worked with athletes in the NFL, NBA, MLB, NHL, MMA,WTA, ATP and Division I universities and colleges throughout the U.S. Dr. Conway has appeared in the *New York Times, Sports Illustrated, Sport Magazine, Chicago Tribune, Boston Globe*. Dr. Conway has worked at Fed Cup in professional women's tennis, Wimbledon Championships and the U.S. Open tennis tournaments.

A graduate of the University of Pittsburgh, Sherman Chiropractic College in Spartanburg S.C., Dr. Conway has completed other post-doctoral work at the Southern California University of Health Sciences in advanced rehabilitation. Dr. Conway has also written several books including, *Alternatives To Back Pain, Advice For People Suffering With Low Back Pain Who Hate Chiropractors*, a contributing author to *Neck Pain, Neck Pain, You Don't Want It, You Don't Need It*, co-written books for the MyoFascial Disruption and Rehab Protocols for the office as well as writing for several popular sports blogs and sports and therapy magazines. Dr. Conway is the co-developer of the MyoFascial Disruption Technique (MFDT) a highly effective soft tissue treatment protocol that has been shown to be 90% faster in relieving pain as compared to conventional treatment. Dr. Conway and his colleagues teach other doctors from around the U.S. these new innovative treatment and rehabilitation protocols. Seeing thousands of patients in his career he has developed a sense of understanding on helping parents assist their children to maximize all of their potential.

CPSIA information can be obtained
at www.ICGtesting.com
Printed in the USA
BVHW081048171221
624277BV00001B/23